BEYOND NIHILISM

WITHDRAWN

Willhoite, Fred
Beyond Nihilism

BEYOND NIHILISM
Albert Camus's Contribution to Political Thought

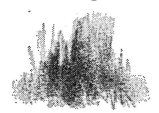

FRED H. WILLHOITE, JR.

LOUISIANA STATE UNIVERSITY PRESS • Baton Rouge

To

GREGORY D. PRITCHARD

Teacher and Friend

Preface

ALBERT CAMUS is not generally thought of as a political theorist. He was not a professional or academic political philosopher, and his worldwide literary reputation was achieved mainly on the strength of his novels. Yet during his entire career as a writer he was persistently concerned with political events, tendencies, and ideas, an interest which he cultivated as indispensable to his effort to comprehend and illuminate the human condition in our time.

The question, then, of whether Camus had an explicit political philosophy must be at least briefly considered. It can only be answered negatively if we seek in his writings a total intellectual system encompassing views on all the significant issues with which political theorists have traditionally dealt. An obvious omission, for instance, would be Camus's failure to supply any coherent theory of political obligation; aspects of this appear in his concern with freedom, democracy, and the limits of the legitimate power of man over man, but these do not add up to a coherent theoretical whole.

However, Camus does confront us with a wide-ranging yet unified vision of man's nature and situation, which is articulated with a thoroughgoing critique of certain prevalent types of politi-

cal ideas and institutions; this is the main thrust of his consideration of specific political issues. The constructive political implications of his view of man are not elaborated nearly to the degree
that characterizes the thought of great political philosophers who,
like Camus, have also employed their fundamental premises as
critical instruments—as, for example, in Plato's critique of undiluted democracy and Hobbes's attack on pretensions to derive
political principles from esoteric divine revelation.

In the final analysis, whether or not one considers a writer to
deserve the title "political philosopher" depends upon how broad
a scope of philosophical issues one expects such a writer to en-
compass, as well as upon the kind of intellectual inquiry which
he has undertaken. In order to avoid the largely verbal quibbling
that writing of Camus's "political philosophy" might entail, I
have deliberately chosen a subtitle which refers to his "contribution to political thought." Whether or not he merits being
called a political philosopher (he made no such claim himself),
Camus, I believe, demonstrated an extraordinary sensitivity to
the central problems of political thought and practice which
makes of his work, taken as a whole, a contribution to contemporary thinking about man's corporate life which is well
worth our careful consideration. Among the elements of his political thought, two themes have been given particular and recurrent emphasis in my analysis: what I have called Camus's existential method and his attempt to overcome the contemporary
threat of nihilism by re-establishing norms for human conduct
in the political realm.

Camus's effort to remain faithfully existential, avoiding generalized or didactic abstractions, accounts, at least in part I
think, for his attempts to illustrate and enrich the content of
his ideas by embodying them in the concrete personages and
events of novels, stories, and plays, rather than presenting his
thoughts solely in philosophical essays. As Roy Pierce (one of
the few political scientists who has written about Camus's political ideas) has remarked, "He was intellectually unsuited to

writing a political treatise of the kind produced by a Hobbes or a Locke or a Rousseau, if only because such a work implies abstraction, and Camus fought against abstractions throughout his entire life." (*Contemporary French Political Thought* [London and New York: Oxford University Press, 1966], 124.) I am not a literary critic, but I hope that I have generally succeeded in maintaining the artistic integrity of Camus's fiction, while at the same time trying to mine it for ideas rather than for aesthetic insights and attainments. This approach is justified, I believe, not only by the consideration that all of Camus's novels and plays (and some of his stories) reveal a conscious philosophic intent, but because the inextricable unity between meaningful thought and the particulars of human existence was one of his fundamental preconceptions.

The reader might consider it somewhat peculiar in a work purportedly dealing with political ideas that discussion of Camus's specifically political views does not appear before the midpoint of the third chapter. My explanation of this apparent anomaly is a conviction that a thorough exploration of Camus's vision of human nature and the human condition is an essential preliminary to any meaningful attempt to comprehend both his philosophical method and his responses to the significant substantive questions of contemporary political inquiry. Camus's political thought would be, I believe, severely truncated—in fact seriously distorted—if no extensive effort were made to explicate his fundamental philosophical and anthropological conceptions.

I have incorporated into this study at many points discussion of ideas presented by a number of contemporary writers, only a few of whom have specifically commented on or responded to the writings of Camus. I have done so in the belief that this approach will help to elucidate Camus's ideas and clarify their implications, and also in the hope that fuller discussion may throw some light on the difficult and controversial issues which he sought to examine.

I am glad to acknowledge the help, both direct and indirect, which I have received in writing this book. The man to whom it is dedicated first introduced me to the intellectual excitement and challenge of political thought; I remain deeply grateful to him, despite the many frustrations that I have experienced in wrestling with difficult ideas. I should also like to thank Professor John H. Hallowell, of Duke University, for first suggesting to me, some time ago, the close study of Camus's political thought. For financial assistance which freed time for writing I am indebted to the Graduate Research Council of Louisiana State University. Finally, I owe more than I can adequately express to my wife, primarily for her patience, but also for her invaluable help in preparing this book for publication.

Unless otherwise noted, translations from French sources are mine. Any errors that may appear in them, as well as in all statements of fact and interpretation, are solely my responsibility.

FRED H. WILLHOITE, JR.

Baton Rouge
May, 1967

Contents

xi

BEYOND NIHILISM

I
Camus and Contemporary
Political Thought

By reason of this attainment of self-consciousness on the part of the will for truth, morality from thenceforward—there is no doubt about it—goes *to pieces:* this is that great hundred-act play that is reserved for the next two centuries of Europe, the most terrible, the most mysterious, and perhaps also the most hopeful of all plays.

FRIEDRICH NIETZSCHE, *The Genealogy of Morals*

This prophetic and terrifying—yet strangely hopeful—remark of Nietzsche's has the utmost relevance for the condition of political philosophy in our time. And the situation of political philosophy is simply, as always, a reflection of the most fundamental preconceptions of contemporary intellectual life. Just as the political theories of Plato, Aristotle, and St. Thomas Aquinas assumed the reality of a purposeful, hierarchically ordered cosmos, so do present-day efforts to produce significant political ideas reflect a grappling with the widespread doubts and diverse but increasingly impotent dogmatisms that have prepossessed Western thinkers in the nineteenth and twentieth centuries.

Whether, in a positive sense, the intellectual climate of these times can be characterized in any summary fashion, it is difficult if not impossible to say; but negatively, at least, it seems beyond

3

dispute that this is not an age of faith and certainty. It is surely an understatement that one would be hard pressed to discern any present or incipient philosophical or religious consensus in contemporary intellectual life. This condition is rooted, as countless writers have pointed out, in the decline since the sixteenth century of traditional religious belief and authority and the rise of modern science to the rank of pre-eminent arbiter of ideas and theories.

In the intellectually pivotal seventeenth century, philosophically minded men confronted a Europe fragmented religiously into several major churches and a host of sects, almost each of which claimed sole custodianship of divine truth. And it seemed that these mutually incompatible claims could be settled only on the battlefield. It was perhaps no mere coincidence that the *Discourse on Method* was produced by a weary participant in the Thirty Years' War. How could certainty, how could true knowledge be obtained, Descartes wondered—knowledge intrinsically true and not dependent for its acceptance or rejection upon the whims, power drives, fears, and wishful thinking of ecclesiastical and political authorities? Descartes's answer is enduringly significant, not so much for its precise content as for its rather tentative presentation of two fundamental attitudes that have acquired virtual presuppositional status in the modern intellectual milieu: first, the rejection (implicit and cautiously qualified in Descartes) of all traditional authorities—religious or secular—as sources of certain knowledge; second, the claim that scientific reasoning and experimentation provide a new and the only reliable pathway to certainty.

This is not the place to rehearse again the much-told story of the rise of modern science and the spread of its assumptions and methods to almost every sphere of scholarly inquiry. Whatever the manifold reasons for these developments, they are today simply facts that must be confronted by anyone who seeks to grapple honestly with the perplexities and potentialities of the human condition. Our supreme problem is the status of moral standards and values. Here the certainty that Descartes and, following him, modern scientists and philosophers have sought has seemed constantly to elude our grasp.

Philosophers as diverse as Hobbes, Marx, and Herbert Spencer have claimed scientific warrant for their perspectives and prescriptions, but, despite the continuing influence of their ideas, this particular claim has survived the tests neither of time nor of sustained critical analysis. Indeed, the dominant view among contemporary philosophers seems to be that the whole enterprise of attempting to establish values by scientific means is misconceived because there is an unbridgeable logical gap between what is (the domain of science) and what ought to be (the province of evaluation). This conclusion and some of its implications are clearly stated by an eminent social scientist:

> Only after fully recognizing that our humanitarian ideals in their most important aspects cannot be extracted from nature solely by scientific means, only then are we mature enough to comprehend our personal responsibility, individually or in groups, in choosing our ultimate standards of measurement, our ultimate norms. . . . No longer then can we take the easy way of "waiting for science to find out what is true." . . . What fundamental attitude to take toward the claim of all men to a share in human freedom and happiness and what limits to set to the legal validity of government measures that disregard this claim, we do not decide by scientific standards . . . but by religious or philosophical convictions or our creative moral and political will.[1]

But for many the basic problem seems to be that a commitment to moral standards on the basis of religious or philosophical preference or the self-conscious "creation" of norms by the "moral and political will" can only be leaps into uncharted darkness, since these alleged pathways to moral truth cannot provide us with knowledge according to the standards of empirical science. Furthermore, Marx's exposure of the interdepen-

---

[1] Arnold Brecht, "The Ultimate Standard of Justice," in Carl J. Friedrich and John W. Chapman (eds.), *Nomos VI: Justice* (New York: Atherton Press, 1963), 68.

dence of economic status and values and Freud's effort to demonstrate that irrational instincts underlie and determine the direction of human rationality have made it appear to many that it is in principle and in practice simply impossible to validate moral principles. Such an enterprise seems destined to end at best in mere wish-fulfillment and at worst in simple futility. For at least a century the specter of nihilism has haunted Western thought. Man seems bereft of externally imposed or intellectually authoritative standards of behavior, to be left entirely to his own devices in the midst of an existence that lacks any intrinsic meaning.

It is unlikely in such a time that we shall see emerge a new common set of moral principles based upon a generally accepted vision of reality, although there are various candidates—Freudian and other advocates of psychoanalysis, many varieties of Marxists, would-be revivalists of the ancient natural law tradition, to mention a few—for the job of averting the conquest of the moral and political imagination by nihilistic defeatism. There are also distinctively individual contemporary thinkers who have wrestled with this overwhelming problem, writers whom it is most difficult and probably unrewarding to categorize with any very exclusive labels. Such a man was Albert Camus.

Camus is best known as a novelist, author of *The Stranger, The Plague,* and *The Fall,* and as the recipient of the Nobel Prize for Literature in 1957. He wrote only one work dealing explicitly with fundamental problems of moral and political philosophy—*The Rebel*; thus it may seem quixotic to single him out for extended treatment within the context of contemporary social and political thought. Further, he said of himself: "I don't think I'm worth a red cent as a philosopher; what really concerns me is knowing how one should act." And in 1945 he noted in his journal: "Why am I an artist and not a philosopher? Because I think according to words and not according to ideas." [2]

²Quoted in Pierre de Boisdeffre, *Métamorphose de la littérature de Proust à Sartre* (Paris: Editions Alsatia, 1952), II, 287; Albert Camus, *Notebooks, 1942–1951,* trans. Justin O'Brien (New York: Alfred A. Knopf, 1965), 113 (entry of September, 1945).

Indeed Camus was not a philosopher in the sense either of an academic teacher and practitioner of philosophic analysis or of a grand metaphysical system-builder. But he was an artist-philosopher in the French tradition of Voltaire, Rousseau, and Gide. As a very young man he wrote in his journal: "People think only in images. If you want to be a philosopher, write novels." [3] And, of course, Camus wrote not only novels but short stories, plays, and a considerable number of philosophical essays.

In an article published four years after Camus's death, Thomas Landon Thorson attempted "to make the beginnings of a case for the inclusion in the tradition of Western political philosophy of . . . Albert Camus," contending that Camus's "thought is 'to the point' in political philosophy in a way that little else is in our time." [4] Thorson concedes that Camus was not a political philosopher if this enterprise is limited to the elaboration of a general metaphysical apparatus from which political prescriptions are allegedly inferred. But Thorson prefers a "functional" definition of political philosophy, as an effort to raise and provide some kinds of answers to questions concerning the proper way to organize politically and to supply criteria for making choices in a political context. And Camus was certainly a thinker who sought "to answer such questions by a careful yet general analysis of their meaning and the consequences of deciding them one way or another . . . ." [5] Thus he is a significant figure in contemporary political philosophy.

Obviously I agree with Thorson's view of Camus's importance, and in a sense this entire study is an extended justification of our common assessment of his significance for twentieth-century political thought. However, this does not mean that we can focus narrowly on Camus's explicit ideas on political organization and decision-making; rather, we must carefully examine the en-

[3] Albert Camus, *Notebooks, 1935–1942*, trans. Philip Thody (New York: Alfred A. Knopf, 1963), 10 (entry of January, 1936).
[4] Thomas Landon Thorson, "Albert Camus and the Rights of Man," *Ethics*, LXXIV (July, 1964), 281, 291.
[5] *Ibid.*, 281.

tirety of his thought as a response to the challenge of nihilism, centering upon his views concerning the nature of this phenomenon and its effects upon political life and thought. That this was a specific major preoccupation of Camus's is apparent in almost everything he wrote, and his private thoughts were directed very early to this situation: "Modern intelligence is in utter confusion. . . . It is a fact that we are suffering from nihilism. . . . There's a whole civilization to be reconstructed." [6]

A preliminary issue that requires some consideration at this point is Camus's relationship to existentialism. This term is notoriously difficult to define, and I shall make no pretense to lexicographical precision in this discussion. Furthermore, merely determining a writer's position in regard to existentialism gives us no direct clue to the character of his political philosophy. There seems to be no single political perspective inevitably attached to existentialist assumptions; logically, an existentialist could be an anarchist, some kind of Marxist, apolitical, an elitist—and perhaps there are other possibilities. Nevertheless, the frequent and casual identification of Camus as an existentialist may have led to a failure to examine carefully and precisely the philosophical underpinnings of his individual perspective.

Camus rather consistently denied that he was an existentialist; this is borne out by two of his remarks from the mid-1940's: "I don't have much taste for the overly celebrated existentialist philosophy, and, frankly, I think its conclusions are wrong." [7] An elaboration of this attitude is found in one of his journal entries from March, 1946:

The whole effort of German thought has been to substitute for the notion of human nature that of human situation and hence to substitute history for God and modern tragedy for ancient equilibrium. Modern existentialism carries that effort even further and introduces into the idea of situation the same uncertainty as in the idea of

[6]*Notebooks, 1942–1951*, pp. 15–16 (entry of March, 1942).
[7]Albert Camus, *Actuelles: Chroniques, 1944–1948* (Paris: Gallimard, 1950), 111.

nature. Nothing remains but a motion. But like the Greeks I believe in nature.[8]

Various writers on Camus's thought have pointed out basic differences between his perspective and that of Jean-Paul Sartre, the quintessential French existentialist. For instance, Thomas Hanna indicates that Camus does not share with Sartre the beliefs that existence precedes essence in the human condition and that the self is therefore in constant danger and uncertainty, ceaselessly questioning itself about its relation to the world and to itself.[9] And further, John Cruickshank points to Camus's dissent from Sartre's view that values do not pre-exist but are simply invented by each man in the processes of acting and choosing. Camus "is not saying that such values are absolute or eternal in the traditional sense. But contrary to Sartre he finds their pre-existence, in some form, essential to his picture of what it means to be a human being." [10]

These remarks—both those of Camus and of the commentators—do not, however, exhaust and dispose of the issue of Camus's relationship to existentialist thought. Although he professed belief in an essential human nature—and this is an important clue to the fundamental character of his perspective— Camus dwelt much more on the human condition than on the precise characteristics that he thought necessary to a comprehension of man's essential being. Camus's starting-point and his philosophical method are profoundly existential; he sets out from his own intensely experienced personal existence and is indifferent to all types of *a priori* categories or concepts as aids to the explication of that existence: "For Camus the brute fact for every man is that he exists and the world exists, and any sort of philosophizing which attempts to explain this fact away or to minimize its importance is either destructive or irrelevant

[8]*Notebooks, 1942–1951,* p. 136.
[9]Thomas Hanna, *The Thought and Art of Albert Camus* (Chicago: Henry Regnery, 1958), xv.
[10]John Cruickshank, *Albert Camus and the Literature of Revolt* (New York: Oxford University Press, 1960), 97n.

to the human situation." [11] Camus's attitude is closely akin to
Kierkegaard's "passionate subjectivity." Furthermore, like Hei-
degger, Camus is profoundly concerned with the meaning for
life of the inevitability and finality of death.

At this point a distinction formulated by Gérard Deledalle may
aid our understanding: "All reflection on the singular and unique
experience that the anguish of living bestows upon a being is
existential. And existentialism is only a particular instance of the
existential." [12] In this sense, existentialism would refer only to a
particular technical philosophy, in France exemplified by Jean-
Paul Sartre and perhaps by Maurice Merleau-Ponty. But existential thought and literature is much more inclusive, incorporating
any writer hostile to a priori conceptions and concerned to attempt an interpretation of the human condition on the basis of
his own experience and the clues he believes that it gives him to
the nature of the experiences of other men. As Glenn Tinder
has pointed out, existential thought represents a revolt against the
abstract impersonalism that has generally characterized Western
philosophy. In the late nineteenth century, "the two principal
philosophical alternatives were positivism and idealism; in one
case the person was lost in the causal regularities of nature, in
the other case in the ideal patterns of a universal mind." Protests—principally those of Kierkegaard and Nietzsche—against
the dominant impersonalist philosophies were uttered but little
heeded in the nineteenth century. But despite the continued as-
cendancy of positivist impersonalism in the present day, "our consciousness of the personal element in society and history has
been renewed above all by the existential philosophers." [13]

Camus is located centrally within this existential current of
thought. In his journal he instructed himself in this typical manner: "Be done with all the rest and state what I most deeply

[11]Thorson, "Albert Camus and the Rights of Man," 284.
[12]Gérard Deledalle, L'existentiel, philosophies et littératures de l'existence
(Paris: Editions Renée Lacoste, 1949), 12.
[13]Glenn Tinder, The Crisis of Political Imagination (New York: Charles
Scribner's Sons, 1964), 288.

feel." [14] Camus sought always to remain faithful primarily to his own most deeply experienced perceptions and emotions—"the value of Camus's processes of thought derives from the very fact that they are lived rather than reasoned. . . . This does not mean, of course, that a philosopher must of necessity speak about what he has not experienced. But in so far as he integrates experience within a system, he transforms. Dialectics gradually take the place of intuition." [15]

Any existential thinker initially confronts an obvious but very serious problem: if his basic perspective is derived solely from his own experiences and perceptions, how can he claim for his viewpoint relevance to anyone or any situation beyond himself and his personal involvements? That Camus sought to speak meaningfully to and about the condition of all men and not merely himself is apparent throughout his work. He clearly stated this universalistic objective in his journal: "Our task: to create universality or at least universal values. Win for man his catholicity." [16] Insofar as such an effort would require for its success the agreement of all men to the values proposed, or even the concurrence by all who are confronted by the existential theorist's writings, the inevitable outcome is failure. The writer can only appeal to others to confront and examine honestly their own experiences and perceptions, hoping that what they discern and the implications they draw will be similar to his own. But, practically speaking, the great diversity of human perspectives and environments appears to render such an outcome, at best, highly unlikely. The most that can be hoped for—particularly by a thinker such as Camus, who was intensely aware of man's limitations, including an inescapable fallibility—is that a climate of full and open communication among men will be established in order to nurture whatever commonness can be discovered.

[14]*Notebooks, 1942–1951*, p. 188 (entry of October, 1947).
[15]Serge Doubrovsky, "The Ethics of Albert Camus," trans. Sondra Mueller and Jean-Marc Vary, in Germaine Brée (ed.), *Camus: A Collection of Critical Essays* (Englewood Cliffs, N.J.: Prentice-Hall, 1962), 72.
[16]*Notebooks, 1942–1951*, p. 120 (entry of November, 1945).

Yet the existential writer must continue to maintain that he can genuinely know only what makes sense to him in terms of his own most intimate experiences, that all abstractions remain alien to him until they acquire validation within the matrix of his personal existence.

At this point it thus becomes necessary to provide some biographical information about Camus. Son of a Spanish mother and a French Alsatian father, Albert Camus was born in the small Algerian town of Mondovi on November 7, 1913. [17] His Algerian origins profoundly shaped his attitudes, both generally and in specific instances. Of equal significance was his class background; his home was not a bourgeois domicile such as those which have sheltered most great modern French writers— for example, Proust and Sartre—in their early years. Camus's father worked as a farm laborer and was killed in 1914 in one of the early battles of World War I. The widowed mother soon moved her family to a lower-class section of Algiers, where young Albert grew up in wretched poverty. Five members of the family lived in a squalid two-room apartment, with the mother supporting them by doing household chores for hire.

Living in poverty apparently did not create in Camus any bitterness against life or against his fellow men, nor did it make of him as a mature man a radical revolutionary. He certainly never romanticized the life of the poor, and he never ceased to view the eradication of poverty as a primary social objective. Yet he always admired the indomitability of spirit found in so many persons in the class of his origins, and he always felt an almost physical fraternity with the working class. As a very young man he confided to his journal: "When I see things clearly, I have only one thing to say. It is in this life of poverty, among these vain or humble people, that I have most certainly touched what I feel is the true meaning of life." [18]

[17]Most of the biographical information presented here is based upon the account of Roger Quilliot, *La mer et les prisons: essai sur Albert Camus* (Paris: Gallimard, 1956), 9–17.
[18]*Notebooks, 1935–1942*, p. 4 (entry of May, 1935).

It is true, however, that Camus's native abilities permitted him to escape both poverty and membership in the working class. Successful in scholarship competition, he was enabled to attend the *lycée* in Algiers and proved to be an excellent student. At seventeen he was first stricken by tuberculosis, which continued to plague him, more or less seriously, the remainder of his life. Very early this brilliant and sensitive young man was brought up against the existential fact of his mortality, and from his first essays until his last writings he sought to discern the implications for man's life of an awareness of its inevitable extinction. Camus's suffering from this serious disease must certainly have sharpened and intensified this concern in his thinking.

In 1930 Camus entered the University of Algiers as a student of philosophy, and in 1936 he was awarded a graduate degree for a thesis on the relationship between Hellenism and Christianity as discerned in a study of Plotinus and Saint Augustine. To support himself while studying he held a series of part-time jobs, as salesman of automobile accessories, ship broker, meteorologist, and clerk at police headquarters, among others: "Thus he learned . . . the dull routine of the workingman's existence. But he also learned the obscure virtues which this uniformity, though it may submerge the worker, does not succeed in stifling in him." [19]

In 1934 Camus became a member of the Communist party in Algiers and retained at least a nominal connection with it until 1937. However, within a year after joining, he became disillusioned when the party's line abruptly shifted on the question of Arab claims. He later remarked of this youthful episode: "If I was once a communist, I have never been a Marxist." [20] When it became obvious to him that the Communists were not primarily concerned with the fate of the wretched Algerian Arabs

---

[19]Albert Maquet, *Albert Camus: The Invincible Summer,* trans. Herma Briffault (New York: Braziller, 1958), 16.
[20]Quoted from a 1957 speech to a group of Paris bookbindery workers, in Pierre Aubery, "Albert Camus et la classe ouvrière," *The French Review,* XXXIII (October, 1958), 20.

but were merely attempting to use their protests as a means to gain power, Camus, in disgust, gave up his assignment of propagandizing the Arab population. He had not become a party member because his intellect had been won over by Marxist doctrine; rather, he had been moved to action by the spectacle of gross human suffering with which he had at first believed the Communists were primarily concerned also.

One of Camus's youthful passions was acting, and in 1935 he led in the establishment of a young actors' group in Algiers, the *Théâtre du Travail*—later the *Théâtre de l'Equipe*—in which he participated for several years, not only as an actor but also as director and playwright. For two years he was also employed as a leading actor in the traveling troupe of Radio-Alger. Reflections on the significance of the actor's mode of life appear in several of his works, principally as an example of the "absurd" life in *The Myth of Sisyphus*.

Forbidden because of his delicate health to study for the highest French degree in philosophy, Camus in 1937 left on a poor student's tour of Southern Europe, traveling to southeastern France, Florence, Genoa, and Pisa; one of the fruits of this trip was a significant essay in one of his early books, *Nuptials (Noces)*. Upon his return to Algiers, he became a reporter on a leading newspaper and for the rest of his life was connected in some way with professional journalism. His initial employment in this field was of short duration, however, for he incurred the wrath of government officials by writing an exposé of French administrators' inhuman treatment of the natives of the Kabylia section of Algeria. This episode caused him to be denied a government post that he had been promised after the outbreak of World War II in 1939.

With all routes to advancement apparently closed to him in Algiers, Camus moved to Paris in 1940 and obtained an editorial position with *Paris-Soir*. In 1942 he entered the Resistance movement, working primarily on the publication of the clandestine newspaper *Combat*. The publication that same year of his first novel, *The Stranger,* brought him to the attention of the

French literary community. In 1944 Camus first met Jean-Paul Sartre, whose works he had read—and severely criticized—while he was still working as a journalist in Algiers. During the forties Camus began to devote most of his working time to his own writing, and the success of his books and plays enabled him to become relatively independent of outside employment. He became, however, one of the directors of *Combat* after it emerged from clandestine status in August, 1944, and under his direction this paper became one of the most eloquent advocates of social reform in postwar France. In 1947 financial difficulties and political differences split the directoral group of *Combat,* but through the editorials he had written for it Camus had already gained a considerable reputation as an idealistic (sometimes, perhaps, naively so) champion of a new humanistic politics.

Camus's second and most popularly successful novel, *The Plague,* was published in mid-1947 and placed him in the front ranks of contemporary French writers. In 1951, after years of arduous intellectual labor, his most important work on politics and society, *The Rebel,* appeared and was greeted by a storm of controversy that swept French intellectual circles for more than a year. It ended with Camus's scathing reply to a derisive review published in *Les Temps Modernes,* a rather sarcastic rejoinder by the magazine's director, Jean-Paul Sartre, and a total break in the relationship between the two writers. Of this incident Simone de Beauvoir, Sartre's companion of many years, has written: "If this friendship exploded so violently, it was because for a long time not much of it had remained. The political and ideological differences which already existed between Sartre and Camus in 1945, had intensified from year to year." From her perspective—and Sartre's—Camus had become increasingly a naive idealist and moralist, in his anticommunism deserting the cause of the working class and becoming a champion of bourgeois values; though he professed dislike for the United States, "he went over, practically speaking, to the American side." Somewhat spitefully, she concludes: "Personally, this break in their relations did not affect me. The Camus who had been dear to me had ceased to exist a long while before." [21] Camus's reaction to this confrontation appeared in his published letter to Sartre and, more obliquely but with greater force, in his short novel *The Fall*, published in 1956.

During the 1950's, Camus's consistent opposition to political oppression was expressed in various ways. In 1952 he angrily withdrew from collaboration with UNESCO when Franco's Spain was admitted to the organization, and in a public speech he denounced Soviet suppression of the East Berlin workers' uprising in June, 1953. Similar public statements followed the Soviet army's crushing of the Hungarian revolt in 1956. During the Algerian War which racked France in the latter half of this decade, Camus sought a tortuous middle way that would transcend the slogans of Right and Left; for his pains he was rejected and denounced by ideologues on both sides of the bloody conflict that was decimating the native country that he never ceased to love with his whole being. In January, 1960, Camus was killed in an automobile crash—he had been honored in his early forties by the world's greatest literary prize, was working strenuously on a new novel, and was esteemed by the literate public in most of the world, especially by young people.

Though only forty-six when he died, Camus left novels, plays, stories, essays, and a posthumously published journal which incarnate a moving and distinctive vision of the world and of the times through which he lived. It was apparent from the many eulogies which followed his death that, in starting from and seeking to remain faithful to what he learned from his own experience, Camus had succeeded in striking a responsive chord in the hearts and minds—if not of men universally or of all his readers—of countless individuals haunted by nihilism and horrified by the bloodiness of the twentieth century, yet, like Nietzsche, strangely hopeful.

---

[21]Simone de Beauvoir, *Force of Circumstance,* trans. Richard Howard (New York: G. P. Putnam's Sons, 1964), 259–60.

II
Human Nature and the Human Condition: The World of Absurdity

No POLITICAL thinker of any consequence can be understood simply through an examination of his views on governmental institutions and policies. To cite only two well-known examples, Plato's sketch of an exemplary *polis* in *The Republic* is incomprehensible apart from a grasp of his understanding of reality and of the relationship between man's nature and the sum total of being. Similarly, Marx's critique of government and his premonitions of the character of a truly communist society cannot be grasped without an initial effort to comprehend his views of man's alienated condition and of the nature of human history. Thus Camus's distinctly political ideas cannot assume the meaning and significance he intended for them unless we first explore his views on man's nature and condition.

There is some danger involved in the approach I have taken of concentrating first on Camus's early works, delaying extensive consideration of the writings he began to publish after his thirtieth year. Camus did not suddenly change his mind on fundamental matters at the age of thirty; not only did he never renounce his youthful works, he continued to reiterate and enlarge upon basic themes that appeared in his earliest essays. The terms "absurdity" and "communion" do not designate two clearly distinct stages in his philosophical development, in which the latter represents an overt or implicit rejection of the former. Writings from these two stages of his career can be roughly distinguished, however, in terms of main emphases; there is discernible development in his thought dealing with the human condition. It should become clear that in a fundamental sense "communion" is the more significant term characterizing Camus's perspective, and its meaning for him warrants extensive development.

Origins of Camus's View of the World

The essays Camus wrote in his early twenties, which were collected in *Betwixt and Between* (*L'envers et l'endroit,* 1937) and in *Nuptials* (*Noces,* 1939), contain in germ almost all the principal motifs in his thought on the human condition and also demonstrate the organic bonds between his personal experience and his ideas. This is especially true of the more philosophically reflective essays in the latter volume, and we shall concentrate on them in seeking to discern the root elements in Camus's perspective. His profound attachment to his native North African soil, his intimate knowledge of and deep communion with nature, his most strongly felt reactions to his immediate experience of the world are nowhere more apparent than in these poetically written essays.

The underlying themes to which Camus continually returned, whether as novelist, short-story writer, dramatist, or essayist, are almost all presaged in this single passage from *Nuptials:*

To feel one's attachment to a certain region, one's love for a certain group of men, to know that there is always a spot where one's heart will feel at peace—these are many certainties for a single human life. And yet this is not enough. But at certain moments everything yearns for that spiritual home. "Yes, we must go back there—there, indeed." Is there anything odd in finding on earth that union that Plotinus longed for? Unity is expressed here in terms of sun and sea. The heart is sensitive to it through a certain savor of flesh which constitutes its bitterness and its grandeur. I learn that there is no superhuman happiness, no eternity outside the sweep of days. These paltry and essential belongings, these relative truths are the only ones to stir me. As for the others, the "ideal" truths, I have not enough soul to understand them. Not that one must be an animal, but I find no meaning in the happiness of angels. I know simply that this sky will last longer than I. And what shall I call eternity except what will continue after my death? I am not expressing here the creature's satisfaction with his condition. It is quite a different matter. It is not always easy to be a man, still less to be a pure man. But being pure is recovering that spiritual home where one can feel the world's relationship, where one's pulsebeats coincide with the violent throbbing of the two-o'clock sun. It is well known that one's native land is always recognized at the moment of losing it. For those who are too uneasy about themselves, their native land is the one that negates them. I should not like to be brutal or seem extravagant. But, after all, what negates me in this life is first of all what kills me. Everything that exalts life at the same time increases its absurdity. In the Algerian summer I learn that one thing only is more tragic than suffering, and that is the life of a happy man. But it may be also the way to a greater life because it leads to not cheating.[1]

This long passage has been quoted in full because it is central to an explication both of the basic themes of Camus's work and of the experiential substance of his reflections. Here we can discern the leitmotifs believed by Camus to be the only "certainties" of life: man's joy in nature, the total this-worldliness of life, the conjunction of happiness and absurdity, and complete honesty to oneself. And elsewhere in these early essays we shall encounter the initial formulation of the theme of man's rebellion against death.

The glorious joy of communion with the earth, the sea, and all the fierce beauty of nature finds repeated expression in these essays. The young Camus speaks of throwing his body into the pungent flowers and, in so doing, "fulfilling a truth that is of the sun and also of my death. . . . I have a wild love for this life

---

[1]Albert Camus, "Summer in Algiers," in *The Myth of Sisyphus and Other Essays,* trans. Justin O'Brien (New York: Alfred A. Knopf, 1955), 151–52.

and want to speak of it freely: it bestows upon me the pride
of my human condition." Against those who would denigrate
this pride, he rejoins that indeed he is rightfully proud of "this
sun, that sea, my heart leaping with young blood, my body that
tastes of salt, and the enormous painting of the sky, where ten-
derness and glory meet in yellow and blue." From such experience he draws this conclusion: "Everything here leaves me whole,
I give up nothing of myself, I assume no mask: it suffices me to
learn with patience the difficult science of living, which is well
worth anyone's knowing how to live." [2]

Camus thus declares that if we can forget our prejudices,
throw aside the masks with which we screen reality from our
vision, and revel in the glory of sun, flowers, and sea, we will
experience the sheer joy of life that man in this happy condition
can know through natural, instinctive—almost animal-like—ex-
altation of the body. Camus derived this attitude not from the
romantic verses of Chateaubriand or Victor Hugo but immediately from the youthful experiences he describes in the essays.
For the young Camus, life at its best was a nuptial feast spread
by nature for the man who would seek simply to enjoy her
bounties. Later, when Camus attempted to elaborate a more in-
tellectualized approach to life, seeking, himself, to know *how* to
live, the fundamental value of life for him remained the exalted
joy which he had tasted in its purest form on the sun-swept
beaches of Algeria.

Significantly, elemental physical happiness recurs in his writing as a supreme value at a time when he had already entered
upon the gray and arduous ordeal of surviving the years of the
German occupation of France:

Purely physical joys with the mind's consent. There lies perfection,
harmony with one's condition, man's gratitude and respect.

Wild and pure sloping dunes! Glory of the water, so black in the
morning, so clear at noon, and warm and gilded in the evening.

[2]Albert Camus, "Noces à Tipasa," in *Noces* (Paris: Charlot, 1939),
18–20.

Long mornings on the dune among naked bodies, and immediately everything has to be repeated, everything said that has been said. There was youth. There is youth and, at the age of thirty, I want nothing else but such youth to continue. But . . .[3]

Yet such bodily joy cannot be the sum of man's existence, because he possesses the inescapable capacity for self-consciousness: "Thought is always out in front. It sees too far, farther than the body, which lives in the present. To abolish hope is to bring thought back to the body. And the body is doomed to perish." [4] This brings us to an elaboration of a second principal motif in Camus's early thought, his refusal to believe in the reality of any life other than the present earthly existence, not because of any alleged scientific or rational disproof of an after-life, but simply because of an intense existential concern with his own knowable bodily existence: "Pointlessness of the problem of immortality. We are interested in our destiny, admittedly. But *before,* not after." [5] In this life we can know such intense happiness as that which he describes, and whatever happens to us here and now is so deeply felt that speculation about a life that we have not experienced seems grossly irrelevant: "Even if I wished it, what have I to do with any truth that does not decay? It isn't cut to my dimensions." [6]

To what criteria of behavior does this deeply felt conviction of mortality lead Camus? Simply to the fully conscious savoring of each precious moment of life:

Few people understand that there is a type of refusal that has nothing in common with renunciation. The words "future," "better-off," "one's place"—what do they mean here? What does the "progress of the heart" mean? If I obstinately refuse all the "later ons" of the world, this is because I don't want to turn my back on my present riches. It doesn't please me to believe that death opens upon another life. For me it is a closed door.[7]

[3]*Notebooks, 1942–1951,* pp. 16–17 (entry of March, 1942).
[4]*Notebooks, 1935–1942,* pp. 104–105 (entry of August, 1938).
[5]*Ibid.,* 36 (entry of June, 1937).
[6]Albert Camus, "Le désert," in *Noces,* 100.
[7]Albert Camus, "Le vent à Djemila," in *Noces,* 35–36.

Camus does not concern himself in these early essays with the
issue of moral imperatives incumbent upon the individual in relation to other men. Communion here assumes the form almost
completely of elemental physical immersion in the plenitude of
nature. This does not mean that Camus was aloof from or hostile to others; he never idolized Rousseau's isolated "happy savage." As a young man he was simply trying to come to grips with
his deepest perceptions of his personal situation. And he never
ceased to believe that the individual cannot be wholly subsumed
under social and political categories or any other kind of abstractions. As he noted in his journal soon after the end of World
War II: "Man is not *only* social. His death at least belongs to
him. We are made to live in relation to others. But one dies
truly only for oneself." [8]

A third theme in *Nuptials* is the conjoining of man's desire
for happiness and his awareness of mortality, resulting in a feeling that the human situation is absurd. Camus writes movingly
of his conviction that it is man's role in nature to be a happy
creature. After a day of unsullied physical enjoyment he felt
that he had fulfilled his vocation as a man.[9] The possibility—
and, at times, the reality—of such a joyous existence leads men
to desire life's everlasting continuance. But the impossibility of
fulfilling this yearning means that we must surmount our trepi-
dation at the prospect of death and, in full cognizance of our
inescapable fate, affirm the happiness that we can know: "What
is happiness if not the simple accord between a being and the
existence that he leads. And what more legitimate accord can
link man to life than the double awareness of his desire to endure
and his destiny of death?" [10]

Life is very good and yields a fierce, tender, bitter-sweet happiness to those who love its beauty with all their hearts and
dedicate themselves to its perishable reality. This passionate af-

---

[8]*Notebooks, 1942–1951,* p. 122 (entry of November, 1945).
[9]"Noces à Tipasa," 24–25.
[10]"Le désert," 94–95.

firmation of life has the effect, however, of intensifying one's feeling of the absurdity of human existence. If life is joyous and good, it is for man the ultimate absurdity that he should be aware of his inevitable extinction. Here we find the experiential origin of Camus's concept of "absurdity"; despite his efforts to treat this idea in logical fashion in *The Myth of Sisyphus,* absurdity for Camus was never an abstract category. Rather, it was always a deeply felt existential reality that does not, as we shall see, yield at all readily to systematized philosophic treatment.

The full acceptance of one's humanity, in its joy and its absurdity, leads to "not cheating," to a whole-souled honesty which is a fourth leading motif in Camus's early writings. In his journal he wrote of his attitude toward the absurd: "The will is nothing. Acceptance everything. On one condition: that, faced with the humblest or the most heart-rending experience, man should always be 'present'; and that he should endure this experience without flinching, with complete lucidity." [11] Camus could conceive of no legitimately human way of confronting his experiences and perceptions except in complete openness and without fear of the consequences. It may appear that Camus here introduces the moral obligation of personal honesty simply as his individual, arbitrary preference. But this is true only to the same extent that his whole position is one of preference and is not based on intellectually compelling logical demonstration. His espousal of personal integrity is simply the inevitable concomitant of his existential stance—his commitment to speak about and act upon the basis only of what he knows through his own experiences and perceptions.

The young writer felt that "everything is simple. It's men who complicate things. Don't let them tell us otherwise. Don't let them say to us about the man condemned to death that 'he's going to pay his debt to society,' but rather that 'they're going to cut his head off.' This may not seem like much, but it makes a bit of a difference. And then there are people who prefer to

[11]*Notebooks, 1935–1942,* p. 143 (entry of September, 1939).

look their fate in the eyes." [12] It is significant that in this early essay Camus illustrates dishonesty by the way people talk about a condemned man. For he continually emphasized that inhumanity, injustice, and terrorism are outgrowths of efforts to evade our naked humanity by using abstract concepts to screen from our vision both the absurdity of our condition and the evils of organized society.

Thus a lucid faithfulness to the experience of the mingled joy and absurdity of life requires a necessary if often difficult and personal integrity—but, strangely, this honesty reinforces, by making genuine, the happiness that we can know:

> I truly feel . . . that the real, the only progress of civilization, the kind to which from time to time a man commits himself, is the creation of conscious deaths. . . .
> As I confront this world I neither want to lie nor be lied to. I want to take my clearsightedness with me all the way to the end and look upon my demise with all the profusion of my jealousy and my horror. It is insofar as I detach myself from the world that I fear death, insofar as I attach myself to the fate of living men instead of contemplating the enduring sky. To create conscious deaths is to diminish the distance that separates us from the world, and to enter joylessly into this awareness, conscious of the exalting pictures of a world forever lost.[13]

A refusal to evade the reality of our fate draws us nearer to the world, makes us aware of the transitory nature of all our achievements, and exalts the joy of immediate experience. For the only happiness we can know is rendered poignant by the awareness of inevitable death.

But, though it cannot be escaped, death must not be either placidly or unthinkingly accepted. It is in this context that the theme of revolt makes its first appearance in Camus's writings; it later became his central concern, as he grappled with the funda-

---

[12]Albert Camus, "Entre le oui et le non," in *L'envers et l'endroit* [1937], trans. Bernard Frechtman, *Partisan Review,* XVI (November, 1949), 1097.
[13]"Le vent à Djemila," 38–40.

mental issues of political life. Camus's concern with the meaning and implications of revolt is traceable to a particular experience that he recorded and commented on both in his journal and in *Nuptials*. In 1937 he visited Italy, seeking to recover from a serious recurrence of tuberculosis. He was haunted by the imminent possibility of his own death.

In Florence he strolled through the Cloister of the Dead of the Santissima Annunziata and observed that the epitaphs seemed to indicate that all those buried there had willingly accepted death. Suddenly, standing against one of the great pillars of the cathedral, he felt intensely fierce rebellion against such resignation well up within him:

Alone against the column, I was like someone who is seized by the throat and who cries out his faith as a final word. Everything within me protested against this kind of resignation. "One must," said the inscriptions. But I said no, and my revolt was true. That joy which goes about the earth, indifferent and absorbed in itself like a pilgrim —I had to follow it step by step. And as for the rest, I said no. I said no with all my strength. These slabs taught me that this was futile. . . . But today I still do not see what futility takes away from my revolt, and I feel keenly what is thereby added to it.[14]

In this moment of instinctive rebellion Camus discovered that his love for the earth, for life in its mingled joy and hopelessness, was so overwhelming that he could not resign himself to the death his lucidity would not permit him to forget. Revolt surged up within him; all the forces of the world which work to obliterate human life must be resisted: "If it is true that all truth bears within itself a bitterness, it is likewise true that every negation contains a manifesto of affirmation. And the song of love without hope to which contemplation gives birth can also serve as the most efficacious rule of action." [15]

Camus's existential sequence: life is very good but mortal; yet when its joy overwhelms us, we rebel against death and all death-

---

[14]"Le désert," 88–89.
[15]*Ibid.*, 99.

bringers; because this revolt is in the name of life, it leads to a keener awareness of the poignant happiness that can be ours if we affirm our allegiance to the earth.

Florence! One of the few places in Europe where I realized that in the heart of my rebellion an affirmation lay dormant. In her sky of mingled tears and sun I learned to consent to the earth and to burn within the dark flame of her celebrations. I experienced . . . what word? what frenzy? how can the union of love and rebellion be hallowed? the earth! In this great temple deserted by the gods all my idols have feet of clay.[16]

Revolt later became for Camus a concept and a richly meaningful standard of value, as he sought in *The Rebel* to deal with the implications of significant political ideas and practices. But whatever additional meanings this term was later to assume in his thought, its rootage in intensely personal reaction to the existentially realized fact of mortality can always be discerned. The connections between his experience and the more universalized implications Camus sought to draw from it are not always logically impeccable, but at least in his own thinking he never strayed far from what his unbending efforts to remain lucid, "not to cheat," had revealed to him as the simple, unquestionable truth.

The "Absurd Man": A Point of Departure

It is important that we keep in mind, in considering Camus's philosophical ideas on the "absurdity" of life, both the experiential basis and meaning of this conception and his attitude toward it in *The Myth of Sisyphus:*

The absurd, hitherto taken as a conclusion, is considered in this essay as a starting-point. In this sense it may be said that there is something provisional in my commentary: one cannot prejudge the position it entails. There will be found here merely the description, in the pure state, of an intellectual malady. No metaphysic, no belief is involved in it for the moment. These are the limits and the only

---

[16]*Ibid.*, 102.

bias of this book. Certain personal experiences urge me to make this clear.[17]

It cannot be too strongly emphasized that Camus never intended to be primarily a "philosopher of the absurd," either in the sense of presenting absurdity as fully descriptive of human existence, as prescriptive of norms for men's actions, or as leading irrevocably to nihilistic conclusions. The absurd was for him always nothing but a point of departure, a place where, bereft of convincing transcendent meanings or imperatives, he felt compelled to take his stand before setting out to chart a path to authentic human existence.

Like the earlier essays, *The Myth of Sisyphus* is experientially rooted and hyper-individualistic in orientation. This is entirely appropriate, as the essay deals with a basic issue confronted by any individual who comes to full self-awareness: "There is but one truly serious philosophical problem, and that is suicide. Judging whether life is or is not worth living amounts to answering the fundamental question of philosophy." [18] This grave and simple question does not imply for Camus any explicit political concern; that is secondary and becomes meaningful to the individual only after he has passed through the personal crisis in which the only question of importance to him is whether or not life is worth the trouble of living.

The experiential source of the absurd in this essay differs considerably from its origins in *Nuptials*. In both instances a conscious awareness of one's inevitable death brings on the feeling of life's absurdity. But in the earlier essays it was the contrast between death-awareness and the great joy of a happy life that gave birth to the absurd. Perhaps because he seeks to address an audience most of whom he assumes have not known the pure physical joys of his own youth, and also to indicate that the absurd lurks universally in the depths of the human condition,

[17]Albert Camus, "The Myth of Sisyphus," in *The Myth of Sisyphus and Other Essays*, 2.
[18]*Ibid.*, 3.

Camus evokes in *Sisyphus* a picture of absurdity emerging from the monotonous round of everyday life. The man who rides the streetcar to work every morning, does his job, eats lunch, works in the afternoon, rides the streetcar home, eats again, and goes to bed—even the man who seems totally enmeshed in and insensitized by such a routine day in and day out—may suddenly one day wonder why he is living as he is.

This sudden, unsought but unforgettable "why" that pierces the weary facade of daily routine is the genesis of the awareness of the absurd for the individual; to begin to think is to begin to be undermined. What is the point of one's activity, one wonders, when the revelatory "why" makes him suddenly aware that only a greater or lesser number of years stands between the present moment and his inevitable death. In an instant when one is wholly caught up in the absurd, he is overwhelmed by the apparent futility of all his efforts and aspirations, for "no code of ethics and no effort are justifiable *a priori* in the face of the cruel mathematics that command our condition." [19]

Camus quickly moves beyond a description of this anguished experience which even the most ordinary man may undergo to a more philosophic consideration of the meaning of absurdity as it confronts the man who seeks intellectually to comprehend the conditions of his existence. First he learns that the world of nature is not cut to man's measure; that is, he cannot truly comprehend the physical universe he inhabits. The scientist's attempts to explain the world end, eventually, in non-sensible myth and metaphor, such as an invisible planetary system in which electrons gravitate around a nucleus, or in light patterns conceived as consisting simultaneously of waves and particles. Thus one cannot truly apprehend through science this world which seems so immediately real to the senses. The physical universe ultimately defies the coherent processes of human rationality.

Yet man instinctively longs for total comprehension, for understanding of that nature in which he participates, and for mean-

[19] *Ibid.*, 16.

ing and eternal duration for his life. Neither the world nor man is, separately, absurd; they are simply incommensurate. Absurdity arises from man's conjunction with and demands upon the world:

This world in itself is not reasonable, that is all that can be said. But what is absurd is the confrontation of this irrational and the wild longing for clarity whose call echoes in the human heart. The absurd depends as much on man as on the world. For the moment it is all that links them together. It binds them one to the other as only hatred can weld two creatures together. This is all I can discern clearly in this measureless universe where my adventure takes place.[20]

Camus has been criticized on this point for asking more of science than it promises or can ever give in explicating the nature of the universe.[21] But such a response misses Camus's essential concern, which is precisely that science has deprived us of a common-sense understanding of nature which it has not replaced and cannot replace with any literally comprehensible vision of the universe. Intellectually, this seems to leave us bereft of any direct relationship to that nature in which our senses make us immediately aware that we participate.

This situation and its origins have been brilliantly explicated by Hannah Arendt. She maintains that the true "Copernican revolution" in Western thought was not a shifting from the earth to the sun as the center of the universe but the distrust of ordinary sensory perception that resulted from Galileo's use of the telescope, which demonstrated that our everyday impressions of nature may well be incorrect. In the quest for more effective ways of dealing with the natural world, mathematical calculations and experimentation were increasingly employed and have proved incredibly successful means of manipulating physical things. Yet such technical achievements cannot "prove" that science deals with an authentic order given in nature; because "scientists for-

[20]*Ibid.*, 21.
[21]See especially A. J. Ayer, "Novelist-Philosophers—VIII: Albert Camus," *Horizon*, XIII (March, 1946), 155–68.

mulate their hypotheses to arrange their experiments and then
use these experiments to verify their hypotheses . . . , they obviously deal with a hypothetical nature." [22]

The very science which is taken as the supreme measure of reality "unfortunately puts man back once more—and now even
more forcefully—into the prison of his own mind, into the limitations of patterns he himself created." The absurdity of man's
condition, in Camus's sense, is that

[t]he moment he wants what all ages before him were capable of
achieving, that is, to experience the reality of what he himself is
not, he will find that nature and the universe "escape him" and that
a universe construed according to the behavior of nature in the
experiment and in accordance with the very principles which man
can translate technically into a working reality lacks all possible
representation. What is new here is not that things exist of which
he cannot form an image—such "things" were always known and
among them, for instance, belonged the "soul"—but that the material
things we see and represent and against which he had measured
immaterial things for which we can form no images should likewise
be "unimaginable." With the disappearance of the sensually given
world, the transcendent world disappears as well, and with it the
possibility of transcending the material world in concept and thought.
It is therefore not surprising that the new universe is not only
"practically inaccessible but not even thinkable," for "however we
think it, it is wrong; not perhaps quite as meaningless as a 'triangular
circle,' but much more so than a 'winged lion.' " [23]

This radical disjunction between the natural world we perceive
every day and the inescapable perspective of modern science is
considered by Camus as one significant evidence of the absurdity of the human condition. The intellect is incapable, even by
employing the most powerful tools it has fabricated, of demonstrating even an essential commensurability between man and the
nature of which he is a part. Intellectual inquiry into the nature
of things cannot quell the feeling of absurdity but merely intensifies it.

[22]Hannah Arendt, *The Human Condition* (Garden City, N.Y.: Doubleday
Anchor Books, 1959), 254–61.
[23]*Ibid.*, pp. 261–62.

The theme of man's communion with the natural world scarcely appears in *The Myth of Sisyphus,* yet when Camus seeks to discern meaning in the world he is caught up in immediate experience of it and his intellect encounters frustration: "Here are trees and I know their gnarled surface, water and I feel its taste. These scents of grass and stars at night, certain evenings when the heart relaxes—how shall I negate this world whose power and strength I feel? Yet all the knowledge on earth will give me nothing to assure me that this world is mine." [24]

Although science seems only to dissect and classify the world, and its attempts at ultimate explanations end in conclusions our senses cannot grasp, Camus reasserts the authority for him of his immediate experience of physical nature: "What need had I of so many efforts? The soft lines of these hills and the hand of evening on this troubled heart teach me much more. I have returned to my beginnings." [25] The absurd, insofar as it involves man's relationship to nature, is only rational or theoretical incommensurability between them; it is still possible to find experiential meaning in immediate enjoyment of the world.

Another significant theme that recurs in *The Myth of Sisyphus* is the refusal of any conception of an after-life, in preference for the known certainty of our present finite existence. This means that we cannot know whether the world has any transcendent meaning:

What can a meaning outside my condition mean to me? I can understand only in human terms. What I touch, what resists me— that is what I understand. And these two certainties—my appetite for the absolute and for unity and the impossibility of reducing this world to a rational and reasonable principle—I also know that I cannot reconcile them. What other truth can I admit without lying, without bringing in a hope I lack and which means nothing within the limits of my condition? [26]

There are two consequences of this resolution to accept the reality only of man's earthly existence. First, the conscientious re-

[24]"The Myth of Sisyphus," 19.
[25]*Ibid.,* 20.
[26]*Ibid.,* 51.

fusal of eternal life gives one the only genuine freedom knowable
to man. And second, a legitimate and essential sphere is demar-
cated within which human reason may operate effectively.

Metaphysical freedom is of no concern to the absurd man; the
ancient philosophical debate between proponents of free will and
of determinism is irrelevant to one who believes neither in a God
who controls his actions nor in an after-life in which he will be
judged according to the use he has made of his capacity for free
choice. The only meaningful conception of freedom is that of the
prisoner or of the citizen in confrontation with political authority, that is, "freedom of thought and action. Now if the absurd
cancels all my chances of eternal freedom, it restores and mag-
nifies, on the other hand, my freedom of action. That privation
of hope and future means an increase in man's availability." [27]

An existential awareness of death and of its utter finality for him
informs the absurd man that "there is no future. Henceforth
this is the reason for my inner freedom." [28] There is no point in
living for the "later ons" of the world, in vain hope of fulfilling
one's proper role in life to qualify for a future reward. The absurd man is free to live with passionate awareness in each successive moment, and "it is clear that death and the absurd are
here the principles of the only reasonable freedom: that which
a human heart can experience and live." [29] It is apparent that
both sheer physical freedom of action and an expanded realm of
free choice brought to consciousness by awareness of the absurd
are of great value to Camus. The nature, value, and limits of
freedom came to be centrally significant in his political theory of
rebellion.

The limitation of Camus's concern to this world and man's
present life implies a certain sphere of efficacy for human reason. True, reason cannot discern the meaning of existence, and
the confrontation of reason with the impenetrability of the world

[27] *Ibid.*, 56–57.
[28] *Ibid.*, 58.
[29] *Ibid.*, 60.

constitutes the metaphysical basis of the absurd. But in its futile quest for the absolute the absurd mind discovers that "reason is useless and there is nothing beyond reason." [30] This implies that reason is essential and to a significant degree effective for dealing with human problems, that men share a common, if limited, rationality. (Camus's limitations as a philosophical thinker are evidenced here by the brevity and lack of precision in his consideration of the meaning of "reason." In practice, he seems to have meant by it a commonsensical rationality more circumscribed than the ontological reason of either philosophical realism or Hegelian dialectics but less restricted than the wholly ends-means calculative rationality of logical positivism. Beyond this generalization it is difficult to discern precisely what his conception of reason entailed.) A French critic has remarked that at this point the absurd appears to become for Camus not so much the incoherent as the inexplicable. It seems, for instance, impossible to explain the existence in a disordered and unjust world of beings who demand order and justice. But if one is such a being, why should he not accept himself as he is? Devoid of ultimate explanations for his existence, he is aware that he is quite capable of understanding many things that are important to him. "From the moment he recognizes 'this efficacious but limited reason,' we can discern what Camus's thought seeks: . . . a positive humanism and a relative optimism." [31]

Camus's concern with happiness reappears in *The Myth of Sisyphus*; in fact, it assumes a focal place in his version of the ancient myth that furnishes the title for this essay. As Camus presented him, Sisyphus is the prototype of the absurd hero. He scorned the gods, despised death, and had a passionate love for life. For his impudence he was condemned by the denizens of Olympus to spend eternity rolling a mammoth boulder to the top of a steep hill, from the summit of which the stone always tum-

[30]*Ibid.*, 35.
[31]Pierre-Henri Simon, *L'Homme en procès* (Neuchâtel: Baconnière, 1950), 107–108.

bled back to the plain below. Camus imagines that Sisyphus' descent to the plain need not take place in despair and monotony—at times he may even be joyful. He is lucidly aware of his fate, that his rock and his task, though his inescapable destiny, are wholly his own. Within this compass—constricted though it may be—Sisyphus is master of his reactions to his fate.

For Camus, Sisyphus, with his meaningless task and his inescapable condition, is like the absurd man, conscious of his ultimately fatal destiny but seeking to exhaust the present potential for happiness. "Happiness and the absurd are ... inseparable. It would be a mistake to say that happiness necessarily springs from the absurd discovery. It happens as well that the feeling of the absurd springs from happiness." [32] As we have seen, it was by the latter route that the young Camus had first become aware of the absurd, as revealed in the irreconcilability of his love for the happy life and his awareness of its ultimate extinction.

Without hope but fully open to immediate experience, the absurd man, like Sisyphus, finds in happiness the mainstay of his existence:

Sisyphus teaches the higher fidelity that negates the gods and raises rocks. He too concludes that all is well. This universe henceforth without a master seems to him neither sterile nor futile. Each atom of that stone, each mineral flake of that night-filled mountain, in itself forms a world. The struggle itself toward the heights is enough to fill a man's heart. One must imagine Sisyphus happy.[33]

Happiness and the absurd are linked by the iron bonds of experiential logic. If life is wholly mortal and if our longing for ultimate meaning can never be fulfilled, joyous exhaustion of that which is immediately given is the most reasonable course to pursue: "From the moment man . . . chooses to play the absurd role, the most absurd thing would be not to desire happiness." [34]

[32]"The Myth of Sisyphus," 122.
[33]Ibid., 123.
[34]André Rousseaux, Littérature du vingtième siècle (Paris: Albin Michel, 1949), III, 80.

A fourth recurring emphasis, even more evident in *The Myth of Sisyphus* than in the earlier essays, is Camus's insistence upon the necessity of absolute personal integrity, of faithfulness to what one truly knows, feels, and experiences. Hence he clings tenaciously to the absurdity which has been revealed to him in experience, insisting that it must be coped with and not evaded. Although he derives some of his concepts, in particular his view of the limitations of reason, from existential thinkers such as Kierkegaard and Karl Jaspers, he criticizes them for failure to remain true to the absurd, which their own experience and reflective intelligence has discovered. Such existentialists, Camus declares, take an unjustified "leap" to some transcendent principle which supposedly gives meaning to the world and to human life; principally they turn to religion, deifying the absurd which they cannot comprehend. This kind of failure to remain true to the absurd by living with its reality Camus calls "philosophical suicide," and he seeks to avoid committing it.

Likewise he responds negatively to the question, with which the essay begins, whether one should literally kill himself. The absurd is the rock-bottom truth about existence that we discover in our experience; to commit suicide would destroy the opposition between the mind and the ultimately incomprehensible universe, negating one of the terms of the absurd and violating the truth of absurdity. From a purely logical standpoint, this conclusion that suicide is unjustifiable is hardly convincing. If, as Camus appears to assume, one has to account for his actions only to oneself, suicide would negate the necessity of accountability; obviously a dead man cannot hold himself responsible. Camus actually rejects suicide not on logical grounds but because he believes that the individual *can* find meaning in life, even if ultimate significance can never be discerned.

Hence he chooses to be faithful to his personal experience of absurdity, in order "to be consistent." He reports seeing in Italian museums small painted screens once used by priests to conceal the sight of the scaffold from the eyes of men soon to be executed. "The leap in all its forms, rushing into the divine or the eternal, surrendering to the illusions of the everyday or of the idea—all these screens hide the absurd." [35] To retain one's integrity it is essential to do without a screen, to live in lucid awareness of death and the absurd: "Reduced to its simplest expression, Camus's thought may be summarized in a single question: in the eyes of the condemned man who refuses supernatural consolation, what values remain?" [36] The quest for these residual values cannot begin, Camus believed, until one is committed to the experience of the absurd and has pledged faithfulness to its mortal certainty.

Finally, there reappears the motif of rebellion—"the certainty of a crushing fate, without the resignation that ought to accompany it." [37] Revolt against the absurd is essential to a continuing awareness of its reality; unless one struggles with the absurd, the experience in which it has come to be known may quickly fade in intensity, and the potential meaning of this discovery for one's life may never be realized. Camus declares: "At this juncture, I cannot conceive that a skeptical metaphysics can be joined to an ethics of renunciation." [38]

Again Camus's effort at logical justification is faulty; on the verbal level he appears simply to depend upon an equivocal word to defend the necessity of rebellion. Even if one accepts his idea of the absurd as the "opposition" between man's rationality and an ultimately incomprehensible world, there is no logically compelling reason for agreeing that this condition necessarily entails "opposition" as revolt against the absurdity of this conjunction of man and the world. Opposition in the first sense simply means incommensurability; it is the conclusion of an ultimately futile struggle to grasp the absolute. It would be just as much—and just as little—a logical response to this per-

[35]"The Myth of Sisyphus," 91.
[36]Rachel Bespaloff, "Le monde du condamné à mort," *Esprit*, XVIII (January, 1950), 1.
[37]"The Myth of Sisyphus," 54.
[38]*Ibid.,* 55.

ception to sink into weary resignation as it would be to continue to struggle against a condition that one knows to be both absurd and inescapable. It is not entirely unfair to state that Camus's revolt in this context "is a blind leap exactly like the passage from the absurd to hope for which he chided the existentialists." [39]

But Camus's rebellion against the absurd is not really directed at the rational incommensurability between man and the universe; that is only a possible intellectual frustration, adding to but not constituting the fundamental absurdity of man's condition— the conjunction of experienced happiness and a lucid awareness of its inescapable cessation in death. Rebellion, which keeps continuously alive an awareness of the absurd, requires a whole-hearted embracing of life, a perpetual struggle against death.

Hence the absurd man seeks to live each moment to the full; this implies a quantitative, rather than a qualitative, standard for living. But Camus does not draw out explicit quantitative principles to guide the absurd man's life; he merely seeks to present examples of how the absurd life may be practiced. And, significantly, he cautions: "Do I need to develop the idea that an example is not necessarily an example to be followed (even less so, if possible, in the absurd world) and that these illustrations are not therefore models?" [40]

At this stage Camus was exceedingly hesitant to offer any advice on how to live, and it is not at all certain that he sympathizes with the exemplary persons he sketches. These quantitative lives are those of Don Juan, the actor, the conqueror, and the artist. The first seeks to make love to as many women as possible, the second to create an endless succession of ephemeral illusions in order to "live doubly," the third struggles for human freedom, and the fourth finds his vocation in imaginative creativity. Each is continuously aware that life has no significance

[39]Emmanuel Mounier, "Albert Camus ou l'appel des humiliés," *Esprit,* XVIII (January, 1950), 36.
[40]"The Myth of Sisyphus," 68.

transcending the particular moments in which he lives it. Of these examples, the conqueror is most portentous for the development of Camus's ideas on politics.

In order to explore more fully the world of absurdity, we shall examine Camus's most full-blown illustration of an absurd life, the narrator of his first novel, *The Stranger*. Parenthetically, I do not believe that my attempt to draw philosophic meanings from this work does violence to its artistic integrity. The principal support for my position on this matter is the simple fact, which should become quite obvious, that Camus's novels are consciously philosophical. And as specific evidence for this position there is this notation from his journal, written when he had just begun to think about the work that was to be published in 1947 as his second novel: *"The Plague* has a social meaning *and* a metaphysical meaning. It's exactly the same. Such ambiguity is in *The Stranger* too." [41]

Meursault, a sub-clerk in an Algerian office, tells a very simple—but absurd—story. It begins with the death of his mother in a rest home several miles from Algiers. Meursault takes the bus to the small town where his mother's body lies, sits all night near her coffin, and the next day walks behind the hearse on the way to the church. Physical sensations of heat and discomfort remain with him as the primary impressions of this experience. After returning to the city, Meursault goes to the beach the following day, picks up a girl whom he had known slightly, takes her to see a comic movie, and brings her home to spend the night with him.

The next day he inadvertently becomes involved with Raymond, a neighbor who is purported to be a pimp. But Meursault is indifferent to Raymond's way of living and does not object to assisting him in a tawdry scheme to get revenge on his mistress. Raymond interprets Meursault's indifferent collusion for a show of friendship and invites the clerk and the girl Marie, now Meursault's mistress, to a weekend at a beach cottage. They are followed to the beach by two Arabs who are relatives of Raymond's

[41]*Notebooks, 1942–1951*, p. 36 (entry of October, 1942).

aggrieved mistress. After an altercation in which one of the Arabs slashes Raymond's arm, Meursault and Raymond return to the cottage. Meursault then decides to take a walk in the blinding mid-afternoon sun. In his pocket is a revolver which he had taken from Raymond to keep him out of trouble. Coming upon one of the Arabs sitting in the shade of a boulder, Meursault tightens his hand around the gun, and when the Arab, without shifting his position, reaches toward his knife, Meursault is suddenly blinded by the intense sunlight and loses all consciousness of his actions. As if by impulse, his finger tightens on the trigger and the gun fires, killing the Arab. Still without any conscious reason, Meursault fires four times more into the inert body.

Arrested and, after several months, brought to trial, Meursault is startled to hear the prosecutor accusing him of cold-blooded, premeditated murder. An effort is made to prove the accused's callous and criminal character by calling witnesses who testify to Meursault's impassiveness and apparent lack of grief at his mother's funeral. The prosecutor declaims that any man who would attend a comic film and take a mistress the day after his mother's burial is obviously a criminal at heart. In effect, the prosecutor ties together events which in Meursault's experience were entirely discontinuous and unrelated. Testifying in his own behalf, Meursault's only explanation for shooting the Arab is that it happened "because of the sun." Against this ridiculous defense the prosecutor easily wins the case, and Meursault is sentenced to be decapitated.

Alone in the death cell, Meursault is at last visited by the prison chaplain, whom he had persistently refused to see. When the priest begins to speak of sin, repentance, and eternal life, Meursault loses his customary impassiveness; he begins to scream out denials and denunciations to the chaplain, and prison guards are barely able to restrain him from striking the priest. In the end Meursault is left in his cell awaiting his execution on the morrow.

It is important to recognize that Meursault is an incarnation

of the absurd life and that even before the story begins he has
gone through some kind of experience that has given him at
least a minimal consciousness of absurdity. That he is not a
Nietzschean intellectual is Camus's way of pointing out that absurdity can strike the most ordinary individual today, that it is
a gray eminence haunting all men. It is also a further indication
that the absurd is an experiential reality, not a conclusion arrived at through ratiocination.

At an early point in the narrative, Meursault's employer asks
him if he would prefer a transfer to the Paris branch of the
firm:

> I said yes, but that, basically, it made no difference to me. He
> asked me then if I wasn't interested in a change of life. I replied
> that one never changes his life, that in any case everything was on a
> par and that my life didn't displease me in the least. He seemed
> rather frustrated and told me that I never gave a direct reply, that
> I had no ambition, and that this was disastrous in business. Then
> I returned to work. I would have preferred not to annoy him, but I
> didn't see any reason for changing my life. In thinking about it
> carefully, I concluded that I wasn't unhappy. When I was a student,
> I had a great deal of ambition of that sort. But when I was forced
> to give up my studies, I came very quickly to the realization that
> that wasn't really important.[42]

Material ambitions, "changing one's life"—these values of the
bourgeois world in which Meursault works are insignificant trifles to him. He had experienced the absurd when he came to
realize that these things were not "really important," that what
is of importance for him is total fidelity to his own feelings and
experience and the immediate, concrete joy of physical sensations. Fifteen years after writing *The Stranger,* Camus remarked
of its central character:

> For me Meursault is not a dolt but a poor and naked man, a lover
> of the sun that leaves no shadows. Far from being deprived of all
> feelings, a profound, because implicit, passion animates him—the

[42]Albert Camus, *L'Etranger,* ed. Germaine Brée and Carlos Lynes, Jr.
(New York: Appleton-Century-Crofts, 1955), 62.

passion for the absolute and for truth. This is still a negative truth, the truth of being and of feeling, but one without which no conquest of self or of the world will ever be possible.

One would not be far off the mark to read in *The Stranger* the story of a man who, with no attitude of heroism, consents to die for truth.[43]

Meursault's utter honesty consists in his refusal to express any sentiment he does not actually feel. The discomfort of his chair and the hot, dusty road impressed themselves upon him most vividly at his mother's funeral; he felt no particular grief—what could he do for the dead? Instead of repentance, he expressed only the bored irritation he actually felt after the pointless event. Likewise he does not plead self-defense when on trial for murder, because he truly feels that the oppressive heat of the sun, and not the threat of the Arab's attacking him, caused him to fire the revolver. Meursault "expresses what he is; he refuses to blow up his feelings, and immediately society feels itself threatened." [44] Meursault finds no meaning or purposes in the disparate events of his life; each is for him an immediate, self-contained, and irreplaceable experience. Society imposes a false meaning upon his deeds—and by implication, upon life—and condemns him for "not cheating."

The radical absence of concern for transcendent meaning in life is a trait which marks Meursault as an absurd man. For example, the inquiring magistrate who interviews Meursault prior to his trial attempts to persuade him to become a Christian. When Meursault says that he does not believe in God, the magistrate is incensed. He asserts that every man actually believes in God, even those who turn away from Him. "This was his conviction, and if he were ever led to doubt it, his life would have no meaning. 'Do you want my life to be meaningless?' he exclaimed. In my opinion this didn't concern me, and I told him so." [45]

[43] "Avant-propos," in *ibid.*, viii.
[44]*Ibid.*, vii.
[45]*Ibid.*, 89.

Meursault experiences his life as sheer quantity of sensation; there are no intrinsically significant details, for to him the question of the meaningfulness of life as a whole is simply pointless: "Prisoner of his limited human condition, life appears senseless to him at every moment, not because of any intellectual reasons, but from immediate evidence." [46]

Certain experiences, however, do mean something to Meursault—though not in the sense of bestowing upon his existence any kind of transcendent significance. As he sits in the courtroom, tired and sweltering in the summer heat, he hears through a window the sound of an ice cream vendor's bell. At once a flood of memories breaks in upon him; he thinks regretfully of things which are now absent from his life—"the poorest and most tenacious of my joys: summer smells, the section of the city that I love, a certain kind of evening sky, Marie's laughter and her dresses." [47]

But Meursault does not reveal himself as a "wholly absurd" man until his decisive act of rebellion. The chaplain who attempts to present to him the consolations of religion becomes for Meursault the embodiment of all the dishonesty and bad faith that condemned him to death for not weeping at his mother's funeral. Meursault clings tenaciously to this life and its physical sensations, and the priest's talk of spiritual love and the after-life are more than he can stomach:

The lives of others, a mother's love—how did these concern me? Or his god, the lives people choose, destinies that others decide upon—what did these have to do with me, since a single destiny was to select me—and along with me millions of privileged people who, like him, spoke of themselves as my brothers. Did he understand, did he really understand? Everybody was privileged. There is no one except privileged people. All the others would also be condemned some day. And he as well—he would be condemned. [48]

[46]Albert Ollivier, "Albert Camus et le refus de l'éternel," *L'Arche,* (October-November, 1944), 159.
[47]*L'Etranger,* 122.
[48]*Ibid.,* 137.

This piercing awareness of men's common destiny of death brings to Meursault a keener realization than ever before that immediate happiness, the simple joys that a person can experience within his condition, no matter how limited, exhaust the goodness that he can know. Although Meursault had experienced "intimations of the absurd" long before this moment and had lived an absurd life, the rationale for his mode of existence is clearly articulated only when he openly revolts against dishonesty and death. After his violently emotional outburst he feels purged of evil, emptied of hope, and exposes himself fully "for the first time to the tender indifference of the world. In finding it to be so similar to myself, in fact so brotherly, I felt that I had been happy and that I yet was." A man indifferent to imposed meanings and ignorant of intellectual puzzles finds a strange immediate communion with an impenetrable and equally indifferent world. Intensity of sensation is all in all: "So that everything might be consummated, so that I could feel less lonely, there remained to me the hope that there would be many spectators at my execution and that they would greet me with cries of hatred." [49]

The interlocking themes of absurdity and concrete sensual happiness give to *The Stranger* its form and substance. The absurd man lives out his simple destiny, exhausting each successive moment of the present, remaining utterly true to his experience, finally rebelling against hypocrisy and death and finding even within the narrow spatial and temporal confines of a death cell the spark of life that continues to nourish his joy. Meursault's story is not intended to supply us with a moral lesson or with a model for living, because he does not go beyond confrontation with the absurd. And for Camus the absurd was always only a starting-point, never the conclusion of his thought.

Even within the confines of his exploration of the world of absurdity, Camus was manifestly not content to settle upon this point of departure as revelatory of fixed standards for human behavior. One of the examples of an absurd life in *The Myth of*

[49]*Ibid.*, 138.

Sisyphus is indicative of the political implications Camus was later to draw more clearly from his existential analysis of the human condition. "The Conqueror" is not a Caesarist ruler but is rather an "absurd" struggler against the dehumanizing forces of the contemporary age. (He is obviously modeled after the heroes of Malraux's early novels, which Camus greatly admired.) The Conqueror proclaims:

"Conscious that I cannot stand aloof from my time, I have decided to be an integral part of it. This is why I esteem the individual only because he strikes me as ridiculous and humiliated. Knowing that there are no victorious causes, I have a liking for lost causes: they require an uncontaminated soul, equal to its defeat as to its temporary victories. For anyone who feels bound up with this world's fate, the clash of civilizations has something agonizing about it. I have made that anguish mine at the same time that I wanted to join in. Between history and the eternal I have chosen history because I like certainties. Of it, at least, I am certain, and how can I deny this force crushing me?" [50]

The Conqueror admits that action is in itself useless, for the only significant action would be the remaking of man and the earth. This more than Herculean task can never be accomplished, but the Conqueror feels a necessity to act as if it were possible. For in the pathway of struggle he is led to the flesh, his only certainty. His futile combat, waged in the name of the poor and the oppressed, is in reality a perpetual active protest against the existence of evil in the world (the germ of Camus's later distinction between historical and metaphysical revolt). But evil can be fought only through historical action which, however, remains fully cognizant of its final impotence: " 'I maintain my human contradiction. I establish my lucidity in the midst of what negates it. I exalt man before what crushes him, and my freedom, my revolt, and my passion come together then in that tension, that lucidity, and that vast repetition.' " [51]

The Conqueror remains ever aware of man's mortal destiny,

[50] "The Myth of Sisyphus," 85–86.
[51] *Ibid.*, 87–88.

but he discovers in the midst of his struggles an amazing grandeur in men. He perceives men's mutilation but also finds one strange " 'luxury' "—" 'that of human relations. . . . in this vulnerable universe everything that is human and solely human assumes a more vivid meaning. . . . Taut faces, threatened fraternity, such strong and chaste friendship among men—these are the true riches because they are transitory.' " [52]

The eternal is irrelevant to the Conqueror's thinking and actions; he draws his opposition from all "churches, divine or political," which claim possession of eternal truth. Truths that he can touch, or that his heart cannot deny, are the only verities that concern him. His struggle has to do only with mortal men in the here and now. Mortality is inescapable but, nevertheless, gives impetus to his efforts: "In the rebel's universe, death exalts injustice. It is the supreme abuse.' " [53]

Although Camus claims to portray the Conqueror "without value judgments," simply as one possible incarnation of a self-consciously absurd life, this man's convictions are among those which characterize the true rebel of Camus's later writings. Rebellion against death and suffering for the sake not of religious or ideological abstractions but of simple common humanity Camus came to see as the most authentic way of living out one's destiny. Even here in *The Myth of Sisyphus,* which focuses almost exclusively on the anguish of the individual bereft of cosmic meaning, a portrait of the clear-sighted rebel engaged in a vocation of political struggle occupies an important place in Camus's thinking.

Indeed, in his earliest years of maturity Camus was never a self-isolated romantic individualist. As a writer for a left-wing newspaper in Algiers in the late 1930's, he became deeply interested and involved in political controversies. He supported the Popular Front movement in France but protested the Blum government's failure to aid the Loyalists in the Spanish Civil War. He

[52]*Ibid.,* 88.
[53]*Ibid.,* 90.

vigorously protested what he saw as a politically motivated pros-
ecution of a grain-distribution official and some of his Moslem
assistants, and his journalistic efforts were probably helpful in
finally securing an acquittal in the case. He led in many attacks
on members of the French government in Algeria for their reactionary and oppressive policies toward the Moslem population
and was one of the first Algerians of French descent to make
broad-scale attacks on colonial policy in North Africa.[54]

In these early years Camus had only begun, in a tentative fashion, to work out a rationale for political involvement and criteria
of evaluation for political life. Characteristically, extensive experience preceded self-conscious philosophizing, for Camus could
never see the legitimacy of *a priori* fabrication of principles in
isolation from the realm to which they are supposed to apply.

That he was grappling intellectually with the problems of man's
corporate existence is evident, however, in an essay written in
1940:

I do not believe in reason enough to subscribe to progress, or to any
philosophy of history. But I at least believe that men have never
ceased to advance in realizing what their destiny amounts to. We
have not overcome our condition, but we are better acquainted with
it. We know that we are within a contradiction, but that we must
refuse this contradiction and do what must be done to reduce it.
Our human task is to find ways of diminishing the infinite anguish
of free souls. We must bind up the wounded, make justice conceivable in a world that is so obviously unjust, and happiness meaningful for people who have been poisoned by the misfortune of
this century.[55]

This "contradiction" in the human condition is, of course, the
disjunction between man's desire for unending happiness and the
inescapable fact of death. But in this essay Camus intimates that

---

[54]For details on these matters, see the fine book on Camus's journalistic
writings by Emmett Parker, *Albert Camus: The Artist in the Arena*
(Madison and Milwaukee: University of Wisconsin Press, 1965), Chaps.
1 and 2.
[55]Albert Camus, "Les Amandiers," in *L'Eté* (Paris: Gallimard, 1954),
71–72.

the contradiction can be made less painful if life is made more fully human—freer, more just, and happier. Apparently this lessening in the intensity of the essential contradiction of human existence is to result from the *struggle* against bondage, injustice, and unhappiness, for Camus had already indicated that anything which makes life more attractive at the same time exalts its absurdity—that is, heightens awareness of the fundamental human predicament. It may not be off the mark to discern in nascent form at this early stage of Camus's intellectual development his mature conviction that fundamental human problems will persist whatever progress may be made in the improvement of social and political institutions and that any effort aimed at perfecting mankind by collective means is doomed to failure.

Camus's play *Caligula,* written in 1938 though not produced for the stage until 1945, also contains intimations of the young writer's concern for man's lot in the modern state. The Roman emperor Caligula is plunged into despair upon the death of Drusilla, his sister and mistress. He emerges from this traumatic experience with the simple but shattering conviction that man is a creature who dies and is not happy; he has become acutely conscious of the ultimate absurdity of human life.

Apparently in a frenzy, yet in reality completely lucid, Caligula sets out to remake the absurd order of things by striving for the impossible; the symbol of this yearning is his desire to possess the moon. He transvaluates the values by which the empire has been governed, and great numbers of "virtuous" men are put to death in his determined quest for the impossible—a world in which men will be happy and will not die. Caligula uses his vast power in an effort to negate the world as we know it, asserting: "This world has no importance; once a man realizes that, he wins his freedom." [56]

Cherea, who becomes the leader of the opposition to Caligula, shares the emperor's belief in the absurdity and horror of a world

[56] Albert Camus, *Caligula,* Act I, in *Caligula and Cross Purpose,* trans. Stuart Gilbert (London: New Directions, 1947), 21.

of unhappy mortals. This commonness of perspective with Caligula makes Cherea's decision to plot against his ruler an agonizing choice; unable to be dogmatic or even very articulately to provide a rationale for himself, Cherea nevertheless elects to head the conspiracy which ends in Caligula's assassination.

This play can be interpreted, without distortion, I believe, as a premonition of Camus's mature views on revolt. Both Caligula and Cherea are rebels against the absurdity of the human condition. Caligula's "metaphysical rebellion," as Camus was later to call it, takes the form of a claim to total freedom—a liberty completely devoid of regulative principles or boundaries. Like Dostoevsky's Ivan Karamazov, a pivotal figure in *The Rebel*, Caligula in effect proclaims that if God is Dead—if there is no discernible transcendent order of things—everthing is permitted; freedom becomes nihilistic destruction and oppression. Cherea, another "absurd man," feels that it makes no sense to react to mortality and unhappiness by taking the side of death and misery. Though unable clearly to articulate the rationale for his decision, Cherea instinctively rebels against the emperor's destructive nihilism by siding with men's desire for happiness. He concludes that true freedom carries within itself inherent limitations, and just before he is killed, Caligula also comes to profess the same belief: "I have chosen a wrong path, a path that leads to nothing. My freedom isn't the right one." [57]

Yet, in the final line of the play Caligula cries out, as he is being stabbed to death, "I'm still alive!" [58] Not only does the absurd survive the death of this particular man who had experienced its full weight, but the threat of nihilism, which intensifies absurdity by consciously adding to the sum total of death and suffering, also persists as a challenge and a threat to mankind. Clearly, in this early work Camus was already groping toward an elucidation of the inner meaning of revolt against absurdity and of the implications of this rebellion for ethics and politics.

[57]*Ibid.*, Act IV, 94.
[58]*Ibid.*, 95.

The absurd was for Camus a wrenching and inescapable existential reality. It was his way of expressing his inability to discern either a cosmic or a divine order of which man is a part and which makes human life ultimately coherent; in his experience Camus could find no such set of transcendent meanings. There are no laws or norms accessible to man through revelation or from nature to govern the manifold complexities of his existence.

But this conviction never entailed for Camus the conclusion, as it does for the nihilist, that no valid standards for the conduct of life can be discerned by man. To find them we must look not to the heavens but to ourselves, exploring the innermost recesses of our being and our experience. In order to cope with the absurd, and move beyond it, Camus believed in using the philosophic method summed up in this notation from his journal: "The greatest saving one can make in the order of thought is to accept the unintelligibility of the world—and to pay attention to man." [59]

Directing our attention in this way would lead, Camus claimed, not to nihilistic passivity or destructiveness but, if we are faithful to our perceptions, to a realm of human significance: "Raising the question of the absurd world amounts to asking: 'Are we going to accept despair, without doing anything?' I suppose that no one honest can answer yes." [60] Increasingly Camus turned to the world of the inter-human in order more fully to grasp and to communicate the meanings which, however paltry they may seem if measured by cosmic standards, are truths that spread around us, as we stand our ground before the ultimate darkness of the human condition, a circle of light.

[59]*Notebooks, 1942–1951*, p. 86 (entry of November, 1943).
[60]*Ibid.*, 89 (entry of November, 1943).

III
Human Nature and the Human Condition: The World of Communion

DURING THE latter years of the Second World War, Camus's thinking turned increasingly to the realm of relationships among men. He sought to express and to work out a rationale for his efforts to move beyond the absurd to the affirmation of regulative human values. The chaotic circumstances of the war years provided the matrix for and additional stimulus to Camus's development beyond his point of departure toward the construction of a positive morality, both for the individual and for society. We noted in the preceding chapter that intimations of such a constructive effort are present in Camus's early works, and *The Plague,* his second novel and obviously an affirmative declaration of values, was begun in 1941, prior even to the publication of the absurdist works, *The Stranger* and *The Myth of Sisyphus.* It is apparent that Camus's postwar concerns and perspective represented no radical break with a youthful nihilism, as some critics have claimed. He was never a nihilist, and the absurd was never more than a starting-point in an attempt to work out coherently the implications of his personal experience and perceptions.

But, as a persistently existential thinker, Camus must have been deeply affected by his involvement in the French Resistance effort.

A profound sense of human solidarity in the struggle against evil and oppression, a visceral contempt for totalitarianism and its degradation of man's existence, an upsurging faith in the potentialities of human sympathy and intelligence—these beliefs began to assume definitive form in Camus's thinking during the difficult years of the Occupation.

Perhaps the fundamental question which Camus addressed to himself and to his readers, and to which he sought continually to provide at least provisional and fragmentary answers, was simply, what does it mean to be a man? In his early works he responded by emphasizing man's alienation from transcendent meanings and by affirming man's desire for happiness commingled with an awareness of mortality that leads to a feeling of the ultimate absurdity of life. But, whatever its final futility, he also stresses the necessity of rebellion against death and absurdity. In the works which followed the absurdist writings he saw with increasing clarity that being a man requires broadening one's rebellion so that it encompasses resistance to forces which threaten the lives of all men and not merely oneself: "What we can see Camus defining, simply but with difficulty, is a way of being a man and of helping the humiliated to become men once more. This is the only way that Sisyphus can reply to the silence of the world." [1]

In the four *Letters to a German Friend*, written and published clandestinely during the Occupation, Camus clearly rejects the nihilistic conclusions which, to many, had seemed latent in his earlier works. In these eloquent essays addressed to an imaginary German compatriot on the side of National Socialism, Camus admits to a deep affinity between his absurdism and the intellectual nihilism that he saw as an important influence in the acceptance, even by many intelligent Germans, of Hitler's regime. After all, if life has no discernible ultimate significance, why not make one's own meaning through personal commitment to the most powerful force on the contemporary historical scene? Camus admits the great—perhaps insuperable—difficulty of presenting a per-

[1] Gilbert Sigaux, "Avec Albert Camus," *Preuves*, IV (January, 1954), 80.

suasive logical refutation of this position. Yet it was a choice which he had refused to make and the results of which he adamantly opposed.

In an effort to justify his own choice, both to others and to himself, he declared:

> I have chosen justice in order to remain faithful to the earth. I still believe that this world has no transcendent meaning. But I know that something in it has a meaning and that is man, because he is the only being who demands one. This world at least has human truth, and our task is to give man his justification in the face of destiny itself. And there are none but human justifications; it is man that we must save if we want to salvage the conception of life to which we cling.[2]

In these "letters," Camus did not work out a coherent rationale for the human values to which he had given his allegiance. Confronted with the pestilence of Nazism, one could not "know" and "cure" at the same time, as the chronicler of *The Plague* was to put it; the initial necessity was to choose the side of victimized humanity and engage all one's energies in fighting the battles thrust upon men by their history. But when the immediate crisis had passed, Camus began an effort to "know" why man is to be defended against oppression: "Camus cannot avoid setting forth a new system of beliefs and acts of faith. Far from negating all transcendence, he gives back a structure to a shrunken world limited to man, but a place wherein things take on meaning." [3] As early as 1945, in an essay entitled "Remarque sur la révolte," Camus had begun to articulate a defense of the existence of moral standards transcending men's fluctuating desires and actions. The source of these values was not, however, divine or cosmic order but significant and fertile human experiences and feelings.

Development and enrichment of Camus's vision of the human condition are clearly evident in *The Plague*, published in 1947.

[2]Albert Camus *Lettres à un ami allemand* (Lausanne: Marguerat, 1946), 72–73.
[3]R.-M. Albères, *Les hommes traqués* (Paris: La Nouvelle Edition, 1953), 206.

This novel can be viewed as a passion play in which suffering humanity is the central figure. It is written as a chronicle of events which take place during a bubonic plague epidemic in the Algerian city of Oran. The chronicler, we learn near the end of the account, is Dr. Bernard Rieux, a young physician who takes a leading role in combating the disease.

The course of events is presented in a straightforward and uncomplicated manner. One day rats begin to die by the thousands in the streets of the city. Soon they disappear, but strange symptoms appear in persons stricken by illness. Within a few days it is obvious that Oran has been struck by plague, and the city authorities, who had at first hesitated to take drastic action, close off Oran from the outside world. The death toll continues to mount, despite concerted effort by men from many callings and backgrounds to halt the course of the plague. After several gray and hideous months the plague begins to slacken in its fury and then disappears, as mysteriously as it had come. The gates of the city are reopened; lovers and husbands and wives who had been separated when the plague broke out are reunited—except for those like Dr. Rieux, whose wife had died in a distant sanitorium during the days when no one was allowed to leave the city.

The Plague is obviously an allegory; Camus specifically indicates as much on the title page. On one level it is an interpretation of the critical events in France during the Occupation and of the whole world of Nazi totalitarianism with its death-camps. On a more general political level, "it is also the age of inhumanity, of the God-State, of the sovereign machine, of irresponsible administration. Hence the anonymous character of *The Plague* assumes meaning—its characters are those whom we encounter every day, the anonymous crowd of the condemned." [4]

On yet a third level, this work represents a renewal of Camus's philosophical exploration of man's nature and situation. Just as this concern was the main thrust of his first novel, so it is of fundamental importance in the second. It would be misleading to

[4] Boisdeffre, *Métamorphose de la littérature de Proust à Sartre,* II, 304.

draw sharp contrasts between the philosophical positions of these
two works, principally because the absurd continues as a live
presence in the consciousness of the leading characters in *The
Plague*—and also, the other recurrent themes of Camus's early
writings reappear in this novel, although in somewhat altered
forms. One important respect in which the later work differs from
the earlier, however, is that Camus shifts from a primary concern
with the situation of the lone individual to that of the community.

This new focus does not mean that Camus hypostatizes the
community or envisions it as composed of uniform human components. He portrays very different kinds of persons and widely vary-
ing human reactions to the common condition of plague-
strickenness. Most citizens of Oran do not actively oppose the
plague but seek desperately to ignore it. As far as official restrictions permit, they go about their daily routines and pursue their
ordinary pleasures; the cinemas are always crowded, even though
they soon must resort to showing the same films over and over
again. Some of the inhabitants welcome the plague and cooperate
with it; black marketeers, smugglers, and other criminals profit
from the hardships and terrors of their helpless compatriots.
The narrator does not condemn these collaborators but pities
them for their alienation from the human solidarity experienced
in common suffering.

Only a minority actively combat the plague. Dr. Rieux, who
Camus later admitted presents his own point of view, is the
physician who first takes note of the appearance of the disease
and calls it to the attention of the reluctant authorities. As the
epidemic runs its course he commits himself wholly to the al-
leviation of the suffering the plague brings and to efforts to
wipe it out. Tarrou, a wandering intellectual who keeps a re-
vealing journal of the plague-time, leads the sanitary squad organization. A Jesuit priest, Father Paneloux, is also an active
plague-fighter. Rambert, a Parisian journalist caught within the
city when its gates are sealed, eventually joins the sanitary squad.

The records for this organization are kept by a middle-aged, self-effacing municipal clerk, Joseph Grand. These are the central characters through whose eyes and experiences we see the human struggle against suffering and death.

That *The Plague* does not represent a radical break from Camus's previous concerns is evident in the reappearance of the central motifs of his early writings. The theme of man's communion with nature is almost entirely absent from this somber chronicle. But in one deeply moving scene which occurs at the height of the plague, Rieux and Tarrou, exhausted by their ceaseless activity, decide one night to swim in the sea. As they emerge from the water they experience a wordless communion, an intuition of brotherhood in their common struggle for man. The caressing waves of the ocean symbolize the bonds that bring them together in lucid devotion to the world of nature, which now explicitly encompasses human nature.

The denial of life beyond earthly existence is steadfastly maintained by Camus, but in *The Plague* this is linked more clearly than before to a rejection of Christianity. God as ordinarily presented in the Christian tradition cannot be accepted by one who has chosen to be true to man and his suffering. (Again, it is not "the world" in general to which one is remaining faithful; it is quite specifically to human beings.) It becomes apparent that Camus cannot believe in the existence of an omnipotent and wholly benevolent deity because of the ubiquity of evil and suffering in the world. The ancient theodicy problem becomes a supreme stumbling block to theistic belief for one who finds meaningful communion with men who long for justice and happiness but suffer in the midst of oppression and misery.

The climactic presentation of this view in *The Plague* involves the principals' reaction to the fate of a small child victimized by the disease. Rieux and Father Paneloux watch in anguish as the young boy fails to respond to an injection of anti-plague serum and, after prolonged and unbearable agony, dies. At once the doctor strides out of the room, "a strange look on his face." The priest tries to halt his exit:

Rieux swung round on him fiercely.

"Ah! That child, anyhow, was innocent, and you know it as well as I do."

He strode on, brushing past Paneloux, and walked across the school playground. . . .

He heard a voice behind him. "Why was there that anger in your voice just now? What we'd been seeing was as unbearable to me as it was to you."

Rieux turned toward Paneloux.

"I know. I'm sorry. But weariness is a kind of madness. And there are times when the only feeling I have is one of mad revolt."

"I understand," Paneloux said in a low voice. "That sort of thing is revolting because it passes our human understanding. But perhaps we should love what we cannot understand."

Rieux straightened up slowly. He gazed at Paneloux, summoning to his gaze all the strength and fervor he could muster against his weariness. Then he shook his head.

"No, Father. I've a very different idea of love. And until my dying day I shall refuse to love a scheme of things in which children are put to torture." [5]

For Camus, a God who permits innocent suffering, even if it is recompensed in another life, is an unjust being who not only is intellectually incomprehensible but, on moral grounds, must be resolutely denied. The only alternative to such rebellion is an attitude of resigned acquiescence in the unjust order of things. When the plague first strikes the city, Father Paneloux sternly preaches to his congregation that the epidemic is just punishment for their sins. But after watching the innocent child die in agony, the priest delivers a much subdued sermon with the central message that what passes our understanding must yet be embraced and accepted. When he becomes ill himself, he refuses medical assistance and passively accepts his death in solitude.

[5]Albert Camus, *The Plague,* trans. Stuart Gilbert (New York: Alfred A. Knopf, 1948), 196–97.

Camus's sympathies clearly lie with the rebel who fights death to the bitter end.

Lucid integrity—an honest fidelity to the human condition—continues to be a fundamental value for Camus; it is in fact a foundation stone of the narrative edifice of *The Plague*. Dr. Rieux remarks of his own attitude: "The language he used was that of a man who was sick and tired of the world he lived in—though he had much liking for his fellow men—and had resolved, for his part, to have no truck with injustices and compromises with the truth." [6] Rieux is much more than another absurdist hero. The human condition is not summed up for him in sheer quantitative experience. He has a great deal of empathy with his fellow men and wants no part of injustice or hypocrisy—the human condition to which one should be faithful here extends to man's social existence and takes cognizance of an instinctive human demand for justice.

Yet inescapable components of cruelty and defeat haunt the vision of a fully honest man; absurdity can be confronted and combated but never completely overcome. Rieux concludes the chronicle by remarking that he could not report a final victory but only give an account of what had to be done in the endless fight against terror and affliction by men who strive their utmost to be healers.

And, indeed, as he listened to the cries of joy rising from the town, Rieux remembered that such joy is always imperiled. He knew what those jubilant crowds did not know but could have learned from books: that the plague bacillus never dies or disappears for good; that it can lie dormant for years and years in furniture and linen-chests; that it bides its time in bedrooms, cellars, trunks and bookshelves; and that perhaps the day would come when, for the bane and enlightening of men, it would rouse up its rats again and send them forth to die in a happy city. [7]

The plague—death and evil—can never be wholly eradicated.

[6] *Ibid.*, 11–12.
[7] *Ibid.*, 278.

But rebellion—the active struggle against pestilence—is the pathway to genuine humanity. Rieux's obstinate refusal to accept a creation in which men suffer is the symbol of revolt in *The Plague*. But this revolt transcends, horizontally, the world of the individual. For the most part, in the early essays rebellion was simply the absurd man's futile but meaningful struggle against *his* death. But in Camus's second novel revolt is clearly justified in the name of *humanity's* opposition to death, suffering, and oppression. The moral solipsism of the absurd man is broken by an awareness that his revolt is grounded in an experience common to his fellows and that the sole authentic response to this experience is enlistment in the struggle against misery and terror. Subsequently we shall examine closely Camus's attempt to elaborate philosophically this broadened—and deepened—conception of revolt. It is the keystone of the entire arch of his political thought, both critical and constructive.

A similar development of another recurrent theme, the quest for happiness, is also present in *The Plague*. Most citizens of Oran seem to remain in the purely absurdist phase of this quest; in the midst of tragedy they continue to be engrossed in their private efforts to obtain sensual pleasure. The chronicler does not fulminate against them and seems to find in their lives, however narrow, a certain naturalness that is not to be despised. But for the principals of the narrative the happiness and health of others who live in misery and are ravaged by disease come to be of overriding importance. The limits of purely egoistic enjoyment are surpassed, as well as the boundaries of private rebellion.

The figure of Sisyphus reappears in the disarming guise of Grand, a retiring and apparently insignificant municipal clerk; his "rock" is his effort to write a novel—more particularly, its first sentence. He has rewritten this one sentence hundreds of times but is never able to satisfy himself that it is perfect. Yet he finds purpose and a strange kind of happiness in this absurd enterprise. Unlike Sisyphus, however, Grand is not bound only to his rock and it does not wholly exhaust the meaning of life for him. He readily joins in the battle against the plague, working long hours in addition to his regular employment in order to keep the vital medical records in order. Significantly, Rieux more than half seriously refers to Grand, "who had to his credit only a little goodness of heart and a seemingly absurd ideal," as the "hero" of the narrative. To so consider him "will render to . . . heroism the secondary place that rightly falls to it, just after, never before, the noble claim of happiness." [8]

The principals in this narrative find it impossible to cling to their personal happiness as the *summum bonum*. The journalist Rambert, caught within the closed-off city, is desperately eager to return to his mistress in Paris. He makes contact with people who specialize in arranging illegal escapes from Oran. Rieux, who has taken a friendly interest in Rambert's plight, advises him to move quickly, before the authorities tighten controls and make escape impossible. The doctor's attitude puzzles Rambert; why should a man who feels and fulfills his responsibility to fight the plague help another man who is seeking to run from it? Rambert asks the doctor why he does not prevent the planned escape by reporting it to the police. Rieux only replies that Rambert's plan is none of his business, that he is incapable of deciding what is the right course in such a case. Rambert rejoins: " 'If that's so, why tell me to hurry up?' It was Rieux who now smiled. 'Perhaps because I, too, would like to do my bit for happiness.' " [9]

But, when the escape plan has been completed, Rambert goes to Rieux and Tarrou to tell them that he has decided to remain in Oran and join their public health team. To leave under the circumstances would, he says, embarrass him in relation to the woman he loves. Rieux replies that this belief is nonsense, that

[8]*Ibid.,* 126–27.
[9]*Ibid.,* 183.

there is nothing shameful in preferring happiness. " 'Certainly,' Rambert replies. 'But it may be shameful to be happy by one-self.' " [10] Rieux debates the point no further.

Clearly Camus feels that it is incumbent upon the man who seeks to be genuinely human to seek to alleviate the misery of others, even at the cost of his own happiness. When Rambert observes to Rieux and Tarrou that they have apparently chosen to act in contradiction to their personal happiness, the doctor admits that although nothing in the world is worth turning one's back on what one loves, that is in fact what he is doing. Wearily, he concludes that all that remains to do is draw the logical con-clusion from this fact: " 'A man can't cure and know at the same time. So let's cure as quickly as we can. That's the more urgent job.' " [11]

The doctor cannot articulate a rationale for turning his back on personal happiness and physical love, but this philosophic in-capacity does not prevent his acting as he feels he must. (Ca-mus's point is weakened somewhat, I believe, by his choice of Rieux's profession; after all, a physician could certainly justify combating an epidemic simply on the grounds of his professional responsibility.) Camus seems to be indicating that many men, in times of crises threatening not merely themselves but others, experience an instinctive obligation toward the victims of "plague," whatever particular form it may assume. Although he made an effort to provide a logical explication of this experience in *The Rebel,* its source as, initially, a *felt* and not a *rational* obligation always gave to it its principal significance. In 1953, Ca-mus told an interviewer:

. . . from my first articles to my latest book I have written so much, and perhaps too much, only because I cannot keep from being drawn toward everyday life, toward those, whoever they may be, who are humiliated and debased. They need to hope, and if all keep silent or if they are given a choice between two kinds of humiliation,

[10]*Ibid.,* 188.
[11]*Ibid.,* 189.

they will be forever deprived of hope and we with them. It seems to me impossible to endure that idea, nor can he who cannot endure it lie down to sleep in his tower. Not through virtue, as you see, but through a sort of almost organic intolerance, which you feel or do not feel. Indeed, I see many who fail to feel it, but I cannot envy their sleep.[12]

The Plague is Camus's most thoroughgoing and probably his most effective depiction of the human situation. An effort to grasp the fullness of his vision requires an initial attempt to clarify the context of Camus's thought. The philosopher Maurice Friedman has pointed out that the problem of "alienation" has been a recurrent theme in nineteenth- and twentieth-century views of man. Thinkers as diverse as Hegel, Feuerbach, Marx, Nietzsche, Sartre, and Erich Fromm have emphasized man's estrangement—from nature, from other men, from himself. Essentially man is viewed as alienated from meaning and finds himself, if he examines his condition closely and honestly, a stranger or an exile—as Fromm puts it, man is "the freak of the universe." [13] This perception has been fostered by the decline of traditional religious belief, in fact by rejection of the orthodox Judaeo-Christian God whose existence, so long as men could assume it without difficulty, gave to human life an intrinsic purpose.

The initial form assumed by the revolt against the traditional deity is that of "the Modern Promethean," [14] who seeks to restore to man all the desirable human qualities from which man has long alienated himself by projecting them onto an imaginary divine being or, in Marx's thought, into that tyrannical institution, private property. The Modern Promethean seeks totally to destroy the existent human condition and end man's alienation through the creation of a radically new order. He is repelled by

[12]Albert Camus, "The Artist and His Time," in *The Myth of Sisyphus and Other Essays,* 211.

[13]Erich Fromm, *The Sane Society* (Greenwich, Conn.: Fawcett Publications, 1965), 30.

[14]Maurice Friedman, *Problematic Rebel: An Image of Modern Man* (New York: Random House, 1963), 175.

the suffering, oppression, hypocrisy, and absence of freedom that characterize the lives of alienated men.

A second kind of reaction to alienation is also pointed to by Friedman:

> If the Modern Promethean is marked by the either-or which holds that man must destroy the reality that faces him in order to recover his alienated freedom, the Modern Job is marked by the "both-and" which faithfully affirms what confronts him as the "given" of his own existence and at the same time does not submit to it but opposes and contends with it. The choice of the Modern Promethean is between submission and rebellion, that of the Modern Job between this very either-or, in which submission and rebellion are the two sides of the same coin, and that other rebellion which holds the tension between the affirmation of oneself and the faithful confronting of what faces one.[15]

The Modern Job, like his Old Testament prototype, begins by radically questioning the meaningfulness of human existence. His perception of and rebellion against its absurdity are as deeply rooted and as genuine as the like reactions of the Modern Promethean. This essential kinship is supplemented, however, by an equally fundamental distinction between the two perspectives. The Modern Promethean's revolt tends to become an ideology, a political program for remaking the world of man. But the Modern Job lacks the cosmic confidence—or arrogance—of the Promethean ideologist. Man must indeed reject an unjust God, but this gives him no warrant for assuming an omniscience and seeking an omnipotence appropriate only to deity. The Modern Job constantly contends with absurdity and injustice but seeks to avoid reinforcing them by joining in the Promethean's ruthless quest for a perfected humanity.

For Friedman the prototypical Modern Job is Camus, and the principal literary expression of this persepective is *The Plague*. At one point in the narrative Tarrou and Rieux engage in a frank extended conversation. Tarrou tells of his years-long strug-

[15]*Ibid.*, 398.

gle with the problem of murder. As a youth, he had experienced total revulsion against killing when he observed his father, a public prosecutor, demand and obtain the death penalty for a wretched, frightened little man charged with murder. To further his revolt, Tarrou had joined a revolutionary workers' movement (undoubtedly the Communist Party). But one day he had been present at an execution ordered and carried out by party comrades, and his revulsion against killing had returned in all its aboriginal force. Deserting the movement, he had since devoted his life to a quest for as much personal innocence as could be obtained in a world that he saw as universally afflicted by the plague of organized and legitimized murder. He seeks to become at least "an innocent murderer."

Tarrou ends his "confession" by summing up the purpose of his life:

"It comes to this," Tarrou said almost casually; "what interests me is learning how to become a saint."

"But you don't believe in God."

"Exactly! Can one be a saint without God—that's the problem, in fact the only problem, I'm up against today. . . ."

"Perhaps," the doctor answered. "But, you know, I feel more fellowship with the defeated than with saints. Heroism and sanctity don't really appeal to me, I imagine. What interests me is being a man."

"Yes, we're both after the same thing, but I'm less ambitious." [16]

Camus made it abundantly clear many times that he intended Tarrou's final remark to contain no irony but to state the simple truth, that he sided not with the would-be saint (who does, however, express certain of Camus's distinctive views) but with the healer who wants to be only, but genuinely, a man. Rieux, the Modern Job, lives within the plague, maintaining a steadfast confrontation with death and absurdity; for him man's "problematic becomes a ground, the paradox of the person a stance, exile and rebellion a way." [17]

[16]*The Plague,* 230–31.
[17]Friedman, *Problematic Rebel,* 480.

Rieux takes his stand in a dialogical relationship with reality, in Martin Buber's meaning of "dialogue." This relationship Friedman describes as one "of openness, directness, mutuality, and presence." [18] Rieux's is "a Modern Job's rebellion within the dialogue with the absurd—contending with the absurd yet trusting in the meaning that arises from this contending." [19] He can accept neither Paneloux's submission to reality as objectively meaningful nor Tarrou's purely subjective rebellion that leads to a frantic quest for personal purity. Eschewing the quest for individual perfection, Rieux seeks to fulfill his humanity through "full involvement, commitment, and response in the situation" in which he finds himself.[20]

The importance of dialogue for Camus is evident in this excerpt from his journal: "What balances the absurd is the community of men fighting against it. And if we choose to serve that community, we choose to serve the dialogue carried to the absurd against any policy of falsehood or of silence. That's the way one is free with others." [21] An open confrontation with the absurdity of the human condition is possible only through the complicity of true inter-human dialogue.

The human tragedy latent in nondialogical relationships is illustrated in a play Camus wrote in 1943, *Cross Purpose.* *(Le Malentendu).* In this drama an old woman and her daughter are proprietors of an inn in a small Central European town. For many years they have dreamed of escaping their dreary and monotonous existence by moving to southern Europe, where they can enjoy the warm sun and the fresh ocean breezes. In order to realize their all-consuming ambition, they have been systematically murdering and robbing all solitary and apparently wealthy travelers who have come their way. Only one victim short of obtaining enough money at last, they receive one evening

[18]Maurice Friedman, "Introduction" to Martin Buber, *Between Man and Man* (New York: Macmillan Company, 1965), xiv.
[19]Friedman, *Problematic Rebel,* 438.
[20]*Ibid.,* 436.
[21]*Notebooks, 1942–1951,* p. 126 (entry of November, 1945).

a richly dressed young man, whom they do not recognize as their long-lost son and brother. He does not reveal his identity to them, but plans to remain incognito until the following day in order to discover through frank conversation what his mother and sister most desire. He is well able to fulfill their wishes, for he has made a huge fortune since leaving home. But when he tries to talk openly and sympathetically with his sister, she coldly replies:

. . . no more talk about your heart, please. We can do nothing about that. . . . Take your key and make yourself comfortable in your room. But remember you are in a house where the heart isn't catered for. Too many bleak years have passed over this little spot of Central Europe, and they've drained all the warmth out of this house. They have killed any desire for friendliness and, let me repeat it, you won't find anything in the least like intimacy here. You will get what the few travellers who lodge with us are used to get, and it has nothing to do with sentiment. So take your key and bear this well in mind: we're accepting you as a guest, in our quiet way, for interested motives, and if we keep you it will be in our quiet way, for interested motives.[22]

That night the two women kill their unrecognized son and brother. Going through his clothing in search of money, they find his passport and discover, in horror, his true identity. The mother, in complete despair, throws herself into the river where she had already helped to cast the body of her son. The sister, intensely bitter at what she sees as her mother's desertion, confronts her dead brother's wife, who soon arrives in hope of joining a joyous reunion. At this point the sister views the whole tragic chain of events as a revelation of the absurdity and injustice of the world and of a God who is surely deaf and either impotent or malign. After the sister has exited to go hang herself, the wife sinks to her knees in total desolation and calls upon God to have pity on those who love each other and have been separated forever. In response, an old manservant who has

[22]Albert Camus, *Cross Purpose,* Act I, in *Caligula and Cross Purpose,* 124.

been mute throughout the play enters and asks if he had been
called. Desperately the wife begs him to be kind and say that
he will help her. In the curtain line, he replies clearly and
firmly, "No."

At first glance this play might be plausibly interpreted as a
purely "absurdist" work, in fact the bleakest and most pessimistic
that Camus ever produced. But he did not himself so understand
it, and, I think, his reasons are apparent even in the admittedly
somber text. Camus certainly did intend seriously the denial of
any possibility of divine aid or consolation for man; as he saw it,
man does confront a deity who, at best, is deaf to his cries for
justice and meaning. But he is not contending that human existence is inevitably and inescapably turned to tragedy by the effects
of absurd cross-purposes. After all, the mother and sister are
murderers and, in pursuit of their ideal, have elected to place an
impenetrable psychic wall between themselves and others whom
they see only as victims to be ruthlessly exploited and not as
persons to be encountered in openness and mutuality. In a moment of frenzied yet lucid insight shortly before she takes her
own life, the sister exclaims: "Crime . . . means solitude, even if a
thousand people join together to commit it." [23] Like Caligula,
the murderesses have chosen "the wrong kind of freedom," a
monological hardness and fanaticism that leads to death, rather
than the genuinely free dialogical attitude that exalts and enhances life. The strong implication is that the truly human
pathway is not to ape a deaf god or an indifferent universe but to
enter freely into communion with other men. Two years after
completing *Cross Purpose*, Camus put down this clue to its
interpretation in his journal: "The whole misfortune of men comes
from the fact that they don't use a simple speech. If the hero . . .
had said: 'Well, here I am and I am your son,' the dialogue would
have been possible and not at cross-purposes. . . . There would
have been no tragedy because the height of all tragedies lies in
the deafness of the protagonists." [24] Even the relatively innocent

[23]*Ibid.*, Act III, 165.
[24]*Notebooks, 1942–1951*, p. 125 (entry of November, 1945).

son was guilty of an antidialogical deviousness, for which he paid an exorbitant price.

Camus's emphasis, especially in his mature works, upon the central human significance of dialogical communion is not a desperate and evasive kind of sentimentality; he was not speaking of a mindless, dependent clinging to one another on a darkling shore. We can best grasp his meaning by turning briefly to the strikingly parallel perspective of Martin Buber.

Buber, the great Jewish existential writer, was the foremost twentieth-century philosopher of dialogue. His fundamental distinction between "I-Thou" and "I-It" relationships is well known but difficult to comprehend, principally because it concerns realities that may often be grasped only at a level that is not primarily verbal. These categories refer to the attitude or stance of the individual toward all other persons and things. Acting within the context of "I-It," one channels his efforts into the appropriation and use of things and people to gratify his desires and advance his self-conceived interests. In such a relationship one has closed himself off from the revelatory potentialities of encounter with that which is not oneself. "I-Thou" cannot be so easily characterized; like "I-It," it can be known only in experience, but since we are ordinarily immersed in the objectified realm of "It," from which we may rarely if ever escape, what Buber means by "I-It" is readily recognizable.

"I-Thou" is "real life," "eternal life," "real meeting," genuine "encounter." It is unplanned, unpreconceived, spontaneous confrontation with some thing or some person, in which one is fully "present," seeking not to appropriate or use, physically or psychologically, what or who confronts one but letting it or him be—and finding in this meeting reality that one had never known prior to this event. "I-Thou," the dialogical relationship, is a revelatory experience; in fact, Buber speaks of it as the inner meaning of the religious term "revelation." [25] This revelation is not a suddenly-heard edict or proclamation from a supernatural cosmic being;

[25]Martin Buber, *I and Thou*, trans. Ronald Gregor Smith (2nd. ed.; New York: Charles Scribner's Sons, 1958), 109.

it is simply what one comes to know and can know genuinely only in dialogical encounter. No specific "content" is given in this revelation but only "a Presence as power" that contains three inseparably interrelated elements: first, "the whole fulness of real mutual action, of the being raised and bound up in relation"; secondly, "there is the inexpressible confirmation of meaning," which, thirdly, "is not that of 'another life,' but that of this life of ours. . . ." [26]

Dialogue in Buber's sense need not be verbal; in fact, full mutual presence may more frequently occur in the absence of articulation than in company with it. Two notations in Camus's journal give indications of his comprehension and profound appreciation of the "I-Thou" relationship: "Now I have learned to expect less of [people] than they can give—a silent companionship. And their emotions, their friendship, and noble gestures keep their full miraculous value in my eyes; wholly the fruit of grace." [27] By "grace" Camus appears to be pointing to precisely the same experienced phenomenon as Buber's "revelation." Fifteen years later Camus wrote: "There always comes a moment when people give up struggling and tearing each other apart; willing at last to like each other for what they are. It's the kingdom of heaven." [28] Again the parallel with Buber's "I-Thou" encounter is unmistakable. Camus's Dr. Rieux in *The Plague* also recounts profoundly communicative though unarticulated "I-Thou" experiences involving himself and his mother and, at one point, a weeping, almost broken Joseph Grand.

That the discernment of a fundamental and significant similarity between the perspectives of Camus and Buber is not an arbitrary intellectual imposition is evidenced by these two writers' expressed attitudes toward one another. R. W. B. Lewis reports that "Camus acknowledges a profound respect for Buber. . . . And Camus is even willing to say that, for himself, 'the sacred' is just

[26]*Ibid.*, 110.
[27]*Notebooks, 1935–1942*, p. 7 (entry of May, 1935).
[28]*Notebooks, 1942–1951*, p. 253 (entry of April, 1950).

that presence felt in the silence during a moment of genuine awareness." [29] And, according to Maurice Friedman, Camus even stated "that he would not mind being called religious in Buber's sense." [30] Elsewhere Friedman reports that, in a letter to him, Buber observed: "I would not call Camus an atheist. He was one of the men who are destroying the old images. You know how I feel about them." [31] As Buber saw Camus's achievement, he had radically called into question the traditional symbols, doctrines, and ideas of religion by judging them quite inadequate to express the experientially meaningful realities of the human condition. Camus's iconoclastic rejection of what he understood to be the Judaeo-Christian God ended not in pure negation but in the affirmation of dialogical Presence, and for Buber this was the essence of true religion—namely, the reality that we meet in fully open confrontation, not a doctrine which we claim to be the conclusion of a logical argument or accept on the authority of those who claim official custodianship of revealed truth.

Camus's mature "religious" attitude is "bodied forth," to use Buber's wonderfully expressive language, in one of his last works, a short story entitled "The Growing Stone." The central figure in this tale is D'Arrast, a French civil engineer who comes to a Brazilian village to direct the construction of a much-needed dam. He arrives at fiesta time, and although the villagers try to make him feel welcome, he is unable to enter fully into their joyous celebrations. At one of the festival events he meets a sailor, a simple ship's cook, who had been shipwrecked off the nearby shore several days before. As the cook floundered in the water, he had prayed desperately to the Virgin, promising that if his life could be spared he would carry a huge stone on his head from his

[29]R. W. B. Lewis, *The Picaresque Saint: Representative Figures in Contemporary Fiction* (Philadelphia and New York: J. B. Lippincott Company, 1959), 103. Report of a conversation between the author and Camus.
[30]Maurice Friedman (ed.), *The Worlds of Existentialism: A Critical Reader* (New York: Random House, 1964), 239.
[31]Friedman, *Problematic Rebel,* 442n.

home in the village to the church, some distance away. A man of honor, he is intent upon fulfilling his promise the following day. D'Arrast cannot understand the cook's fidelity to his desperate vow but sympathizes with his feeling of gratitude.

After a night of wild dancing, from which D'Arrast is kindly but firmly excluded, the cook is exhausted but still determined to make good his promise. In the intense heat of the day, D'Arrast sees him struggling under the weight of the huge stone, barely able to move as he approaches the church. Finally the man can bear his load no longer, and, with all the villagers looking on, collapses short of his goal. Hardly conscious of what he is doing, D'Arrast suddenly strides through the crowd to his suffering friend, picks up the stone, and carries it not to the church but all the way back to the cook's hut, where he dumps it into the glowing fire.

And there, straightening up until he was suddenly enormous, drinking in with desperate gulps the familiar smell of poverty and ashes, he felt rising within him a surge of obscure and panting joy that he was powerless to name.

When the inhabitants of the hut arrived, they found D'Arrast standing with his shoulders against the back wall. . . . With eyes closed, he joyfully acclaimed his own strength; he acclaimed, once again a fresh beginning in life. At that moment a firecracker went off that seemed very close. The brother moved a little away from the cook and, half turning toward D'Arrast but without looking at him, pointed to the empty place and said: "Sit down with us." [32]

Through an almost instinctive act of fidelity to a simple man whose credence in a supernatural deity he cannot share, D'Arrast is able to enter into deeply meaningful communion with men whose perspectives and culture differ completely from his own. His turning from the church, which represents to him only a dead image, and back to the circle of poor and humble men whom he has come to help in a concrete way, gives birth to the possibility of dialogue, filling D'Arrast's life with newfound meaning.

[32]Albert Camus, "The Growing Stone," in *Exile and the Kingdom,* trans. Justin O'Brien (New York: Alfred A. Knopf, 1957), 212–13.

Of the meaning revealed in dialogical relationship, Buber remarks: "You do not know how to exhibit and define the meaning of life, you have no formula or picture for it, and yet it has more certitude for you than the perceptions of your senses. What does the revealed and concealed meaning purpose with us, desire from us? It does not wish to be explained (nor are we able to do that) but only to be done by us." [33] This passage explicates perfectly the observation of Dr. Rieux in *The Plague* that one cannot cure and know at the same time and that the more important task is to cure. For in that curing there comes to light a meaning that no abstractly patterned claim to "know" can ever provide. "Camus' dialogical rebel Doctor Rieux stands, like Camus himself, for the meeting with concrete everyday reality rather than for any particular ideology or point of view." [34]

In order fully to comprehend Camus's dialogical rebellion, we must examine carefully its most explicit and detailed elaboration, found in his most significant philosophical work, *The Rebel*. Here we discover the core of Camus's vision of human nature and the human condition and of his existential ethic. "What is a rebel? A man who says no, but whose refusal does not imply a renunciation. He is also a man who says yes, from the moment he makes his first gesture of rebellion." [35] The prototypical rebel is a slave, heretofore submissive, who suddenly decides that he cannot obey some new command from his master. His refusal is obviously negative, but it simultaneously affirms the existence of a limit, a borderline, that the command-giver has exceeded. Perhaps inarticulately, but certainly, the slave feels that he is right, that there is in him something "worthwhile" which it is unjust for the master to violate or ignore. The slave, victim of systematic oppression, asserts at least a right not to be oppressed beyond what he can tolerate.

In changing suddenly from a state of silent acquiescence, the

[33]Buber, *I and Thou,* 110.
[34]Friedman, *Problematic Rebel,* 437.
[35]Albert Camus, *The Rebel: An Essay on Man in Revolt,* trans. Anthony Bower (New York: Vintage Books, 1956), 13.

rebellious slave tacitly invokes a value. Or, more precisely, a state of awareness comes into being in the midst of the act of revolt—"the sudden, dazzling perception that there is something in man with which he can identify himself, even if only for a moment." [36] Prior to his revolt, the slave had never really experienced this identification, but when awareness of it breaks upon him, his refusal to obey a particular command becomes simultaneously a rejection of slavery. That part of him for which he seeks respect becomes the supreme good, to which he is willing to be faithful even at the cost of his life. He desires either to identify himself completely with this good of which he has suddenly become aware or to be finally annihilated by the oppressor who confronts him. It now seems infinitely preferable to die for freedom than to live in slavery.

Strangely, rebellion, "though it springs from everything that is most strictly individualistic in man, questions the very idea of the individual." [37] If the rebel chooses the possibility of his death rather than submit to oppression, he demonstrates a willingness to subordinate his personal fate to a common good that transcends in significance his individual existence. He acts on behalf of yet indeterminate values which he feels are common to himself and all other men. Careful analysis of the experience of revolt leads to awareness of a common human nature: "Why rebel if there is nothing permanent in oneself worth preserving?" [38]

The objection has been made that revolt may well be purely egoistic, that "there is no reason to suppose with Camus that when a slave revolts he is asserting the freedom of mankind rather than just rebelling against his personal oppressor." [39] Camus admits that rebellion may be egoistically motivated, but whatever the rebel's conscious motives, implicit in his act are

[36]*Ibid.*, 14.
[37]*Ibid.*, 15.
[38]*Ibid.*, 16.
[39]Judith N. Shklar, *After Utopia: The Decline of Political Faith* (Princeton: Princeton University Press, 1957), 141–42.

values which transcend his own desires. Moreover, one may rebel against lies as well as against oppression, and the rebel's willingness to die resisting oppression is evidence that revolt demands rights for all men. For the individual rebel who perishes in the midst of his revolt can never enjoy those rights himself. His act demands respect for himself only insofar as he identifies himself with a human community.

The nonegoistic elements in revolt are further elucidated by taking note of men who are roused to revolt not by their own suffering but by knowledge of oppression of which other persons are the victims. This phenomenon is based not on empathetically imagining oneself in the victim's place, for one may find himself unable to bear the sight of offenses committed against others that one has borne himself without rebelling—for example, suicides by imprisoned Russian terrorists protesting the whipping of their comrades. Nor is rebellion against the suffering of others the result of rational calculation of common interests, for men may be deeply repelled by injustices inflicted upon those whom they consider enemies. "Therefore the individual is not, in himself alone, the embodiment of the values he wishes to defend. It needs all humanity, at least, to comprise them." [40] The experiential logic of rebellion leads to the conclusion of a "metaphysical" human solidarity.

Rebellion is often, but mistakenly, confused with resentment. But resentment is founded on envy, which desires what it does not have, while the rebel seeks to defend what he is. Also, externally directed resentment always springs from resentment against oneself. The rebel, however, in his revolt has found a new respect for himself and, in fighting for the integrity of one part of his being, seeks not to conquer his opponents but only to compel them to respect his essential human nature. Unlike the resentful man, the rebel desires to inflict pain or humiliation on no one and will even accept pain himself so long as his integrity is respected.

[40]*The Rebel,* 17.

This does not imply that no rebellion is motivated by resentment, but in its "widest sense" rebellion far surpasses resentment. Resentment is wholly negative, though it may sometimes assume the shape of an abstract love for mankind based on a theoretical confidence in human nature. But revolt, though it begins as negation, is primarily significant as passionate affirmation: "Rebellion, though apparently negative, since it creates nothing, is profoundly positive in that it reveals the part of man which must always be defended." [41]

Camus strives mightily in his analysis of rebellion to avoid hypostatizing it as a timeless abstract category. He points out that men living in a "sacred world" where all meanings seem to be "given" and are taken for granted cannot even conceive of rebellion. The problem of rebellion is—or has been heretofore—meaningful only within the context of Western thought, particularly in recent centuries which have been characterized by massive secularization of ideas, assumptions, and patterns of life. "The rebel is a man who is . . . determined on laying claim to a human situation in which all the answers are human— in other words, formulated in reasonable terms." [42] Rebellion, though certainly not the sum total of human experience, is of great significance today because "sacred" answers are no longer compelling. Rebellion is an essential dimension of man in our historic situation, and honest confrontation of reality compels us to seek our values within it.

Faithfulness to the meaning of revolt makes us aware that human solidarity is based upon rebellion and that this solidarity alone justifies rebellion. Any revolt which negates this solidarity is not true rebellion but acquiescence in murder. "In order to exist, man must rebel, but rebellion must respect the limit it discovers in itself—a limit where minds meet and, in meeting, begin to exist." [43]

[41]*Ibid.,* 19.
[42]*Ibid.,* 21.
[43]*Ibid.,* 22.

Revolt represents movement beyond the experience of the absurd. For the absurd man, suffering is individual, but in rebelling he perceives suffering as a collective experience, "a mass plague." Within the human condition revolt assumes the same place as Descartes's *cogito* in the realm of abstract thought; rebellion reveals the initial certainty luring the individual from his solitude. "It founds its first value on the whole human race. I rebel—therefore we exist." [44]

In order to prevent Camus's conception of revolt from assuming the appearance of a quite unexistential abstraction, let us employ it in an effort to elucidate a recent social and political phenomenon of the greatest importance in the United States. This is the massive protest by Negroes against their long-standing subservience to whites and the Negroes' efforts to bring about a reordering of American society so that they might become persons with rights, status, and opportunities equal to those which white Americans have long enjoyed. The origins of this movement are diverse and extremely complex, and I do not pretend to be able to provide any definitive interpretation of them. However, I do believe that in some crucial respects the Negroes' efforts to attain full citizenship point up the meaningfulness of Camus's "true rebellion." This is particularly true of the nonviolent, direct-action components of the "freedom movement."

The organized bus boycotts which began in 1956 and the "sit-ins" which started in 1960 can be viewed as originating in spontaneous protests against subhuman treatment, implicitly in the name of a common human nature and to protect an essential human dignity with which the protestors identified themselves. The initial impulse of these movements seems to have been neither envy nor a desire for vengeance but rather the rebel's instinctive conviction that the oppressive treatment to which he has long been subjected exceeds the intrinsic limits of genuinely human behavior. Also contributing to the appearance of this movement as rebellion in Camus's sense has been the participation within it

[44]*Ibid.*

of many white persons, impelled not by rational calculations of self-interest but simply by "identification of one's destiny with that of others and a choice of sides." [45]

In opposition to this view, it might be maintained that this rebellion took place within a cultural context of official commitment to liberal democratic norms and that many of its partisans have sought to justify it by appealing explicitly to humanistic or to Christian principles. But it appears at least equally justifiable to conclude that these norms and principles were, prior to the first stirrings of the Negroes' revolt, largely dead formalisms without power to alter the oppressive system of racism. To a considerable degree the central values of the "freedom movement"—especially its resolute nonviolence and its leaders' determination to defend an essential human nature common to all men across racial lines—appear to have sprung to life from the experiential core of rebellion against racist oppression. This example may serve, at least in part, to illustrate the real-world relevance of Camus's existential analysis of rebellion.

We have noted in Camus's works, beginning with his youthful essays and reappearing persistently, a preoccupation with revolt. And its formulation in *The Rebel* is the existential ground on which he stands in order to interpret political phenomena and to suggest prescriptions for the regulation of man's corporate life. At this point arises a pivotal question in the interpretation of Camus's thought—namely, the inner meaning for him of revolt. More particularly, did he employ a single term as a common label for very different concepts, or are there discernible links between the early and mature formulations of rebellion?

The young Camus rebelled against his own inevitable death, more precisely against the absurdity he perceived in the condition of a man who yearns for the unending perpetuation of the happiness he experiences but who is lucidly aware of his inescapable mortality. Is there any relationship between this traumatic experience of revolt against death and absurdity and the rebel-

[45]*The Rebel,* 17.

lion against oppression, injustice, and suffering that assumes the center of the stage in the *Letters to a German Friend, The Plague,* and *The Rebel*? One critic sees a stark contrast between these two formulations of revolt, claiming that rebellion in the latter works "is very different from the lucid, personal revolt in *Le Mythe de Sisyphe*. It is unreasoned and emotional, originating in a primitive feeling of human solidarity and of human dignity." [46] There is some limited validity in this observation, but it overlooks the origin of Camus's youthful personal revolt in soul-shaking, emotion-laden existential awareness, not in lucidity in the sense of coldly rational calculation.

Undoubtedly there was a broadening of Camus's formulation of revolt, from apparently egocentric concern in its early expressions to involvement of and with all men in its later form. But it would be a mistake, I believe, to view this development as reflecting two quite distinct attitudes. In 1958, Camus's first collection of essays was republished, with a new preface by the author. Here he spoke of the life-long influence upon him of the environment in which he grew up. The poverty of his family, he declared, had never been a misfortune for him; the brilliant Algerian sunlight had enriched his childhood and youthful years beyond calculation: "Even my revolts were illuminated by it. Almost always, I think I can say without dishonesty, these were revolts on behalf of everyone, in the hope that the lives of all men might be enhanced by illumination." [47]

One might say of this passage, of course, that in hindsight Camus wanted to see a consistency in the development of his central concern, whether it was discernible in his writings or not. But this hardly seems fair to the man, who was deeply involved in the struggle against injustice and misery inflicted upon others even while he was thinking out and writing his "absurdist" works. And further, it is an injustice to the thinker to claim that he

[46] Philip Thody, *Albert Camus, 1913–1960* (New York: Macmillan Company, 1961), 85.
[47] Albert Camus, "Preface" to *L'envers et l'endroit* (Paris: Gallimard, 1958), 13–14.

intentionally or unintentionally distorted the truth about his own development in his remark about the meaning of his "early revolts." I believe that there is in Camus's various presentations of revolt an underlying unity that reveals a persistent faithfulness to an existential approach and perspective and a generally successful effort to prevent moral concern from degenerating into abstract moralism.

The thread of continuity is that Camus's revolt was always directed against death on behalf of life. Clarification of this point will require, however, some effort at unwinding the thread. In October, 1946, Camus wrote in his journal: "Relation of the absurd to revolt. If the final decision is to reject suicide in order to maintain the confrontation, this amounts implicitly to admitting life as the only factual value, the one that allows the confrontation, 'the value without which nothing.' Whence it is clear that to obey that absolute value whoever rejects suicide likewise rejects murder." [48]

Yet, as we have noted, a few years later Camus declared that the rebel is willing even to lose his life in defending "a part of his being," his essential human nature, with which he identifies himself in the act of rebellion. Does this represent a change of mind about the ultimate value of human life? A convincing case might be made for this position, but I think it would seriously distort Camus's point of view. It seems to me that he meant by "life," or at least came to mean in his mature thought, more than simply the continuance of biological functioning.

His struggle with the bare natural fact of mortality, so strikingly dramatized in his early works, is illuminated by passages from his posthumously published notebooks. These remarks appear to reveal a growing conviction that natural death is not in itself man's supreme enemy, or at least not one that can meaningfully engage his powers of resistance. An entry from 1943 seems to indicate a belief that the fact of death may even lend a certain coherence to the world of human experience: "Death gives its

[48] *Notebooks, 1942–1951*, p. 149 (entry of October, 1946).

shape to love as it does to life—transforming it into fate. . . . What would the world be without death—a succession of forms evaporating and returning, an anguished flight, an unfinishable world. But fortunately here is death, the stable one." [49]

Death is to be confronted, not suppressed or denied, so that personal freedom and meaning may be born: "There is no freedom for man so long as he has not overcome his fear of death. But not through suicide. In order to overcome, one must not surrender. Be able to die courageously without bitterness." And later: "Revolt. Freedom in regard to death. Considering the freedom of murder, there is no freedom possible other than freedom to die; in other words, suppressing fear of death and giving that accident its place in the natural order of things. Strive toward this." [50] It appears that Camus was seeking to establish, in his personal existence, a dialogical relationship with death. Mortality as such is not our malevolent enemy but an inescapable adversary that can teach us the meaning of inner freedom if we stand our ground in openness and lucidity before it. This attitude did represent a rejection of and development beyond Camus's youthful rebellion against even that death which is part of "the natural order of things."

Revolt in Camus's later formulation of it is refusal to side with or to foster death and all the actions and attitudes which he saw as death-forces, because they diminish the possibility of a fully human life. Oppression, aggression, the infliction of misery upon human beings diminish life, both quantitatively and qualitatively, and the rebel resolutely resists them in order to defend that essentially human part of his being which his revolt reveals as transcending in significance even his individual existence. He finds that what links him to all men is, if necessary, worth dying for.

Camus's identification of death and oppression appears to be based solely on personal observation, interpretation of his own

---

[49]*Ibid.,* 68 (entry of March, 1943).
[50]*Ibid.,* 98 (entry of September, 1944), 154 (entry of 1947).

experience, and common sense, especially upon his perception
that the most extensive and systematic killing in our age has
been inflicted upon mankind by Nazi and Communist tyrants.
However, the similarity between his view and Freudian analyses
of this issue is too striking to pass unnoticed. Freud's derivation
of aggressiveness from the death instinct is well known—for
example: "This aggressive instinct is the derivative and the main
representative of the death instinct which we have found
alongside of Eros and which shares world-dominion with it." [51]
Camus's revolt can be interpreted as combat against what the
Freudian theorist Norman O. Brown has called "death-in-life," [52]
or what Herbert Marcuse, the eminent Freudian social philosopher, has termed "surplus-repression." [53] For these terms refer to
socially manifested aggressiveness which suppresses men's usually unconscious longing for a fully gratifying human existence.

Perhaps a brief comparison between Camus's conception of
the links between death and oppression and that of Marcuse
will further illumine the relationships between the former's perspective and Freudianism. There are both striking similarities and
significant differences between the viewpoints of the two writers.
Camus expresses an attitude that Marcuse would hope to see
generalized in a future "non-repressive civilization." In such a
society death would cease to be an instinctual goal manifesting
itself in oppression and become only a natural fact, the domain of which men would continually struggle to reduce. But at
present, Marcuse says, it is "not those who die, but those who
die before they must and want to die, those who die in agony
and pain, [who] are the great indictment against civilization." [54]
Death, when feared as an omnipresent threat, glorified as a
noble sacrifice, or accepted with resignation, reinforces surren-

[51]Sigmund Freud, *Civilization and Its Discontents,* trans. James Strachey
(New York: W. W. Norton, 1961), 69.
[52]Norman O. Brown, *Life Against Death: The Psychoanalytical Meaning
of History* (New York: Vintage Books, 1959), *passim,* especially Chap. 15.
[53]Herbert Marcuse, *Eros and Civilization: A Philosophical Inquiry into
Freud* (New York: Vintage Books, 1955), 32.
[54]*Ibid.,* 215.

der and submission to oppression and makes meaningful revolt impossible. Camus certainly did not think, with Marcuse, that death can be made wholly rational and painless, the result only of free choice by men who have lived lives of complete gratification and know that what they love will be preserved after their demise. But Camus did see the dark, subterranean, and insidious connection between death and all the forces oppressing mankind which Freudian theorists have made a valiant effort to elucidate. Nor did Camus possess Marcuse's hope for a wholly non-repressive social order; yet Camus's revolt converges in spirit, if not wholly in substance, with the utopian writer's vision of a meaningful form of human confrontation with death.[55]

The unity of revolt against death and absurdity and revolt against oppression is further clarified by Camus in *The Rebel,* where he indicates how rebellion is bound up inextricably with men's experience of true communion with one another. The rebel's experience discloses the essence he shares with other men, an innate inter-human solidarity. Turning to further consideration of the master-slave relationship, Camus declares that it is in itself destructive of this commonness; servitude raises a barrier that definitively obstructs dialogical communication. The rebel rejects injustice not because it contradicts some abstract eternal norm but "because it perpetuates the silent hostility that separates the oppressor from the oppressed. It kills the small part of existence that can be realized on this earth through the mutual understanding of men." [56] Lying is also ruled out by the rebel's existential value-standard, since untruth dis-

[55]So far as I can discover, Camus never thought within a Freudian framework or even employed psychoanalytic terminology. At one point in his journal, however, he records an insight that is strikingly similar to Marcuse's contention that Eros and the death instinct are manifestations of a single Nirvana principle which impels the psyche to seek release from tension: "The mad thing about love is that one wants to hurry and lose the interim. In this way one wants to get closer to the end. In this way love in one of its aspects coincides with death." (*Notebooks, 1942–1951,* p. 255 [entry of May, 1950].) Cf. Marcuse, *Eros and Civilization,* Chap. 11.

[56]*The Rebel,* 283.

rupts communion. And most obviously, rebellion proscribes murder and violence, which impose complete silence upon their victims.

Every rebel, solely by the movement that sets him in opposition
to the oppressor, therefore pleads for life, undertakes to struggle
against servitude, falsehood, and terror, and affirms, in a flash, that
these three afflictions are the cause of silence between men, that
they obscure them from one another and prevent them from redis-
covering themselves in the only value that can save them from
nihilism—the long complicity of men at grips with their destiny.[57]

Life-in-communion is the supreme value for the rebel; existential awareness of it provides him with criteria for his actions. It is not, therefore, inconsistent for him to risk his own
life in defense of rebellion against death and on behalf of life.

Close attention to the movement and impulses of rebellion
discloses that in no sense is it a demand for total freedom.
Rebellion is directed against the master's claimed freedom to
oppress the slave and the tyrant's claimed freedom to terrorize
his subjects. The rebel cannot remain faithful to the meaning of
his revolt by fostering oppression and murder. His act implicitly
claims for all men a limited freedom: "It is then possible to
say that rebellion, when it develops into destruction, is illogical.
Claiming the unity of the human condition, it is a force of life,
not of death." [58] Rebellion resolutely refuses to legitimize murder,
for in principle revolt is directed against death.

But rebellion can also become inauthentic if the rebel shrinks
from his felt obligation to oppose falsehood, injustice, and violence
and seeks a purely personal sanctity, "sainthood without God."
The rebel cannot claim absolute immunity from participation in
killing and lying, for these evils are inherent in the condition in
which the rebel lives. These means of combat cannot be definitively eschewed without giving up rebellion and simply acquies-
cing in the unbroken reign of falsehood, bloody-mindedness, and

[57]*Ibid.*, 284.
[58]*Ibid.*, 285.

terror. If he remains faithful to his revolt, the rebel lives in near-unbearable but inescapable tension. He knows the good—to create life-in-communion in place of "death-in-life"—but in its pursuit he may be compelled to do evil which he cannot, in principle, justify: "In any case, if he is not always able not to kill, either directly or indirectly, he can put his conviction and passion to work at diminishing the chances of murder around him. His only virtue will lie in never yielding to the impulse to allow himself to be engulfed in the shadows that surround him, and in obstinately dragging the chains of evil, with which he is bound, toward the light of good." [59]

Camus's fertile conception of revolt was further clarified by what was to be his final novel, *The Fall,* published in 1956. This might well not be the impression one receives from the book upon a first reading, but I believe that careful analysis will bear out my claim.

The story is presented as a monologue (this is a significant clue) by a man who makes his headquarters in a sailors' bar on the Amsterdam waterfront. He begins by introducing himself to a bourgeois lawyer from Paris who has wandered into the bistro, with whom he enters into a largely one-sided conversation that eventually lasts five days. The monologuist has given himself the alias of Jean-Baptiste Clamence, a heavily ironic name, since he is anything but a prophet of mercy (*la clémence*). Rather, he considers himself to be a *vox clamens* in the desert of his times, not to offer to it a redeeming hope but to intensify its utter sterility.

Clamence's "fall" was not really from innocence, but from an ignorant and cheerful complacency into a self-knowledge with which he has since sought incessantly and variously to cope. He had once been an eminent Parisian lawyer, with a reputation for nobility and humanitarianism gained by eloquent defenses of widows, orphans, and poor people who ran afoul of the law. He was physically attractive, successful with women, a partisan of

[59]*Ibid.,* 285–86.

"progressive" causes who joined readily in constant denunciations of men of power. Furthermore, he was a compulsive performer of "good deeds," even pushing other people out of the way in order to be the first to offer a blind man help in crossing the street. He was a paragon of virtue—and he knew it. In fact, he admits, the whole point of his noble deeds was to gain adoration for himself. After helping a blind man across the street, Clamence would tip his hat in response to the man's thanks—obviously to make certain that his kindness would be recognized and appreciated by the passersby.

In great detail, Clamence makes very clear that he was always "a monster of pride":

I was always bursting with vanity. I, I, I is the refrain of my whole life. . . . I admitted only superiorities in me and this explained my good will and serenity. When I was concerned with others, I was so out of pure condescension, in utter freedom, and all the credit went to me: my self-esteem would go up a degree. . . .

It is not true, after all, that I never loved. I conceived at least one great love in my life, of which I was always the object.[60]

Clamence frankly confesses that his championing of the underdog and his numerous charities were all calculated to increase his prestige and self-esteem—he had a "passion for summits," an intense desire to be elevated above other men. He goes so far as to declare himself an "enlightened" advocate of slavery; this form of social organization alone conforms to the requirements of human nature, for it permits some men at least to gratify fully their "passion for summits."

But eventually the serpent of self-knowledge slithered into Clamence's ignorantly prideful paradise; its façade crumbled and finally collapsed. His first moment of uneasiness came one fine autumn evening at the close of an especially satisfying day; he had helped a blind man, secured a reduced sentence for a properly grateful client, and delivered to his friends a brilliant improvisation on the beastliness of the governing class. Walking along the

[60]Albert Camus, The Fall, trans. Justin O'Brien (New York: Alfred A. Knopf, 1956), 48, 58.

Left Bank, he paused on the Pont des Arts—"I dominated the island"—and began to luxuriate in a feeling of vast power and plenitude. Suddenly, he heard a laugh from somewhere behind him. Wheeling around, he saw no one, but again he heard the laughter, which seemed to come from the river below. Dazed and shaken, he hurried home. Regarding his smiling face in the mirror, he seemed to see a double countenance.

Soon he recalled an event which had taken place two or three years previously and which he had repressed from his consciousness. Hurrying home late one night after a pleasurable rendezvous with his mistress, he saw a young girl standing on a bridge over the Seine. After he was well past her, he heard the unmistakable sound of a body striking the water, then several cries for help. He paused, trembling, telling himself to run to the girl's rescue, but then, succumbing to an irresistible weakness, he walked slowly away and told no one of what he had heard and seen. At the time he had coped with the situation simply by not reading the newspaper for the next few days.

The mocking laughter continued to haunt Clamence, and memories of his cowardice when no one was watching to censure him for it, plus other repressed memories which kept returning to his consciousness, drove him to desperate self-knowledge. He became fully aware that his virtue was purely self-serving, that he had been all along an egomaniacal fraud. Thenceforth the life he had been leading seemed utterly pointless, and he found himself unable to continue it either convincingly or effectively. Without his former belief in his own nobility, he became a rather poor lawyer and soon lost most of his clients. Seeking to find a new meaning for his life, or to narcotize himself against awareness of its pointlessness, he turned to romantic love, to gross debauchery, then to chastity; he even tried speaking the bitter truth about the legal profession to a group of younger colleagues (they decide, somewhat uneasily, to take his caustic remarks as an insider's joke). But nothing helps the fallen man, until at last he finds "salvation" in assuming the role of a "judge-penitent."

For Clamence now devotes himself to the service of a new

certainty that has replaced his former conviction of his absolute righteousness: "we cannot assert the innocence of anyone, whereas we can state with certainty the guilt of all. Every man testifies to the crime of all the others—that is my faith and my hope." [61] Before his "fall," Clamence, as a defense attorney, used to wonder how any man could have enough confidence in his own righteousness to permit his assuming a position in the judiciary. But, in his quest for a new life, he has become not a man whose official function is adjudication but one whose whole being and purpose are judgmental to the very core. All men must be polluted, hypocritical, and guilty—though in respect to what law they are no longer sure—for that he himself is, Clamence is certain. And furthermore, contemporary men judge one another ceaselessly and mercilessly, each seeking desperately to escape the judgment of the other: "God is not needed to create guilt or punish. Our fellow men suffice, aided by ourselves. . . . For them, no extenuating circumstances; even the good intention is ascribed to crime. . . . Don't wait for the Last Judgment. It takes place every day." [62]

The meaning of "judge-penitent" is gradually revealed in the course of the monologue. Clamence at last observes that every judge must some day be penitent, so he starts as a penitent in order to finish as a judge. As he says, he retains his "passion for summits"; he is still a monster of pride. The whole point of his protracted confession is to awaken in his auditors, whom he chooses with great care, a consciousness of their own hypocrisy and guilt. They then pour out to him their self-debasing reminiscences, and he passes judgment on their lives.

The Fall has been interpreted in various ways, many, I believe, erroneous. For example, Philip Thody writes: *"La Chute* can be read as a kind of critique of *La Peste,* for until he discovered how impure his motives were, Clamence had been living as a legal equivalent of Doctor Rieux." [63] This observation

[61]*Ibid.,* 110.
[62]*Ibid.,* 110–11.
[63]Thody, *Albert Camus, 1913–1960,* p. 184.

seems at best highly dubious, and Thody makes no real effort to substantiate it. Rieux was in no sense a "monster of pride"; he made no attempt through his "good deeds" to call attention to himself and, as narrator of *The Plague*, carefully refrained from passing judgment on men who were either indifferent to the city's distress or who profited from it. Moreover, the contrast between Clamence and Rieux points up Camus's belief that "doing good" is not in itself sufficient to enable one to fulfill the vocation of "being a man." Rieux seeks to stand in dialogical relationship with his fellows, while Clamence, both before and after his "fall," tries frantically to stand above, and never "with," them.

Though proceeding somewhat along the same lines as Thody's, R. W. B. Lewis's interpretation is even wider of the mark. He identifies Camus's point of view with Clamence's and opines that Camus was groping "toward a new basis for solidarity with his fellows: to what might be called the fellowship of those ashamed, the democracy of the guilty. . . . It is as though Dr. Rieux had fallen; and, for Clamence himself, the experience is at the same time a kind of 'rise'—he is at least a much fuller human being, and a more real one." [64] In response to this view, it should first be noted that Camus himself declared that although he shared the "great feeling of friendship for the first Christian" which the narrator of *The Fall* expresses, "that, I may say, is the only point which I have in common with this Jean-Baptiste Clamence with whom people want to identify me." [65]

But even more significantly, it is clear from the narrative itself that Clamence is anything but "a much fuller human being" after experiencing his "fall"; he has elected a way of life which diminishes rather than enlarges his humanity:

To be sure, my solution is not the ideal. But when you don't like your own life, when you know that you must change lives, you don't have any choice, do you? What can one do to become another?

[64]Lewis, *The Picaresque Saint,* 107.
[65]Interview in *Le Monde,* August 31, 1956, quoted in Thody, *Albert Camus, 1913–1960,* p. 175.

Impossible. One would have to cease being anyone, forget oneself for someone else, at least once. But how? Don't bear down too hard on me. I'm like that old beggar who wouldn't let go of my hand one day on a cafe terrace: "Oh, sir," he said, "it's not just that I'm no good, but you lose track of the light." Yes, we have lost track of the light, the mornings, the holy innocence of those who forgive themselves.[66]

When he came to self-awareness, Clamence had at least a faint intimation of another way in which he might have "changed his life," the polar opposite of the course he chose—which was really no change at all. This is the way of dialogue and communion, not of monologue and judgmental self-exaltation. Unable to "forget himself" by seeking honest openness with his fellow men, he loses all opportunity for a genuinely human life. One critic has accurately noted that "Jean-Baptiste Clamence is to be viewed as representing in the universe of Camus' fiction the absolute antithesis of the true rebel." [67] The contrast between Clamence and D'Arrast (in "The Growing Stone," published a year later than *The Fall*), for example, demonstrates that Camus did not, in the years following the appearance of his extended analysis of revolt, change his view of the "true rebel" as the embodiment of the most genuinely human life. Recognizing, like Tarrou but even more extravagantly, that everyone is radically infected by "plague," Clamence elects not to join in struggling against the evil in himself and in society but rather to side with the plague and intensify its misery.

In spite of his mordant, apparently ultra-realistic cynicism, Clamence is unwilling to face up squarely to the human condition. For what he desires is self-deification, the consolation of a shabby godhood. His reaction to an acute awareness of his mortality is evasive self-deception: "I was too much in love with myself not to want the precious object of my love never to disappear. Since, in the waking state and with a little self-knowl-

---

[66]*The Fall,* 144–45.
[67]Nathan A. Scott, Jr., *Albert Camus* (New York: Hillary House, 1962), 85.

edge, one can see no reason why immortality should be conferred on a salacious monkey, one has to obtain substitutes for that immortality." [68] Fearing to confront openly his "finitude anxiety," Clamence settles on the illusory surrogate-immortality of total self-centeredness. He wills to give himself alone ultimate significance by negating the human significance of everyone else.

Furthermore, he denies and rejects solidarity with his fellows. His failure to aid the drowning woman reveals to him that he had never acted out of spontaneous concern for human need but always on the basis of calculated self-advantage. Instead of learning from the guilt he feels for his failure that genuine solidarity is a fundamental human reality, he universalizes his guilt as the only quality men have in common. And he seeks to elude even this commonness by exalting himself finally as a judge proclaiming the guilt of others, indicating that solidarity in guilt alone is illusory and issues only in solitude.

Finally, Clamence refuses genuinely human freedom and chooses inhuman freedom. That he recognizes the former, and that it is identical with the freedom the "true rebel" seeks to defend and nurture, is apparent in a statement he makes:

> . . . freedom is not a reward or a decoration that is celebrated with champagne. . . . It's a chore, on the contrary, and a long-distance race, quite solitary and very exhausting. . . . that's why freedom is too heavy to bear, especially when you're down with a fever, or are distressed, or love nobody. . . .
> The essential is being able to permit oneself everything, even if, from time to time, one has to profess vociferously one's own infamy. I permit myself everything again, and without the laughter this time. [69]

Careful consideration of *The Fall* leaves one with the overwhelming impression that Clamence is spiritually dead, for he has taken the side of death against life by locking himself irretrievably in a judgmental solitude. He is indeed guilty, but his

[68] *The Fall*, 102.
[69] *Ibid.*, 132–33, 141–42.

guilt consists not so much in his pre-fall hypocrisy as in his free and conscious choice of monological self-isolation as a mode of existence. The antirebel languishes in an earthly hell.

There is one additional dimension of *The Fall* which is particularly relevant to this study, namely its explicit political meaning. It can be comprehended primarily within the framework of *The Rebel,* but it is also essential in this connection to refer once more to Camus's publicly expressed disagreement with Jean-Paul Sartre. In the early 1950's, Camus came to view Sartre as the leader of "the Parisian left-wing literary Establishment," [70] whose policy of political collaboration with the Communist party Camus found totally repugnant. In a sense *The Rebel* was a kind of declaration of his independence from this Establishment, and through its principal outlet, Sartre's *Les Temps Modernes,* he was reciprocally excommunicated. In his reply to this journal's review of *The Rebel* by Francis Jeanson, one of Sartre's disciples, Camus gave what seems to me, in retrospect, an invaluable clue to the political implications of *The Fall.* He wrote of

. . . these bourgeois intellectuals who wish to atone for their origins, even at the cost of contradiction and of doing violence to their intelligence. In the present instance, for example, the bourgeois is Marxist, while the intellectual propounds a philosophy which cannot be reconciled with Marxism. And it is not his own doctrine that the author of this singular article [Jeanson's review] defends . . . ; it is the viewpoint of the penitent bourgeois. From a certain point of view, this seems pathetic. . . .

But one cannot be communist without being ashamed of one's bourgeois condition, and inversely; one's attempt to combine the two only involves him in two kinds of difficulty. Thus the author of your article finds himself caught in a double embarrassment; the first results from his bourgeois position; the second causes him to suppress what he really thinks and consequently obliges him to falsify the views of others. The result, rather than doctrine and action, is a curious complex in which repentance and submission are mingled. This double effort must be so exhausting that I cannot

---

[70] This is the apt phrase employed in Parker, *Albert Camus: The Artist in the Arena,* 115.

see how it can ever become involved in reality, except as submissiveness.[71]

The French left-wing literary intellectual, of whom Sartre is archetypical, was viewed by Camus as a judge-penitent, and Clamence is a satirical portrait of such a person. Additional evidence on this point is presented by Sartre's long-time companion, Simone de Beauvoir, though she admits it only grudgingly and indirectly. In her memoirs, she declares that in the first part of *The Fall* she recognized the Camus she had known and admired during the war years and "was deeply touched by the simplicity with which he talked about himself now." But suddenly his sincerity waned, and "he switched from the role of penitent to that of judge; he took all the bite out of his confession by putting it too explicitly at the service of his grudges." [72] Obviously, Mlle de Beauvoir finally realized, with great distaste, that Camus was not writing primarily about himself but about her and Sartre's coterie.

Camus believed that such leftist intellectuals were morbidly obsessed with their bourgeois origins but dwelt on their personal penitence only in order to justify becoming merciless judges of their society *en masse*. Sartre sets forth a philosophy which proclaims absolute freedom and total responsibility for one's choices as the essence of the human condition—"no extenuating circumstances are taken into account"—and uses this doctrine as a club to administer verbal beatings to all those insufficiently penitent bourgeois who have not made choices identical with his own. Camus considered this stance especially ironic because Sartrean existentialists present no criteria for evaluating personal choices, much less for justifying their own political and ideological alliance with proponents of a determinist view such as Marxism.[73]

That Camus intended to communicate this message in *The*

[71]Albert Camus, "Lettre au directeur des *Temps Modernes,*" *Les Temps Modernes,* VIII (August, 1952), 329, 331–32.
[72]Beauvoir, *Force of Circumstance,* 349.
[73]For a discerning account of Sartre's philosophical effort to reconcile Marxism and existentialism, see Wilfrid Desan, *The Marxism of Jean-Paul Sartre* (Garden City, N.Y.: Doubleday, 1965).

Fall is evident in the text. Near the conclusion of his monologue, Clamence speaks of modern intellectuals who, like him,
cannot bear the weight of true freedom: "Hence one must
choose a master, God being out of style." Believing that all choices
are arbitrary, they nevertheless cannot refrain from judging; bereft of a foundation for morality, they moralize all the more. In
quest of security for their threatened egos, they run from the
freedom they find onerous and embrace, or at least collaborate
with, a force powerful enough to impose an arbitrary order upon
the world: "In short, you see, the essential is to cease being free
and to obey, in repentance, a greater rogue than oneself." This
submission is a perverse and distorted form of the quest for
communion: "Death is solitary, whereas slavery is collective.
The others get theirs, too, and at the same time as we—that's
what counts. All together at last, but on our knees and heads
bowed." [74]

The principal difference between Clamence and the Sartrean
intellectuals, as Camus saw it, was the former's complete knowledge and admission that he is a proponent of submissiveness:
"I invite the good people to submit to authority and humbly
to solicit the comforts of slavery, even if I have to present it as
true freedom." [75] This, for Camus, was precisely the ultimate
meaning of Sartre's existentialism *cum* Marxism. Those who set
out from the premise of a limitless human freedom, denying the
reality of any permanent human nature or the possibility of
men's discerning any common meaning, are most likely to be
mastered by a "passion for summits." They seek to actualize their
boundless freedom by aligning themselves with a movement
which claims the authorization of history for its exercise of total
freedom, expressed as an effort to remold men through the creation of a perfect society. This submission—as Camus regarded
it—gives to the Sartrean intellectuals, in their own view, a plat-
form elevated well above the heads of their bourgeois neighbors

[74] *The Fall,* 133–36.
[75] *Ibid.,* 137.

and of all insufficiently progressist writers. From this height they play the role of judge-penitents. Their normless judgmentalism, Camus concluded, amounted to a peculiar, shabby, and personally vicious form of antirebellion.

Before moving on to detailed consideration of Camus's specifically political ideas, an effort must be made to draw together in summary form his variously stated reflections on human nature and the human condition. For it should now be quite apparent that he was persistently concerned with the basic questions of philosophical anthropology and of ethics: what is man, and how should he live?

Camus never wrote a treatise on human nature, but in a real sense he wrote almost nothing except observations and commentary on the nature of man. We know from his explicit remark in *The Rebel* that he did believe in the reality of a common, enduring human nature, but, as an existential thinker, he was most reluctant to characterize it by a series of abstract descriptive terms. Furthermore, man's nature cannot be truly comprehended apart from the conditions—natural, historical, and social—of his existence in the world. But although Camus left us with no complete, thoroughgoing, analytical depiction of human nature—such as, for example, Freud's great effort—he did not leave us wholly unenlightened about his views on this important subject.

Let us consider first Camus's position on the problem of human evil—specifically, the question of whether it stems entirely from remediable error or manifests in whole or in part an ineradicable destructive and aggressive tendency in man's nature. A British writer's comment typifies the view of a number of critics: ". . . Camus falls victim of the extreme humanist fallacy of a perfect, or perfectible, human nature." [76] One must grant that there are numerous remarks in and aspects of Camus's works which appear to justify such a conclusion. But nevertheless I believe it is wrong, and I hope to demonstrate that

[76]Cruickshank, *Albert Camus and the Literature of Revolt,* 176–77.

Camus's response to the question of the source of human evil is essentially agnostic, though with optimistic overtones.

The work which has drawn the most commentary and criticism of this variety is *The Plague*. Many critics have remarked that bubonic plague is a wholly inadequate symbol for the German occupation of France, for Nazi totalitarianism, and more generally for the evil which men do to one another. Typical of critiques from a Christian perspective is the observation that, "having made of the plague an allegory of the evil in the world, Camus cannot . . . limit it to the mystery of the physical suffering of children. . . . The real scandal is all the violence that men do to children. And this is most certainly the problem of man and not of creation." [77] And, from an existentialist point of view, it is claimed that "to treat the Occupation as the equivalent of a natural calamity was merely another means of escaping from History and the real problems. Everyone fell in only too easily with the abstract morality expressed by this fable." [78]

There is some justice in these criticisms, but Camus was well aware of them and made an effort to defend the symbolism of the plague. For him it was an apt symbol of ideological abstraction, which he viewed as the truly evil, anti-human root and essence of totalitarianism. Such abstractions are diseases of the soul which have descended upon twentieth-century men, even though the overwhelming majority of them are victims rather than instigators of this disaster. When a French critic asked Camus what he would do if faced with the destruction of human oppressors rather than of microbes, he answered that he and his fellows in the wartime Resistance had already replied to that question. They had admitted, though with great pain, that resistance to evil sometimes requires the taking of human life, and if faced again with such terrorism they would no doubt respond similarly. "Indeed, he had not specifically named the Nazi terror in *La Peste*

[77] Bertrand d'Astorg, *Aspects de la littérature européenne depuis 1945* (Paris: Editions du Seuil, 1952), 193–94.
[78] Beauvoir, *Force of Circumstance,* 129.

'in order to be better able to strike at all [kinds of terror]. Undoubtedly, it is precisely for this reason that I am being criticized, since *La Peste* can justify all forms of resistance against all forms of tyranny.' " [79]

Insofar as Camus intended the plague, on the political level of the allegory, to stand primarily for ideological abstraction, his choice is partially justified, but not completely—abstractions, after all, are created by men, and even if the originators' intentions are good, their creations are exploited by other men to justify the tyranny and oppression which they inflict upon their victims. In this context, *The Fall* can be interpreted as an effort to rectify a certain tendency toward naive optimism which is not altogether absent from *The Plague*, at least on the symbolic level. The later novel shows Camus's awareness that men can and often do choose evil, a choice for which they must be held responsible.

But why do men so choose? For this question Camus claims inability to provide a definitive answer, but he does grapple with the problem in a valiant and searching way. At one point in *The Plague* the narrator remarks:

The evil that is in the world always comes of ignorance, and good intentions may do as much harm as malevolence, if they lack understanding. On the whole, men are more good than bad; that, however, isn't the real point. But they are more or less ignorant, and it is this that we call vice or virtue; the most incorrigible vice being that of an ignorance that fancies it knows everything and therefore claims for itself the right to kill. The soul of the murderer is blind; and there can be no true goodness nor true love without the utmost clearsightedness. [80]

Anyone who asserts that human evil "always comes of ignorance" would appear to be a throwback to the most simple-minded attitudes of the Enlightenment. But a serious effort to grasp Camus's meaning on this point precludes, I believe, considering him a naively rationalistic "child of light," in Reinhold

[79] Parker, *Albert Camus: The Artist in the Arena*, 112–13 (Camus quoted from "Lettre à Roland Barthes sur *La Peste*," in *Club*, February, 1955, p. 7).

[80] *The Plague*, 120–21.

Niebuhr's well-known phrase. Camus, speaking through his narrator, does say that men are more good than bad, and elsewhere
in *The Plague* he declares that there are more things in men to
admire than to despise; but in neither instance does he claim that
there is really no evil in man or that there is essentially nothing
in him that is despicable. We gain an important clue to what
he means by that "ignorance" which produces evil by noting the
narrator's characterization of a petty gangster who turns to prof-
iteering during the plague-time as a man with "an ignorant, that
is to say lonely, heart." [81] It is blindness, a lack of "the utmost
clearsightedness" in regard to the human condition, which produces evil. This is much more a spiritual than it is an intellectual defect; it is failure to discern and be faithful to the essential unity among men known through the experience of
dialogical communion. And one of the most common causes of
this blinding is captivation by ideological abstractions which provide their adherents with a false sense of knowing ultimate, total
truth. This is "the most incorrigible vice" and the one most
pregnant with human evil.

Beyond this point Camus did not go in seeking to explicate
the origins of evil. Of this problem he remarked: "We are faced
with evil. And, as for me, I feel rather as Augustine did before
becoming a Christian when he said: 'I tried to find the source of
evil and I got nowhere.'" [82] About the same time he noted in
his journal: "What is man worth? What is man? All life long,
after what I have seen, I shall have a suspicion and basic worry
about him." [83] Whether man's nature is in an ultimate sense in-
nately good or evil, or, more precisely, what is the primal cause
of human evil, was for Camus finally an unanswerable question
and hence probably not extremely relevant to our real concerns.
It is certain, however, that the view put forth by Clamence in
The Fall, that man is totally evil and totally guilty, was never

[81]*Ibid.,* 272.
[82]Albert Camus, *Resistance, Rebellion, and Death,* trans. Justin O'Brien
(New York: Alfred A. Knopf, 1961), 73.
[83]*Notebooks, 1942–1951,* p. 155 (entry of 1947).

Camus's and that his last novel was an effort to show the in-human consequences of such a belief. In 1954, responding to a question about original sin, he observed: "People have insisted too much upon the innocence of the creation. Now they want to crush us with the feeling of our own guilt. There is, I believe, an intermediate truth." [84] It is this "intermediate truth"—that man retains a relative innocence but is unquestionably capable of "losing track of the light" and sinning grievously against him-self and his fellows, for what ultimate cause we do not know, although intermediate reasons are discernible—that Camus finally presents as his view of human evil.

A second aspect of human nature, according to Camus, is that man possesses an efficacious but limited and fallible reason. On this point also he stood for an "intermediate truth" between the extremes of a world-encompassing rationalism and a vitalistic ir-rationalism. He never renounced the allegiance to reason pro-claimed in *The Myth of Sisyphus*, and in much of his writing, especially the *Reflections on the Guillotine*, he made effective use of straightforward logical and evidential reasoning. However, the political problems which he considered especially critical he viewed as largely the result of an excessive and inflated rationalism. It is sufficient to note here that Camus attributed the totali-tarian impulse to philosophic claims to comprehension of the ultimate order of things, and particularly to what he saw as Hegel's pretension to knowledge of the inevitable course of his-tory. Such claims take us far beyond the certainties of our ex-perience and result in neglect of concrete, existentially perceived human truth.

In the third place, it is necessary here only to recall Camus's profound conviction that men are linked to one another by a common capacity for dialogical communion. From awareness of this existential certainty there emerges a meaning for life which

[84]Interview in *La Gazette Littéraire* (March, 1954), quoted in Philip Thody, *Albert Camus: A Study of His Work* (London: Hamish Hamilton, 1957), 78.

abstract reason is incapable of providing. A creature who desires happiness, man finds his greatest fulfillment in relationships of openness, directness, mutuality, and presence with nature and with his fellow men. These are, I believe, the three aspects of human nature with which Camus was most concerned and which were especially important in giving form and substance to his political thought.

Just as he never composed a systematic treatise on the nature of man, so Camus failed to produce a set of ordered analyses and prescriptions in the realm of ethics. But, as we have seen, he was intensely concerned with knowing "how one should live." Seeking to remain faithful to an existential perspective and approach, he could not accept or advise others to accept ethical principles simply on grounds of claims to authority external to the individual, whether that authority was religious, philosophic, or political. Of religious claims he noted in his journal: "Christ died perhaps for someone, but it was not for me. Man is guilty, but he is so for not having been able to derive everything from himself—this is a mistake that has grown since the beginning." [85]

A Protestant theologian has recently interpreted Camus's perspective on this point as typical of "urban-secular" man, who asks: "What are the sources of meaning and value by which man lives his life? Are they created and imposed by God, or does man invent them himself?" And who replies: "Man . . . doesn't simply discover meaning; he originates it." [86] This view is well taken, insofar as it points up Camus's refusal to acknowledge a cosmic being who arbitrarily imposes an order upon mankind. But it is incorrect in implying that Camus was a "Modern Promethean" who sought to take the place of such a deity by inventing *ex nihilo* and arbitrarily a universe of meaning. This interpretation overlooks Camus's profound appreciation of "given" meanings that he claimed to discover, not to manufacture, through his ex-

---

[85]*Notebooks, 1942–1951,* p. 85 (entry of November, 1943).
[86]Harvey Cox, *The Secular City: Secularization and Urbanization in Theological Perspective* (New York: Macmillan Company, 1965), 72, 74.

perience and perceptions—pre-eminently in dialogical openness to the world.

A penetrating analysis of Camus's ethical perspective has been provided by Serge Doubrovsky. He points out that Camus "had a certain happy experience of being which appeared basic to him: he passed it on to us." In this experience, "he places happiness, . . . the reconciliation of man and nature, above ethics and simultaneously rectifies the indifference inherent in nature, his own nature, through an ethic: solitude exploding in the movement of the heart toward his fellow-man." Camus's ethic is *"existential* in the full sense of the word," for it is founded upon the assumption that "no formula, no effort of discursive thought can absolve us from recreating experience ourselves within ourselves." This effort leads to no closed, fully coherent ethical system, but to "an ethic of 'openness' to the world and to others, an ethic of participation." [87]

Camus's distrust of ethical abstractions was ever apparent, for example in his remark, "One must encounter love before having encountered ethics. Or else one is torn." [88] One must have fully and openly encountered life in existential awareness and found it, even if in some respects absurd and harrowing, essentially good and meaningful, before ethical reflection can be humanly fruitful. Otherwise ethics can all too easily become a closed system increasingly isolated from experience and inspire fanatical efforts to crush human realities inconsistent with the reign of abstract ideals. "One must love life before loving its meaning, Dostoevsky says. Yes, and when the love of life disappears, no meaning consoles us for it." [89]

It is a tenacious love of life here and now, "a happy experience of being," that is basic to all of Camus's ethical reflections, from his earliest through his final works. Such a stance includes foremost the conviction that there are limits man must observe

---

[87]Doubrovsky, "The Ethics of Albert Camus," 83, 84, 76.
[88]*Notebooks, 1942–1951,* p. 199 (entry of September, 1948).
[89]*Ibid.,* 218 (entry of September, 1949).

if he is to avoid violating human nature and remain faithful to the human condition. These boundaries are discovered to be inherent in the widespread modern experience of revolt. Camus never claimed that there is a moral imperative to rebel against "death-in-life" incumbent upon men, although this was his own reaction to oppression and suffering and, he believed, the inevitable response of any normally sensitive person.

In his meditations upon the human condition, Camus was increasingly attracted by what he understood to be a central theme of the ancient Hellenic tradition:

Greek thought always took refuge behind the conception of limits. It never carried anything to extremes, neither the sacred nor reason, because it negated nothing, neither the sacred nor reason. It took everything into consideration, balancing shadow with light. Our Europe, on the other hand, off in the pursuit of totality, is the child of disproportion. She negates beauty, as she negates whatever she does not glorify. And through all her diverse ways, she glorifies but one thing, which is the future rule of reason. In her madness she extends the eternal limits, and at that very moment dark Erinyes fall upon her and tear her to pieces. Nemesis, the goddess of measure and not of revenge, keeps watch. All those who overstep the limit are pitilessly punished by her.[90]

Camus's admiration for classical Greek values centered principally upon the congruence he thought he discerned between the Greeks' advocacy of "moderation" (*sophrosyne*) and his own attachment to "modesty" (*mesure*). Richard Cox has recently pointed out some difficulties in Camus's attempt to claim that these two conceptions are identical. Cox asserts that *sophrosyne* reflected a "cosmic philosophy" which assumed a discernible order of being in the totality of the universe, while *mesure* emanates from a "humanistic philosophy," which finds no such universal order but rather a rationally "absurd" disjunction between man and nature. Cox takes Camus to task for retaining an

[90]Albert Camus, "Helen's Exile," in *The Myth of Sisyphus and Other Essays*, 187.

"historicist" perspective which leads him to restrict his inquiries to the significant experiences of contemporary man; by insisting "that the problem of ideology must be understood in terms of a consciousness of the radically historical character of the human condition, [Camus] undermines and then consigns to oblivion that form of inquiry for which 'revolt' is one form of contemporary replacement: political philosophy in the original sense of an inquiry into the nature of political life and its place in the whole or *cosmos*." [91]

While it may well be true that Camus's claim to emulation of classical Greek ethics is insupportable, it is simply beside the point to accuse him of "undermining" and "consigning to oblivion" cosmic-style political philosophy. This work of "undermining" was begun long before Camus, by the nonteleological perspective that characterizes modern science. Camus, in common with most contemporary thinkers, could discern no cosmic order in which man is to occupy a given niche. For him the only hope of redeeming human existence from total, nihilistic absurdity was to turn from seemingly unanswerable cosmic questions to distinctly human concerns and experiences; faithful exploration of the latter realm was sufficient, he concluded, for the discovery of human limits that cannot be exceeded without inhuman consequences.

It should already be apparent, and it will become even more obvious when we examine Camus's attitude toward political ideologies, that his ethical perspective has much in common with humanism. The latter is impossible to define specifically but can be considered as a category that encompasses the mundane, everyday virtues—such as honesty, fair dealing, and due process of law—which the majority of post-Christian Western men profess to respect. Not long after the war Camus noted in his journal: "The values I ought to defend and illustrate today are average values. This requires a talent so spare and unadorned that I

[91]Richard H. Cox, "Ideology, History and Political Philosophy," *Social Research,* XXXII (Spring, 1965), 96–97.

doubt I have it." [92] His talent did prove equal to the task, but his relationship to humanism always remained equivocal. Also in 1946 he remarked: "It seems that I still have to find a humanism. I have nothing against humanism, of course. I just find it inadequate." [93]

Though scarcely distinguishable in conclusions from liberal humanism, Camus's ethical perspective derives from distinctly different premises. As Philip Thody points out, traditional humanism finds the world to be rational and not absurd. Man is naturally at home in it, and human values are rationally defensible and certain. But Camus's experience of the absurd made it impossible for him to accept these comforting assumptions, and he was thrown back upon the experience of the individual as the only possible source of values. "Setting out from a philosophical *tabula rasa,* he recreated a humanism which starts out from the loss of faith which characterises our time." [94]

This distinctive humanism, the product of an arduous effort to derive conclusions from a lucid, open, existential awareness of the human condition, was the stance from which Camus looked with a critical eye upon the political turmoil of his time and sought to point the way toward a politics of hope.

[92]*Notebooks, 1942–1951,* p. 144 (entry of October, 1946).
[93]*Ibid.,* 135 (entry of March, 1946).
[94]Thody, *Albert Camus, 1913–1960,* pp. 144–45.

IV

The Critique of Ideologies

FOR CAMUS, the supreme challenge to political thought in our time was posed by the dominance and pervasiveness of ideologies in modern political life.[1] He sought first to understand and to explain this condition, and then to define a personal stance toward it. Approaching this complex subject not as a social scientist or historian, but as an artist and existential thinker deeply concerned with the human situation, Camus disavowed any pretension to providing a total interpretation of ideological thinking or of the regimes he viewed as its historical offspring, fascist and communist totalitarianisms. He sought primarily to elucidate the nature of the fundamental human experiences and perceptions which have given rise to ideological world-views and to suggest some explanations of why these perspectives eventually manifested themselves in political forms quite at variance with the intent of their philosophical progenitors. For Camus this sad his-

[1] I use ideology here not in Marx's sense but rather to designate a type of world-view which is simultaneously a total interpretation of human existence, a thoroughgoing indictment and repudiation of existing society, and a program for creating, by means of violent revolution if necessary, a perfect social order which will produce a new humanity in accord with the ideologist's vision of perfection.

tory was the tale of modern rebellion and of its miscarriage and betrayal.

The spiritual impulse for ideological thinking has been provided by what Camus called "metaphysical rebellion"—"the movement by which man protests against his condition and against the whole of creation." [2] Such revolt, like that of the prototypical rebellious slave, is a reaction against felt oppression and frustration. But, for the metaphysical rebel, the oppressor is not another man but rather the human condition afflicted with death and evil. More precisely, the oppressor is a god alleged to be both all-good and all-powerful but who yet permits men to suffer and die. Also, like the revolt of slave against master, metaphysical rebellion is a distinctly Western phenomenon; it could occur only in conjunction with Christianity. The metaphysical rebel "finds in himself" the principle of justice and opposes it to the injustice common in the world. His initial impulse is to strive for the unitarian rule of justice, but "if he is driven to extremes" he may madly seek the reign of total injustice. What he cannot abide is the contradiction between his desire for fulfillment and for justice, and the incompleteness and wastefulness that result from death and evil. The metaphysical rebel is no mere dispassionate theoretical atheist; he is a dedicated blasphemer, "denouncing God as the father of death and as the supreme outrage." [3]

A frontal attack upon the orthodox deity was not conceivable so long as the West was thought of as a unified Christendom. Medieval men considered it a fulfillment, not a violation, of justice that men should be divided between masters and servants; by nature and by divine prerogative man's earthly lot was not easy. God himself had entered history and suffered as a man, the supreme demonstration that man was created to be a suffering creature. But the ubiquity and persuasiveness of

[2] *The Rebel*, 23.
[3] *Ibid.*, 23–24.

these assumptions declined in the post-medieval era, and some eighteenth-century rationalists dared to assert that Christ was only a man and that hence his death justified none of the horrors of man's condition. If there was a god, he was fully responsible for suffering and injustice and had not shared with men the victim's status. A religion brought into question could no longer convincingly justify a master-slave social order or make evil seem ultimately beneficent or even necessary. Metaphysical rebels began to think: if there is a god, he is cruel and must be denied in the name of the human demands for justice and happiness; if there is no god, we are wholly free to remake the world so that it will accord with those basic human desires.

Camus traces the development of metaphysical rebellion in the perspectives of various eighteenth- and nineteenth-century literary figures, such as the Marquis de Sade, Lautréamont, and Rimbaud. But the incarnations of such rebellion most pertinent to his interpretation are Dostoevsky's Ivan Karamazov and Friedrich Nietzsche. Ivan, a pivotal figure in *The Brothers Karamazov,* proclaims that if evil is a necessary ingredient of the created world, he will reject creation itself. He explicitly elevates the principle of justice to a position superior to God and condemns the creator in the name of this principle. Ivan poignantly symbolizes the fundamental enterprise of metaphysical rebellion—an effort to replace the "Kingdom of Grace" with the "Kingdom of Justice."

But, in Camus's interpretation, Ivan betrayed the initial impulse of his own revolt, in his famous assertion that if God is dead, everything is permitted. He erroneously concludes that no values can be affirmed outside the realm of grace, although his rebellion was occasioned by a spontaneous revulsion against suffering and a demand for justice. Furthermore, Ivan acts out his metaphysical conclusion of nihilism by permitting his father to be murdered. For Camus he is also symbolic of totalitarian translations of metaphysical rebellion into historical action; in practice Ivan

and the totalitarians attempt to place themselves upon the vacant
throne of deity by claiming a total freedom. They lack fidelity
to the initial impulses of metaphysical revolt.

The supreme philosophical exemplar of modern rebellion
against God and the human condition, Camus declares, is Nietzsche, in whose thought the nihilistic potentialities in revolt were,
for the first time, plainly articulated. Nietzsche's approach, a kind
of passionate reincarnation of Descartes's methodical doubt, emphasized radical and systematic negation; he sought to unmask
all contemporary idols camouflaging what he considered the essential fact of the death of God. Nietzsche did not "murder"
God; he found rather that God had died in the soul of his time,
that most men were hiding this devastating truth from themselves
with a variety of more or less hypocritical stratagems. Sensing the
explosive impact that a full awareness of this truth would make
upon mankind, Nietzsche sought to transform the apocalypse
which would result into a renaissance, so that at least some men
would respond affirmatively and creatively to the question: "Can
one live without believing in anything?" For Nietzsche not only
rejected Christianity, he scorned the secular messianism of socialism. He charged that socialism, in clinging to a belief in ultimate
historical ends, obscured real and immediate human needs and
was nothing but degenerate Christianity. Socialism is only one
means of disguising the true seriousness of the death of God, for
it continues to hold to "superior" values toward the realization
of which history is supposed to be progressing.

What then does the death of God mean to Nietzsche? Simply
that there is no law superior to or apart from man, nor any law-
giver other than man—no external standards can judge human
values. But the absence of an eternal law does not mean that
there is no law of any kind—if nothing is prohibited eternally,
neither is anything permitted apart from human denial or per-
mission. No liberty is possible except in a world where both
the permitted and the prohibited are defined. Since man must
create his own values, Nietzsche proposes to replace all value

judgments with "absolute assent, and by a complete and exalted allegiance to this world. . . . Total acceptance of total necessity is his paradoxical definition of freedom." [4] In effect, Nietzsche's doctrine of eternal recurrence means that fate is divine and the world, as the ultimate, is God. As creatures of the world, men partake of its divinity by wholeheartedly accepting and affirming its fatalistic reality: "To say yes to the world, to reproduce it, is simultaneously to re-create the world and oneself, to become the great artist, the creator. . . . Divinity without immortality defines the extent of the creator's freedom." [5]

Nietzsche's relationship to nihilism is equivocal; he implies that man lives without restraints, except for those which are self-imposed, and that man can re-create the world in whatever form he has sufficient will and strength to seek unflinchingly to bring into being. And although Nietzsche did not so conclude, it is possible to use his teaching to justify, as did the Nazis, the view that to affirm the world in an unqualified way means admitting the legitimacy of murder. Nietzsche goes beyond nihilism by leaping from the negation of the ideal to its secularization: he concludes that since men cannot attain salvation through God, they must save themselves from meaninglessness through their own earthly efforts. "Philosophy secularizes the ideal. But tyrants appear who soon secularize the philosophies that give them the right to do so." [6] Such was Nietzsche's fate, comprehensible though unjust, at the hands of Hitler and his ideological camp-followers.

A century and a half of metaphysical rebellion and nihilism has disclosed the persistence of human protest against the injustice and absurdity of creation and the human condition. Nihilism concludes that men are enclosed in solitude and that morality is nonexistent. But few have been able to live quiescently with these conclusions, and many have sought to re-create

[4] *Ibid.*, 72.
[5] *Ibid.*, 74.
[6] *Ibid.*, 78.

the world and human values in their own image by unleashing passion and the will to power; all too frequently the results have been suicide, madness, murder, and destruction.

This does not mean that metaphysical rebellion is in itself evil and to be suppressed. Camus admired and participated in its essential impulse, which is to struggle against death and suffering. The rebel fights death not necessarily because he is afraid to die, but because it seems to deprive life of meaning; likewise he protests against suffering for which he can see no justification. The aims of metaphysical rebellion are noble, but the process of its unfolding has been too often marked by tragedy. The root problem is that the rejection of the traditional god has frequently been accompanied by a quest for a new deity, of the desire for which the rebel himself has often been unaware. This can result, as in the case of Ivan Karamazov, in deification of the total rejection of what exists; complete negation produces human destruction. Or, as with Nietzsche, total affirmation of what exists, absolute assent, can lead to acceptance of terror and destruction. "Hatred of the creator can turn to hatred of creation or to exclusive and defiant love of what exists. But in both cases it ends in murder and loses the right to be called rebellion. One can be nihilist in two ways, in both by having an intemperate recourse to absolutes." [7] True revolt does not deify, by absolutizing, either negation or assent, but seeks meaning for life in a protracted struggle against injustice and suffering while seeking conscientiously to avoid adding to the crushing and repulsive weight of human misery.

Rebellion against a god claimed to be creator and preserver of an evil and absurd world, as Camus viewed it, was the beginning of both tragedy and triumph for modern man. The triumph is refusal passively to accept injustice and suffering. The metaphysical rebel pledges himself to build the only kingdom —that of justice—which can replace the realm of grace, to reconstruct the human community upon the debris of the divine com-

[7]*Ibid.*, 101–102.

munity: "To kill God and to build a Church are the constant and contradictory purpose of rebellion." [8] The tragic aspect of this effort is twentieth-century totalitarianism, offspring of a marriage between metaphysical revolt and political revolution. Totalitarians have drawn the practical consequences from the dictum of the nihilistic rebel, who adds to the "I rebel, therefore we are" of the original experience of revolt, a second postulate: "And we are alone."

Modern efforts to embody the aims of metaphysical revolt in worldly reality Camus labels "historical rebellion." As a young man, he had already concluded that revolutionary ideologies are essentially spiritual phenomena: "The spirit of revolution lies wholly in man's protest against the human condition. . . . A revolution is always carried out against the Gods—from that of Prometheus onwards. It is a protest which man makes against his destiny, and both tyrants and *bourgeois* puppets are nothing but pretexts." [9] Revolution can never be understood as an inevitable outcome of the simultaneous presence in a society of mutually incompatible material forces. Camus did not deny the enormous significance of social and economic conditions, but, claiming no expertise in their study, he attempted to give the closest attention possible to the workings and fate of the rebellious spirit as revealed in the ideas and lives of modern revolutionaries.

Camus's conception of the link between metaphysical rebellion and the totalitarian spirit is dramatized in *The Just Assassins (Les Justes),* a play he wrote while also working on *The Rebel.* Based upon historical events, the play is set in Russia in 1905; its protagonists are members of the terrorist wing of the Social Revolutionary party. Most of these terrorists seek to live within the tension of true rebellion. They realize that taking human life cannot be justified, but their feeling of solidarity with one another and with the slave-like Russian masses impels them

[8]*Ibid.,* 103.
[9]*Notebooks, 1935–1942,* p. 84 (entry of February, 1938).

to commit political assassinations in order to provide an opportunity for the emergence of a more nearly just regime.

But they do not kill heedlessly and callously in the name of an abstract, wholly futuristic version of justice. They kill, sparingly and conscious of their guilt, for the sake of true human dignity, because they love life and have dedicated themselves to making life more abundant and more genuinely human for men presently victimized by oppression. They feel that only by putting their own lives in jeopardy when the advancement of their cause compels them to kill, indeed by being willing to give up their own lives to pay for those they have taken, can they justify a revolt that is onerous but for which they feel a responsibility they cannot in good conscience evade. For this band of dedicated rebels, and in particular their principal spokesman, the young poet Kaliayev, the ends which they seek do not justify suspending judgment on the means employed to attain them. Kaliayev voices this explanation of their purpose:

> I believe, like the others, in the idea of the revolution. Like them, I want to sacrifice myself for it. I too can be clever, close-mouthed, two-faced, and pragmatic. It's just that life continues to look wonderful to me. I love beauty and happiness! That's why I hate despotism. How can I explain it? The revolution—certainly! But the revolution for life, to give life a chance, do you understand? . . . We kill in order to build a world free of killing. We accept our guilt so that the earth may at last be covered with the innocent.[10]

Kaliayev expresses the majority sentiment of the group, but he is not unopposed within its ranks. Stepan, a terrorist who has recently rejoined the revolutionary movement upon returning from forced exile in Switzerland, obviously symbolizes the totalitarian spirit, in contrast to Kaliayev's true rebellion. For, in response to the latter's explanation that he is serving the revolutionary cause out of a love for life, Stepan declares: "I don't love life—I love justice, which is above life." [11]

[10]Albert Camus, *Les Justes, pièce en cinq actes* (Paris: Gallimard, 1950), Act I, 40–41.
[11]*Ibid.*, 36.

This contrast becomes even more marked as the drama unfolds. Kaliayev is assigned by the terrorists' leader to assassinate the archduke Sergei by throwing a bomb under his carriage as it moves down the street toward a theater. But Kaliayev returns to headquarters, his mission unfulfilled. Sorrowfully he explains that just as he had braced himself to hurl the bomb at the approaching vehicle, he had seen two childish faces peering through its windows. He had been unable to persuade himself to murder two innocent children; to do so seemed to him inherently dishonorable and utterly unjustifiable.

Stepan explodes: "I can't stomach this kind of nonsense any longer. When we make up our minds to forget children, that's when we will become masters of the world and the revolution will triumph." [12] When Dora, a woman terrorist, protests that even in destroying there is a certain order, that there are limits which must not be ignored, Stepan violently exclaims:

There are no limits. The truth is that you don't really believe in the revolution. If you believed in it totally and completely, if you were certain that through our sacrifices and our victories we will create a Russia liberated from despotism, a land of freedom which in the end will cover the whole earth, if you did not doubt that man, liberated from his masters and his prejudices, will then turn toward heaven the visage of a true god, why would the death of two children matter in the least? [13]

In this play, and for the time being, Kaliayev wins out over Stepan. But in the subsequent history of the twentieth century the self-sacrificing rebels have given way to the totalitarians, for whom the distant end of perfect justice excuses any means employed to attain it—the murder of two or of two million children. Thus Kaliayev's response to Stepan contains a note of doleful prophecy: "I have agreed to kill in order to overturn despotism. But behind your words I can see the coming of a despotism which, if it is ever established, will make of me an

[12] *Les Justes,* Act II, 69.
[13] *Ibid.,* 74.

assassin, even though I tried to be a servant of justice." [14] Our time, Camus believed, has witnessed this tragic miscarriage of rebellion; the reign of totalitarianism has brought assassins to power but has negated, not universalized, justice.

In *The Rebel,* Camus attempts, through analysis of various efforts to embody metaphysical rebellion in revolutionary ideas and action, to summarize the history of revolt's betrayal. The year 1789 was the first critical turning point; the leaders of the French Revolution overturned physically a regime claiming to be founded on divine right; these revolutionaries sought to make historically effective the forces of negation and rebellion which had inspired most of the significant intellectual efforts of the eighteenth century. The Jacobins "added to traditional tyranni-cide the concept of calculated deicide." [15] The Church and the *ancien régime* were linked in such complicity that the monarch presented himself as the earthly representative of the Kingdom of Grace, and the King was killed in the name of justice in its war upon arbitrariness and evil. For abstract grace and abstract justice have one common feature: both crave to be total and absolute. In the French Revolution they became locked in mortal combat; if one denied the God of the Church, logically one had to kill the King: "It is the philosophers who are going to kill the King: the King must die in the name of the social contract." [16]

It was Camus's belief that the frenzy of the Jacobins to establish fully the principle of absolute and total justice had been inspired to a considerable degree by Rousseau's *Social Contract.* In effect, Rousseau's rebellion against traditional authority which he felt to be oppressive took the form of submission to a new god, reason confounded with nature. The new divine vicar is the people, considered to be the embodiment of the "general will": "It is evident that, with *The Social Contract,* we are assisting at

[14]*Ibid.,* 74–75.
[15]*The Rebel,* 112.
[16]*Ibid.,* 114.

the birth of a new *mystique*—the will of the people being substituted for God Himself." [17] This new deity apes all the old divine attributes; it is sovereign, infallible, totally free in respect to itself, and indivisible. The body politic as defined by Rousseau displaces the mystical body of Christendom. It is fitting, therefore, that *The Social Contract* concludes with the prescription of a civil religion, which prohibits not only opposition to the state but a neutral attitude toward its institutions and purposes. Rousseau was the first in modern times—but not the last—to propose the creation of a profession of political faith. He was the first—but again only the forerunner of many—to justify the death penalty for those who refuse to worship the state or to agree to absolute submission of the subject to the sovereign. He truly inaugurated our present age of "sainted Humanity."

The Jacobin extremists, in particular Saint-Just, sought to incarnate Rousseau's ideas in the flesh of history. And in carrying his theories to their logical conclusion they went much further than Rousseau would have desired, particularly in their execution of the monarch and in carrying out a reign of terror. But this is a paradigm of the usual fate of metaphysical rebellion acted out in the political realm. Although the revolutionaries had rejected God and the realm of grace, they were not irreligious. They worshipped at the altar of Truth, Justice, and Reason, the new triune godhead. But abstract principles have little inherent power within the flux of human affairs: "To ensure the adoration of a theorem for any length of time, faith is not enough; a police force is needed as well." [18] If experience indicates that men corrupted by the old order of injustice will not yet act virtuously on their own initiative—virtue is defined, of course, by the new wielders of power—they must be forced to be good in order to make of the Republic the total incarnation of virtue. The terror is but a necessary means for the attainment of a virtuous national unity.

[17]*Ibid.*, 115.
[18]*Ibid.*, 122.

The French revolutionary terror was the first important instance in modern history of metaphysical rebellion carried to
excess through marriage with revolutionary politics. Revolt in the
name of justice and order became subservient to the abstract
ideal of a totally just order; it had to become full historical
reality even at the cost of massive injustice perpetrated against
great numbers of particular persons. The tragic legacy of this
first great revolution was its legitimation of political terrorism.

But even in their extremism, the Jacobins still clung to certain transcendent values—Truth, Justice, and Reason—as sur-
rogates for absolute deity. The most influential nineteenth-century thinkers, however, made a concerted attack upon this pale
shadow of transcendence. In Hegel's thought all values, including
the Jacobin triumvirate, lose eternal status and are wholly incorporated into the flux of history, into the "becoming," rather
than the "is." But Hegel also asserts that these principles will
ultimately come to full realization in the course of the historical
process; thus they become absolute ends or goals and no longer
serve as regulative criteria of means in the historical present.
In practice the Jacobins had traveled far along this road, as
their moral "theorems" had proved impotent for the evaluation
of their own revolutionary policies, but Hegel makes such moral
judgment, in principle, impossible. For him, the good and true
become only that which survives the inexorable dialectical movement of history, in effect the successful, the efficacious. The only
ethical guide to the choice of means is the criterion of pure
pragmatism, as the end of history becomes an all-consuming
passion, the gratification of which justifies any means that will
help to attain it. "The conqueror is always right; that is one
of the lessons which can be learned from the most important
German philosophical system of the nineteenth century." [19]

Hegel himself was, of course, no partisan of political revolution. His only suggestion for a provisional ethic was conformity
with the customs and spirit of the times. But more revolutionary

[19]*Ibid.*, 137.

minds than his were to accept his basic premises while rejecting his conformism in the name of a more "active fatalism" which sought to help along at breakneck speed the "inevitable" movement of history toward its sublime consummation. To the Jacobin legacy to totalitarianism—the principle that the state as the incarnation of virtue may be protected and aggrandized by terror, if necessary—Hegel adds immeasurably by philosophically reinforcing the principle that the end justifies the means. For if the historical process is in itself the ultimate measure of human activity, and if one believes that history is proceeding, tortuously but inexorably, toward a future incarnation of freedom and virtue perfected in all mankind, how can one incur guilt for employing any means—systematic murder, concentration camps, total regimentation of human lives—which seem necessary in the present for the ultimate realization of man's sublime and glorious destiny?

But before such immanent ends could inspire the totalitarian spirit, Hegel's philosophical idealism had to be materialized, conjoined with rebellion against immediate injustice, and rationalized to conform to the revolutionary aspirations of the modern age. For contemporary "rational" totalitarianism, therefore, Karl Marx is the great prophet. Marx's indebtedness to Hegel is well known, but Camus contends that he was also profoundly—and unfortunately—influenced by the Christian heritage of the West and by the bourgeois spirit of his time. Initially Marx rebelled against the nineteenth-century capitalists' treatment of their workers as subhuman implements. This revolt against oppression Camus interprets as a manifestation of the genuinely human impulse of the true rebel. But, when Marx attempted to rationalize and systematize his rebellion, philosophic, religious, and environmental influences turned his thinking into a prophetic ideology; and his concern for realistic social criticism gradually receded in importance as prophecy became a consuming passion.[20]

[20]This interpretation of Marx, like all Camus's interpretations of political thinkers, is open to question. Robert Tucker, for example, has attempted

From Christianity Marx appropriated both the idea of linear history progressing toward a goal and a spirit of totality. The former view, Camus contends, had led Christians to conclude that nature is only the raw material of history and to assume a purely utilitarian attitude toward the natural world. No longer was man to contemplate and joyfully participate in nature, as had the Greeks (and the young Camus), who had revered and respected its given beauty. Nature was solely to be utilized by men, to be transformed and mastered. Marx secularized and extended this perspective; in his thought man became not only master of nature but also lord of history. Long before completing *The Rebel*, Camus had developed this interpretation: "Origins of the modern madness. It was Christianity that turned man away from the *world*. It reduced him to himself and to his history. Communism is a logical successor to Christianity. It is a history of Christians." [21]

The Christian belief that God is absolutely sovereign over every aspect of human life was also secularized by Marx, in whose thought revolutionary ideology claims omniscience and omnipotence. This Christian conviction, cut loose from its transcendent religious moorings, has in fact, Camus declares, become murderous: "Those who claim to know and regulate everything end by killing everything." [22] This secularized spirit of totality, incorporated into contemporary totalitarianism largely through

---

to demonstrate that Marx's initial impulse was a desire to solve the philosophical problem of man's self-alienation, a concern central to the thought of the young Marx's most important philosophical mentors, Hegel and Feuerbach. This would seem to indicate that Marx was originally inspired not by existential identification with downtrodden workers but by a theoretical vision of the proletariat as the most obvious prototype of alienated humanity. Whatever the precise truth may be on this point—and the evidence is most ambiguous—there can be no doubt that much of Marx's continuing influence has been the result of his relentless insistence on the inhuman effects upon the working class of nineteenth-century industrialism. (*See* Robert Tucker, *Philosophy and Myth in Karl Marx* [Cambridge: Cambridge University Press, 1961].)

[21] *Notebooks, 1942–1951*, p. 128 (entry of November, 1945).
[22] *Actuelles*, 198.

Marx's influence, has given to this movement its distinctive features.

Marx also appropriated, in modified form, at least two distinctively bourgeois attitudes prevalent in his time. First, he shared the faith in scientific progress endemic to the nineteenth-century Western *Zeitgeist*. Although Marx railed against rationalistic optimism, he retained its guiding belief in the conception of a difficult but irreversible journey toward a future when man will be fully reconciled with himself and his fellows (the final conquest of "alienation"). To the bourgeois theme of praise for technical and scientific progress, Marx added the contrapuntal embellishment of inevitable social progress toward the goal of a classless society. Secondly, from bourgeois economic theory Marx accepted the belief in a direct correlation between increasing and improving industrial production *per se* and the development of human nature. In particular, he appropriated from Ricardo, a staunch defender of laissez-faire capitalism, the labor theory of value.

Camus maintained that these bourgeois influences caused Marx's thought to reflect a tragically ironic anomaly: he retained the root error of modern industrial society, which is, in the formulation of policy, to regard persons primarily as commodities. And this latent tendency in Marx's ideas has been manifested most fully by the totalitarian regimes which claim to champion the cause of perfected humanity, a result not at all intended by Marx. Camus saw a genuine and moving ethical grandeur in Marx's vehement protests against the indignity and meaninglessness of work in modern society.

But Marx shared the common fate of most prophets: his message was truncated and distorted by his ostensible disciples to make it conform to their immediate intentions. And it must be recognized that a basic premise of Marx's thought can in fact justify the totalitarian Marxists. For Marx the single overriding value was absolute justice (or, as Tucker puts it, triumph over alienation), which could become reality only in the society of mature communism. This perfected social order in turn could appear only in the aftermath of violent and bitter class warfare. One does not concern himself greatly about ethical judgments of his tactics when engaged in mortal combat; we see emerging once more the principle which invariably subverts true revolt— the conviction that the end justifies any means believed neces- sary to its attainment. Camus points out that Marx explicitly repudiated this principle, but his espousal of revolutionary vio- lence for utopian ends makes it quite understandable that his disciples should have given little attention to marking out the boundaries of justice as a criterion of political means. In prac- tice, Marx and his followers overlooked a fundamental truth of human experience, that "the demand for justice ends in injus- tice if it is not primarily based on an ethical justification of justice. . . ." [23]

Marxist socialism became therefore a religion of history—a faith for which the immanent *parousia* was the classless society that would lead to idyllic communism and the provisional ethic nothing but the doctrine of success in its most unvarnished form. With the victory of Marxists in the 1917 Bolshevik revolution, "the new religion is once more confronted with Galilee: to pre- serve its faith, it must deny and humiliate free man." [24]

Lenin's theories and policies represent a decisive turning-point in the development of historical rebellion; in his writings and active leadership during the formative years of the Soviet Union, he showed an overriding concern for the attainment of revolu- tionary goals. Compelled by circumstances to be more practical than Marx, he formulated the conception of an "elite guard" of dedicated professional revolutionaries, whose tasks were to plan the insurrection and govern for an indefinite period in the name of the proletariat, after the destruction of the old regime. In practice this has meant that a self-perpetuating oligarchy, or even an all-powerful dictator, determines which means are most effi-

[23]*The Rebel,* 209.
[24]*Ibid.,* 212.

cacious under given conditions for advancement toward the final realization of revolutionary ends. The familiar and sorrowful result of this mode of operation has been widespread injustice, the wholesale infliction of suffering upon the subject masses, and systematic murder, all in the guise of service to justice and humanity. Totalitarian communism emerged as a potent ideology and historical force when Marx and his revolutionary socialist followers, in their rebellion against the absurdity and injustice of the world, failed to be faithful to the contradiction experienced by the rebel who recognizes that his passion for just ends does not warrant resorting to means which disrupt the solidarity he feels with all men through their participation in a common human condition. The Marxists who became totalitarian rulers took the "easy way" out of the human predicament through the "immediate use of human unhappiness for the sake of happiness in the distant future, rather than in relieving as much and as soon as possible the suffering of millions of men." [25]

Some penetrating observations which reinforce and amplify Camus's analysis of Marxism-Leninism have been offered by Martin Buber. He maintains that Marx's theorizing is fatally deficient as socialist thought in one crucial respect. Of three possible approaches to the consideration of public affairs—economic, social, and political perspectives—Marx compelled himself to attain methodical mastery of the first and was passionately and almost incessantly involved with the third. But he failed, strangely for a socialist, to give anything like adequate attention to the social dimension, that is, to consider the place and character of men's relationships with one another in a truly human society. For Marx the political act of revolution and the political preparations for it remained the principal concern. The sketchiness of Marx's—and Lenin's—vision of the classless society and of pure communism is well known, but even more unfortunate, in Buber's view, was their belief that the elements of a genuinely renewed social order could not even begin to emerge this side

[25]*Ibid.*, 216.

of a revolutionary apocalypse. Hence, "every concrete decision about the practical attitude to such re-structural elements as were actually present, in the process of formation or to be constituted anew, was reached only from the standpoint of political expediency." [26]

The basic aspiration of modern socialism, Buber contended, was historical realization of open and genuine life in community. But for Marx's theory and for Lenin's theory and practice, the success of socialist revolution appeared to demand total centralization of authority, both for doctrinal uniformity and for action in the name of socialism. This policy fatally undermined nascent socialist community, for "the socialist idea points of necessity, even in Marx and Lenin, to the organic construction of a new society out of little societies inwardly bound together by common life and common work, and their associations." [27] Socialism became only an abstract idea, cutting loose from, and negating, the impulse toward life-in-communion which had originally inspired it. Buber's analysis explicates somewhat more specifically than does Camus's the latter's view that Marxist-Leninist totalitarianism represents a tragic miscarriage of modern man's rebellion.

In contrast to the "rational," that is, ultimate goal-directed terror of the historically actualized Marxist state, Camus also considers the "irrational" terrorism of the fascist state.[28] He was convinced that despite their profound differences both of these totalitarian phenomena sprang from the same philosophical and spiritual seeds. As an ideology, Nazism represented horrendous vulgarization of some of the ideas of Hegel and Nietzsche, but despite (or perhaps because of) its intellectual degeneracy, Hitler's movement was nevertheless deadly effective in implementing the view that the death of God and the nonexistence of trans-

---

[26]Martin Buber, *Paths in Utopia*, trans. R. F. C. Hull (New York: Macmillan Company, 1950), 96.

[27]*Ibid.*, 99.

[28]Camus employs the term 'fascism" indiscriminately to refer either to German National Socialism or to Italian Fascism.

cendent values mean in practice that might makes right. Hitler and Mussolini were "the first to construct a State on the concept that everything is meaningless, and that history is only written in terms of the hazards of force." [29]

The fascists did not attempt to escape nihilism by positing an absolute and rational end of history, as did the Marxists. Instead, fascism incarnated an overt nihilism that proved fatally attractive in a Germany shaken to the depths by defeat in the First World War and by economic distress. "To those who despair of everything, not reason but only passion can provide a faith, and in this particular case it must be the same passion that lay at the root of the despair—namely, humiliation and hatred." [30] Ends, within the fascist scheme of things, are nothing more than the proximate and unstable goals of the most degraded passions. But although the ends of communism and fascism are divergent, the two totalitarianisms share the operative principle that the end justifies the means: "the success of an action is set up as an absolute goal." [31] Brute terrorism and naked coercion thus became the definitive modes of operation for fascist regimes. The lack of any serious attempt to justify these means in terms of an ultimate state of things made fascism a wholly "irrational" terror, as contrasted with Lenin's and Stalin's Soviet regime. For the fascists the only "meaningful" realities were strength, force, despotic power, and persistent militancy.

Camus considered fascism also to be a form of degenerate rebellion. Both the true rebel and the nihilist have been inescapably impressed by an experience of the absurdity and injustice of the human condition. But their responses to this perception are radically different, as Camus pointed out to his imaginary German friend:

What were the differences [between us]? You lightly accepted despair and I have never given in to it. You recognized the injustice of our

[29]*The Rebel*, 178.
[30]*Ibid.*, 178–79.
[31]*Actuelles*, 150.

fate only to decide to add to it, while it seemed to me that man had to affirm justice in order to struggle against eternal injustice and to create happiness in protest against an unhappy universe. You have become intoxicated by your despair; you have given yourself over to the destruction of man's works and to intensifying his wretchedness. But I have refused to accept this despair and this tortured world, desiring only that men rediscover their solidarity so that they may return to the struggle against their repulsive destiny.[32]

Camus regarded communist and fascist totalitarianism as but two sides of the same coin—rebellion miscarried and betrayed. Offspring of a generations-long revolt against God and the realm of grace, the totalitarians have "gone awhoring" after new gods and have ended by enthroning themselves as cruel and implacable deities on the once-toppled seat of heavenly power. Rather than bringing to fruition a reign of justice, the communists have relegated it to a future that seems to recede ever farther from the human grasp. And in the fascist state disillusionment with the unjust condition of man led to total cynicism about human values, culminating in a paroxysm of impetuosity, brute force, and irrationality. In suppressing the awareness of genuine human values which come to light in the experience of rebellion, "the prophetic dream of Marx and the over-inspired predictions of Hegel or of Nietzsche ended by conjuring up, after the city of God had been razed to the ground, a rational or irrational State, which in both cases, however, was founded on terror." [33]

Both forms of totalitarianism express an essential nihilism, the most pervasive spiritual malady of our times. This is more apparent of fascism, which possesses neither regulative nor ultimate values. But it is also the case with communist regimes, which have suppressed evaluation of tactics in ethical terms. They overlook the need for valuation in the here and now, the only hope for a life that is meaningfully human. Camus's conviction of the demonic spiritual kinship between the two representative types

[32]*Lettres à un ami allemand,* 70–71.
[33]*The Rebel,* 177.

of twentieth-century totalitarianism had already been formed shortly after the Second World War, and some remarks he uttered in
1946 serve well to summarize his point of view:

> Now that Hitler has gone, we know a certain number of things.
> The first is that the poison which impregnated Hitlerism has not
> been eliminated; it is present in each of us. Whoever today speaks
> of human existence in terms of power, efficiency, and "historical"
> tasks spreads it. He is an actual or potential assassin. For if the
> problem of man is reduced to any kind of "historical task," he is
> nothing but the raw material of history, and one can do anything
> one pleases with him. Another thing we have learned is that we
> cannot accept any optimistic conception of existence, any happy
> ending whatsoever. But if we believe that optimism is silly, we also
> know that pessimism about the action of man among his fellows is
> cowardly.
>
> We oppose terror because it forces us to choose between murder-
> ing and being murdered; and it makes communication impossible.
> That is why we reject any ideology that claims control over all of
> human life.[34]

The institutions of totalitarian states are designed to suppress
dissent and guard against subversion, while perpetuating and
adapting to shifting circumstances the official ideology. The
nihilistic Nazi leaders, as believers only in sheer force and crude
success, always required enemies, of whom the conquest and an-
nihilation gave to the fascists' existence its only, albeit degraded,
significance. Erratic and incoherent movement was the pervasive
characteristic of Nazism. The craving for conquest was directed
both inward at the German populace and outward against the
other nations of Europe. Appropriately, propaganda and repression became the defining characteristics of relationships between
the rulers and the ruled in Nazi Germany; all problems, domes-
tic and foreign, were envisioned in military terms, consonant with
the nihilism of leaders who posed every question as a test of raw

---

[34]Address delivered by Camus at Columbia University, reconstructed
from notes made by Nicola Chiaromonte and quoted in his article,
"Albert Camus: In Memoriam," in Brée (ed.), *Camus: A Collection of
Critical Essays*, 15.

will and virility. "In this way the first and sole principle of this degraded form of mysticism is born, the *Führerprinzip*, which restores idolatry and a debased deity to the world of nihilism." [35] Absolute dictatorship is a logical corollary of the wholly militarized world-view; there must be a supreme leader to direct the battle which life becomes once nihilism has destroyed all regulative values.

The institutionalization of terror is perhaps the most grisly manifestation of the inner dynamics of a regime which seeks in an unlimited way to realize absolute historical ends. For example, agricultural life in Russia failed to fit Marxist economic categories. This embarrassing gap did not, however, restrain the Bolshevik doctrinairies from using mass murder and deportation to force the kulaks—five million "historical exceptions"—into the Procrustean bed which Marxist theory had become. Maintaining forced labor camps filled with political prisoners was justified by Soviet leaders and their apologists on grounds of historical necessity; the camps were merely an institutional means to the attainment of the ultimate end of history. But the inescapable conclusion, even more tragic than ironic, is that a regime proclaiming fanatical dedication to ultimate and perfect human freedom depended heavily in its operations upon a massive kind of slavery.

From his own distinct perspective, Camus interpreted the organized terror systems of totalitarianism as more than means to make secure these regimes and help them along the road to utopia; he saw systematic terror as primarily an instrument which perverted rebellion employs in order to achieve forced unanimity, which it confuses with genuine human unity. The metaphysical rebel's conclusion that "We are alone," though basic to historical nihilism, implies in its extreme versions a solitude for man the horror of which not even nihilists can persistently endure. The glimpse of human solidarity within the shared condition of men, as revealed in the personal vision of the true rebel,

[35]*The Rebel*, 182.

remains to tantalize the totalitarians, who have distorted and degraded the meaning of genuine fraternity: "Terror and concentration camps are the drastic means used by man to escape solitude. The thirst for unity must be assuaged, even in the common grave.... Terror is the homage that the malignant recluse finally pays to the brotherhood of man." [36]

The fatal confusion between true unity of men and forced unanimity also disastrously affected totalitarian policies toward art and science. An obvious example was Lysenko's genetics, which, though discredited by all competent biologists, the Soviet regime long forbade its scientists to challenge. His theory of the inheritance of acquired characteristics faithfully conformed to the totalitarian belief in the infinite plasticity of human nature.

The principal instrument employed by totalitarian regimes to implement their all-embracing policies and to maintain absolute uniformity of thought and action is enormously swollen, all-pervasive bureaucracy; it is the operative arm of the ideology and the submissive servant of the rulers. Camus's observations on the general phenomenon of bureaucratization and on the peculiar characteristics of totalitarian bureaucracy make evident his critical attitude not only toward "successful" historical rebellion but also toward an ever-advancing tendency in contemporary nontotalitarian societies.

Determined to remain faithful to concrete and directly encountered human experience, Camus was deeply disturbed by the ubiquitous depersonalization of man's social existence, what Martin Buber has called "a progressive augmentation of the world of *It*." [37] This phenomenon is seen in its most advanced phases under totalitarian regimes, which make a settled policy of treating all persons as wholly unsacrosanct replaceable parts in a bureaucratized social machine. Bureaucratization is not in itself the prime culprit in this development but is rather a symptom of a deep-rooted sickness in modern society: "We live in a world of

[36]*Ibid.*, 247–48.
[37]Buber, *I and Thou*, 37.

abstraction, of bureaus and machines, of absolute ideas and of unsubtle, unyielding messianisms. We are being smothered by people who believe themselves to be absolutely in the right, whether because of their machines or their ideas. And for all who cannot live except in dialogue and friendship with men, this silence is the end of the world." [38] Depersonalization results from reducing human relationships to the level of abstract order and routine and from a penchant for subjecting whole societies to ideas for which absolute historical truth is claimed. These are the antihuman fruits of contemporary industrial society and of grandiose ideologies.

Camus's play *Cross Purpose* may be considered in one of its aspects as a parable dealing with depersonalization. The sister's refusal to talk personally with the guest, who she does not know is her own brother, reflects her determination to present herself solely in her socially functional role of innkeeper. Her steadfast refusal to encounter guests as persons makes it relatively easy for her to treat them as victims. Hers is an individual instance of the "logical crime"; she does not hesitate to employ the most extreme methods to attain her goal of a personal utopia. Of course, the ends served by coldly rationalized, impersonal behavior need not be malign, but Camus seeks to make the point that depersonalized relationships have penetrated to the heart of contemporary society and have often served to cloak horrendous injustices. It is not so difficult to bring oneself to manipulate, even to kill, human beings if one regards them from an abstract and impersonal point of view rather than as concrete and particular persons.

So profoundly have machine technology and ideological thinking affected the modern world that Camus saw no fundamental differences between the economic values of bourgeois and totalitarian socialist societies. Both, he maintained, have been pervasively influenced by nineteenth-century illusions of the inevitable

[38]*Actuelles,* 144.

beneficence of scientific and technical progress, which have given birth to a common

> . . . civilization of the machine-tamers, which can, through the stresses of competition and the desire for domination, be separated into enemy blocs, but which on the economic plane is subject to identical laws: the accumulation of capital and rationalized and continually increasing production. The political difference, which concerns the degree of omnipotence of the State, is appreciable, but can be reduced by economic evolution. Only the difference in ethical concepts—formal virtue as opposed to historical cynicism—seems substantial. But the imperative of production dominates both universes and makes them, on the economic plane, one world.[39]

Camus was not a romantic primitive calling for the abandonment of industrial technology. His concern was simply that production seemed to have become an end in itself, the social priority to which human nature was usually subordinated: "It is worth specifying that productivity is only injurious when it is considered as an end, not as a means, in which case it could have a liberating effect." [40]

But in fact workers are generally treated as impersonal components of the industrial machine, and as a result their whole mode of existence has taken on a distinctly nonhuman cast. This was Camus's impression upon first encountering conditions in the working-class suburbs of Paris: "Such a sight is the condemnation of the civilization that produced it. A world in which there is no more place for the human being, for joy, for active leisure, is a world that must die. No group of people can live devoid of beauty." And years later he remarked that even growing up in a poor working-class district in Algiers had not prepared him for the hideous cold misery of French industrial workers' living conditions.[41]

---

[39]*The Rebel*, 218.
[40]*Ibid.*, 218n.
[41]*Notebooks, 1942–1951*, p. 69 (entry of March, 1943); "Preface" to *L'envers et l'endroit*, 17.

The fundamental problem remains, even though Marx pointed it out long ago, that industrial work is almost wholly without dignity and meaning for those who must perform it. Camus declares: "When work is a degradation, it is not life, even though it occupies every moment of a life. Who, despite the pretensions of this society, can sleep in it in peace when they know that it derives its mediocre pleasures from the work of millions of dead souls?" [42]

Industrial societies, as presently organized, have negated the possibility of creativity in work and seek to avoid directing attention to this condition which has been a potent force in rendering life ugly and pointless for countless numbers of men. Camus claimed no ability to provide a definitive solution for this massive and enormously complicated problem, though he did offer some admittedly inadequate suggestions. He was deeply concerned, however, that this difficulty not be overlooked, that the genuine human meaning and purpose of production be recognized and that persistent efforts be made to restore creativity and significance to the realm of work.

Within the industrial system a more recent development, which Camus also viewed as a serious problem, has been the rise of a new class—the technocrats, those who coordinate the work of human beings and of machines. Although Marx envisioned the disappearance of the degrading distinction between intellectual and manual work, the necessities of production, which he exalted, have thwarted the attainment of this objective. Marx saw only the need for a "director" at the level of maximum concentration of industrial property, but he did not believe that extensive concentration would survive the abolition of private ownership. He thought that the systematic division of labor and its hierarchical form of organization were coterminous with private enterprise. However, developments since his time have demonstrated that it is the unrestrained productive imperative *per se* which bureaucratizes society and produces the regime of technocrats. In fact

[42]*The Rebel*, 209.

this imperative has extended its influence farthest in the society which supposedly was founded on Marxist principles: "The ideal regime based on collective property could be defined, according to Lenin, as justice plus electricity. In the final analysis it is only electricity without justice." [43]

Although in no society has industrialism been judiciously employed within a framework of respect for the real needs of the human beings who tend its machines, it is only in the totalitarian state that the productive imperative and depersonalized bureaucratic relationships become all-encompassing, as agents of "horizontal religion"—the official ideology. Camus viewed this phenomenon as a result of treason against true rebellion, which teaches that man's essential humanity ought not to be violated. However, "the concentration-camp system of the Russians has, in fact, accomplished the dialectical transition from the government of people to the administration of objects, but by identifying people with objects." [44]

The total bureaucratization of society, consummated in the name of all-embracing ideology, has radically distorted ordinary human relationships:

Dialogue and personal relations have been replaced by propaganda or polemic, which are two kinds of monologue. Abstraction, which belongs to the world of power and calculation, has replaced the real passions, which are in the domain of the flesh and of the irrational. The ration coupon substituted for bread; love and friendship submitted to a doctrine, and destiny to a plan; punishment considered the norm, and production substituted for living creation, quite satisfactorily describe this disembodied Europe, peopled with positive or negative symbols of power. [45]

Even the bureaucratic virtue of political neutrality is denied by totalitarian doctrinaires. The bureaucrat must be wholly committed to the official faith in the ultimate beneficence of history or he might impede the attainment of these splendid goals, as

[43]*Ibid.*, 215.
[44]*Ibid.*, 238.
[45]*Ibid.*, 240.

well as the more proximate ends the rulers proclaim as ideological revelations. In order to guard against political lukewarmness and ensure crypto-religious fervor, totalitarian leaders may find it advantageous to employ as administrators men with the minds and hearts of executioners: "In a civilization in which murder and violence are already doctrines and are on the way to becoming institutions, executioners certainly have a right to enter the administrative system . . ." [46]

Camus's most sweeping indictment of the treatment of persons by totalitarian regimes is presented in his play *State of Siege* *(L'Etat de siège)*. Critics concur in calling this the poorest of his plays, but as an angry polemic the work discloses very clearly Camus's political ideas and attitudes. When he was criticized by Gabriel Marcel for setting the action of the play in Spain, Camus replied:

I wasn't trying to flatter anyone in writing *State of Siege*. I wanted to make a frontal attack upon a type of political order which has been organized on the right and on the left on totalitarian lines. No spectator could, in good faith, doubt that this play sides with the individual, with the nobility of the flesh, and with earthly love against the abstractions and terror of the totalitarian State, whether Russian, German, or Spanish. . . . The evil of our time is the police or bureaucratic State. [47]

A brief summary of the play makes apparent Camus's political concerns. One night a comet, a sign of evil fortune, illuminates the sky above the city of Cadiz. Soon The Plague—in human form and with "the look of a noncommissioned officer" (not the will-less, ambiguously symbolic disease of *The Plague*)— appears and proclaims himself dictator of the city. The new ruler reigns as a merciless judge. His palace is a barracks, and a lawless court is the hunting ground on which he seeks human prey; he proclaims a state of siege. At once the stigmata of The Plague begin to appear on people's skin; at the first suspicion

[46] *Actuelles,* 257.
[47] *Ibid.,* 242–43.

of disease the victim is suspect; when two marks appear he is condemned; and when the third becomes visible he is eradicated. Terror pervades the atmosphere, and everything, including death, is regulated. Denunciations, mass executions, and concentration camps proliferate under skillful management: "The all-powerful machine of bureaucracy pitilessly crushes the palpitating flesh of life and liberty." [48]

Only one man in the city, Diego, conquers his fear. At the onset of the pestilence he had donned the face mask of a physician, and finally he snatches from their mouths the gags which had silenced the humiliated populace. He is not content until he has succeeded in rousing his fellow citizens to proud and wrathful revolt against The Plague. In leading the rebellion, Diego sacrifices his personal happiness with his betrothed, Victoria; with full self-awareness, he surrenders his life in order to free his fellow citizens. His actions illustrate a theme to which Camus continually recurred: "If we reject oppression and falsehood . . . this is because we reject solitude. Every insubordinate person, when he rises up against oppression, reaffirms thereby the solidarity of all men." [49]

When Diego's sacrificial leadership has brought about The Plague's expulsion from the city, citizens who had fled at the beginning of the state of siege return. The stodgy, the optimistic, and the comfortable are in the vanguard of the returning, and it is doubtful that they have acquired any knowledge or courage which will empower them to prevent a recurrence of The Plague's regime. Nada, a nihilist who had served as chief administrator for the Plague, commits suicide, symbolizing the self-destructiveness of a revolt against the absurd which, in serving totalitarianism, had cut itself off from human solidarity and concern.

The Plague's bureaucratic rule is ruthlessly thoroughgoing in attempting to transvaluate and annihilate human feelings and values. At the outset of his regime, the dictator declaims to the

---

[48]Maquet, *Albert Camus: The Invincible Summer,* 111.
[49]*Resistance, Rebellion, and Death,* 104.

frightened populace: "When I come, pathos . . . is forbidden, along with other such trifles as the poignancy of happiness, the stupid expressions of lovers, selfish contemplation of the countryside, and guilty irony. To replace all of that I bring organization . . . a good organization is worth much more than bad pathos." [50]

The bureaucratic penchant for considering rationalized order pre-eminently important is carried to its logical conclusion by totalitarianism. Its leaders seek to reduce persons to the status of manipulable objects by standardizing even the most intimate aspect of the individual's fate. The Plague tells his subjects that they have been dying haphazardly and without serving any overarching purpose: "It is much more dignified to kill for the pleasures of logic. Yes, you used to die badly. . . . But fortunately this disorder will henceforth be administered . . . you will no longer die capriciously. From now on destiny will be wiser; bureaus have been established to take care of that." [51]

The proliferation of complicated regulations which hopelessly entangle the ordinary citizen who seeks to work his way through the bureaucratic maze is portrayed in a grimly humorous sequence. A fisherman cannot obtain a health certificate which he must have to enter his own home; an existence certificate must be shown before the health certificate will be issued, but the rules forbid granting an existence certificate to anyone without a health certificate. The Plague's secretary, Death, can scarcely contain her joy at this wonderful example of how the city is beginning to be administered.

A feature common to all bureaucracies but carried to its utmost limits by totalitarian organization is the adoption of an official technical vocabulary and of tortured, virtually incomprehensible prose. The point of this is clearly explained by the nihilist who heads The Plague's administration: "We want to

[50]Albert Camus, *L'Etat de siège, spectacle en trois parties* (Paris: Gallimard, 1948), Pt. 1, p. 92.
[51]*Ibid.*, 93.

make certain that no one will be understood, even while everyone still speaks the same language. And I assure you that we are approaching the state of perfection when everyone will speak without ever finding a response, when the two tongues which confront one another in this city will each destroy the other so thoroughly that everything will progress toward the final goal— silence and death." [52]

The concern of totalitarian bureaucracy with mass data and its consequent failure to recognize that the mass with which it deals is composed of unique persons is vehemently denounced by Diego:

Ah! You care about nothing but groups! A hundred thousand men, that's what you think significant. That's a statistic, and statistics can't speak! You make curves and graphs with them, don't you! You plan according to whole generations, that's easier! And the work can be done in silence and tranquillity, scented by the odor of ink. But I warn you, a single man is more bothersome; he cries out his joy and his pain. And as long as I live I will keep on sabotaging your lovely order with my cries.[53]

The people, though submissive to the regime, long for a more human way of life—especially for the sweet joys of nature, which Camus never ceased to consider essential for true fullness of life: "We have become wise. We are administered. But in the silence of offices we hear the long-continued cry of hearts torn asunder, which speaks to us of the sea under the noonday sun, of the sweet arms of our wives. Our faces are stamped with an official seal, our steps are numbered, our moments organized, but our hearts refuse this silence." [54]

That a nihilistic irrationalist serves faithfully as chief of The Plague's thoroughly rationalized administration illustrates Camus's belief that "rational" and "irrational" totalitarians find common ground in their efforts at total regulation of their sub-

[52]*L'Etat de siège,* Pt. 2, p. 128.
[53]*Ibid.,* 174.
[54]*Ibid.,* 134.

jects' lives. And it is this chief bureaucrat who, before committing suicide, sardonically declares that what he represents will survive his death: "Even if the city folded up, the sky split asunder, and men deserted the earth, the government offices would open at their appointed time to administer nothingness. I am eternal, and my paradise is furnished with archives and desk-blotters." [55] Camus appears to be saying not only that bureaucracy is a permanent feature of depersonalized social order, but that bureaucracy intensifies its impersonality.

Certainly it is easy to sympathize with Camus's indictment of totalitarian bureaucracy, but it is much more difficult to see in his wholly negative presentation of bureaucracy per se anything more than a romantic aversion to modern society. It is scarcely news that bureaucracy tends to reinforce impersonality and standardization, but before we can seek to cope with these problems, "we must first realize that the organization is here to stay. There is simply no other way to run a world brimming with three billion people in the midst of an industrial epoch." [56] One need not accept uncritically Harvey Cox's view that modern organization is inherently superior to previous modes of collective action because it is "flexible, future-oriented, secularized, and limited in its scope," to agree with him that our real problem is not how to abolish bureaucracy but how to control it for the common good. [57]

A variety of efforts to grapple with this problem have been made by contemporary political thinkers; one whose analysis and proposals seem worthy at least of passing notice is the American socialist writer Michael Harrington. He points out that massive bureaucracy was originally created not by socialism, totalitarian or otherwise, but by industrial capitalism. On this point he is in agreement with Camus, but he goes beyond it in a more specific way than Camus ever did: "Socialism . . . is . . . the

[55]*L'Etat de siège,* Pt. 3, p. 202.
[56]Harvey Cox, *The Secular City,* 173.
[57]*Ibid.,* 175.

one political movement that seeks to represent the claim of the individual as against the bureaucracy by making the latter subject to the democratic will." [58] Harrington maintains that the real difficulty presented by bureaucracy today is its lack of responsibility to the people whom it allegedly serves, because of the absence of democratic control of industrial operations in most Western countries and the total nonexistence of democratic processes in countries of the communist bloc. He sees some hope for reducing the number of intermediaries between the people and policy-makers through the increased use of computer techniques for the bulk of administrative work and of systems approaches which may render broad policy alternatives comprehensible to a democratic electorate.

Such an approach may well be our best hope for bringing some degree of human meaning into a world of organizations. But this route certainly cannot guarantee protection of individual personhood. The most refined mechanized techniques must, for the sake of efficiency and effectiveness, deal with masses and abstractions. Overreactions to organization, such as Camus's, ought at least to be kept in mind, so that the unique humanity of the persons whom bureaucracy is designed to serve may not be, even inadvertently, negated.

Of more enduring significance, I believe, is Camus's analysis and critique of totalitarianism. He does well to remind us that this phenomenon had its origins not in a gangster plot to enslave and exploit humanity, but in the most deeply human impulse of modern man—revulsion and revolt against injustice and servitude. The context in which this movement sprang to life gave to it the form of revolt against a sovereign deity whose responsibility for evil and suffering could no longer be justified. But, tragically, this metaphysical rebellion, in almost all its historical incarnations, metamorphosed into calamitous inhumanity. This outcome, Camus contends, was the result of cutting loose from the experien-

[58]Michael Harrington, *The Accidental Century* (New York: Macmillan Company, 1965), 291.

tial roots of revolt and repressing the truths that constitute the inner meaning of rebellion—that there are limits to the manner in which men may be treated without negating that which makes them human, and that revolt expresses a desire for dialogical communion among men to make fleshly reality of their quest for meaning within their confrontation with death and absurdity.

But metaphysical rebellion turned from existential knowledge to theoretical abstractions; against the totalist claims of Christendom it posed its own "godless theologies," all-encompassing ideologies: "Demonstration. That abstraction is evil. It causes wars, tortures, violence, etc. Problem: How does the abstract view continue in the face of physical evil, ideology in the face of the torture inflicted in the name of that ideology?" [59] These murderous abstractions first appeared as the formal virtue which the Jacobin terrorists claimed to serve. But nineteenth-century philosophers sought to abolish all formal standards by reducing man to historical existence. Abstraction reappeared in this historicism, however, as claims to knowledge of the total meaning of history and, in Marx, certainty of a final benevolent goal at which history must arrive as the outcome of men's chaotic and bloody struggles with nature and with one another.

Men as metaphysical and historical rebels vested themselves with an illusory divinity, claiming a total knowledge that only an omniscient deity could possess. In so doing they lost sight of significant kinds of purely human experiential knowledge: "Historicity leaves unexplained the phenomenon of beauty; in other words, relations with the world (sentiment of nature) and with persons as individuals (love). What to think of a supposedly absolute explanation that . . ." [60] (Camus did not complete the final sentence of this passage; its point, however, is clear.) Neglect of existentially known truths in favor of historical abstractions has caused rebellion directed originally against concrete human suffering to become the ideological justification for regimes

[59]*Notebooks, 1942–1951*, p. 102 (entry of September, 1944).
[60]*Ibid.*, 136 (entry of March, 1946).

which have inflicted suffering on men more massively and efficiently than ever before: "Responsibility toward history does without responsibility toward human beings. That is its comfort." [61]

To Camus, totalitarian ideologies and practices appeared as mortal threats to the basic values which, from his early writings until his final works, he sought to validate and defend—man's capacity for joy through participation in and contemplation of nature, the legitimacy of man's desire for happiness, fidelity to the earth and to concrete persons rather than to a metaphysically or historically abstract humanity of the future, and rebellion in the name of life against death and the "death-in-life" of oppression and monological solitude. Camus's treatment of totalitarianism is, it seems to me, at the very least a significant example of genuinely existential political criticism.

A critic might well respond that although Camus's analysis may tell us something about the spiritual sources and atmosphere of fascism, and perhaps also of Stalinism, *The Rebel,* viewed in retrospect, discloses a significant limitation of an existential perspective. Namely, this work failed to envision the possibility of the Soviet and other communist regimes developing in a more humanly hopeful direction. By steadfastly concentrating on the present situation, the existential writer fails to recognize within it the potentialities which a more future-oriented approach might lead him to take into account. After all, since Stalin's death terror has declined strikingly as an instrument of the Soviet government, the camps for political prisoners have been largely abolished, and the once monolithic Soviet bloc has shown unmistakable signs of disintegration. Perhaps "rationalized totalitarianism" is not so impregnable or so uniform over time as Camus seemed to imply.

There is some justice in this criticism, but I believe it is still possible to defend the continuing relevance of Camus's critique of ideology and its historical manifestations. Five years after the

[61]*Ibid.,* 196 (entry of July, 1948).

publication of *The Rebel,* events in Hungary appeared to bear out his fundamental theses in a dramatic and tragic way. Camus made a scathing attack on the Soviet suppression of the Hungarian rebellion; the only fitting descriptions of the Kadar regime, in his view, were "counter-revolutionary" and "socialism of the gallows." Compelling people to inform on members of their own families, hanging young girls, decapitating members of workers' committees, deporting and imprisoning writers—"is this socialism, the great celebration of liberty and justice? No, we have known, we still know this kind of thing; these are the bloody and monotonous rites of the totalitarian religion! Hungarian socialism is in prison or in exile today." [62]

Camus was particularly disgusted—but not surprised—by the orthodox French Leftist response to events in Hungary, which went along with the Soviet contention that the rebellion had been a fascist plot. Members of the Left who held this opinion demonstrated in a definitive way their utter submission to the claim by the leaders of the most powerful communist state to represent ultimate historical truth. What further proof could be needed that "if absolute truth belongs to anyone in this world, it certainly does not belong to the man or party that claims to possess it. When historical truth is involved, the more anyone claims to possess it the more he lies. In the final analysis, he becomes a murderer of truth." [63]

But, post-Hungary, can Camus's interpretation of totalitarianism be defended? I certainly would not want to deny the possible significance of whatever loosening of rigid control has taken place in the Soviet Union and elsewhere in Eastern Europe, especially the marked decline in physical terror. Nor, I believe, did Camus intend to rule out the possibility of changes for the better in such countries, although the fate of the Hungarian revolt, inclined him toward skepticism. However, despite the indeterminate degree of "thaw" that has occurred in the Soviet Union, ideological indoc-

[62]*Resistance, Rebellion, and Death,* 158.
[63]*Ibid.,* 165.

trination remains a basic practice and prop of the regime, there is no meaningful freedom of association, and the continued persecution of "deviant" writers indicates that ideological terrorism has not yet gone completely out of style. At this point Camus's thought is exceedingly valuable; a thorough understanding of his presentation of the origins, development, and spiritual pretensions of totalitarian ideology should counteract any tendency of ours to succumb to a prematurely optimistic view of the evolution of long-established communist regimes. The question of whether their rulers can ever permit a hearing for views other than the "true faith" of Marxism-Leninism, or encourage diversity, spontaneity, and self-determination, certainly cannot now be answered in the affirmative. And any effort to maintain a clear-sighted political realism requires us not to suppress this question, which Camus's analysis poses so sharply and persistently that it puts almost insuperable obstacles in the way of efforts to evade the issue.

Furthermore, it is obvious beyond dispute that in the contemporary world, especially outside Europe and North America, ideological passions and movements which claim to be bearers of ultimate historical truth and justice are ubiquitous and in many cases politically potent. In this context, it is certainly defensible to see continuing relevance in Camus's warning: "None of the evils that totalitarianism (defined by the single party and the suppression of all opposition) claims to remedy is worse than totalitarianism itself." [64]

But protest against betrayed rebellion was by no means Camus's only political concern. He sought also, in many specific ways, to point out the lessons of true revolt for men in quest of a politics that would not leave them in despair.

[64]*Ibid.*, 171.

V
Toward a Politics of Hope

CAMUS OUTLINED no detailed plan, predictive or prescriptive, of man's political future. To have taken that route would have been inconsistent with his fundamentally skeptical, even hostile, attitude toward ideological thinking. This raises the preliminary question of whether Camus made any positive contributions to political thought. One generally admiring commentator on his writings has remarked: "Basically, the discontinuous intuitions powerfully restated by Camus, once elucidated, reveal less what we should do than *what we should not do.*" [1] There is much truth in this observation, but the obvious truth should be pointed out also, that negative criticism can be made in a meaningful way only from an implicitly positive critical standpoint and thus in itself points toward the discovery of what we *should* do.

In one place in his journal Camus notes that a friendly critic had told him that he had "no head" for politics, that his only fitting role was the noble task of "sounding the alarm." But, he remarks, it is by no means clear precisely what a "political mind" is—and, "as to the 'noble' role of sounding the alarm, it would require a spotless conscience. And the only vocation I feel in myself is telling consciences that they are not spotless and rea-

[1]Doubrovsky, "The Ethics of Albert Camus," 83.

sons why they lack something." [2] This was, of course, what Camus attempted to do in his sustained critique of ideology and of totalitarianism, and I would strongly maintain that that effort must be counted as a positive contribution to our efforts to comprehend and cope with contemporary political life.

Yet some critics maintain that Camus's affirmative efforts were insignificant, even nonexistent. For instance, Michael Harrington writes: "Positively, he could find nothing more than a romantic syndicalism to counterpose against his own corrosive skepticism. He died as he lived: a victim." [3] But I believe that this is a serious misestimation of Camus's achievement. Because Harrington evaluates Camus's thought according to the criterion of his own interest in drawing up a new social and political blueprint, he quite naturally overlooks Camus's genuinely positive emphases. Emmett Parker wisely responds to a similar criticism, that Camus's political views were not sufficiently "practical," by asserting that the politically practical cannot be limited to specific policy proposals and that there is a profound practicality in Camus's never-flagging insistence that man's corporate life must transcend mere political efficiency. "Camus's words are a constant reminder that political institutions are conceived by men to serve man, to enhance his grandeur and offset his weaknesses, to help him achieve, as an individual and as a member of society, his just ambitions. Above all he reminds us that life is too precious a gift to be taken away without the gravest justification." [4] This is, I think, a fair summary evaluation of Camus's positive achievement as a political thinker.

It must be kept in mind, however, that Camus never thought of himself as primarily a political theorist and thus felt no obligation to analyze all important political phenomena. In fact, it was only with some difficulty that he brought himself to the point of considering political life worthy of serious philosophical in-

[2]*Notebooks, 1942–1951,* p. 216 (entry of September, 1948).
[3]Harrington, *The Accidental Century,* 169.
[4]Parker, *Albert Camus: The Artist in the Arena,* 168.

quiry. Several entries in his notebooks indicate a youthful disgust with politics (it is easily understandable why any sensitive
observer would have held this attitude during the final years of
the Third Republic). For instance: "Every time I hear a political speech or I read those of our leaders, I am horrified at having,
for years, heard nothing which sounded human. It is always the
same words telling the same lies." And later that same year he
noted: "Men who have greatness within them don't go in for politics. . . . We must make our men of action into men of ideals,
and our poets into captains of industry. We must learn to live
out our dreams—and to transform them into action." [5] In the
latter entry there is a note of earnest romanticism that was to
become much less apparent in Camus's thought as he matured;
we have explored his cogent arguments against regarding the political sphere as an arena where we transform our dreams into
action.

By 1940 Camus's career as a crusading radical journalist in Algiers ended, and, facing the bleakness of war, he succumbed to a
wholly antipolitical attitude: "More and more, when faced with
the world of men, the only reaction is one of individualism. Man
alone is an end unto himself. Everything you try to do for the
common good ends in failure. Even if you like to try it from
time to time, decency demands that you do so with the required
amount of scorn. Withdraw into yourself completely, and play
your own game." [6]

That Camus could not long rest content within this perspective
of individualistic condescension is made evident by the translator
of his Notebooks, who writes of the passage just quoted that "the
word 'idiot' was written across this remark in red pencil by Camus himself." Although Camus never came to view politics as a
means of salvation for man, either individually or collectively,
he did come to believe in the necessity of considering the politi-

[5]Notebooks, 1935–1942, pp. 48 (entry of August, 1937), 78–79 (entry
of December, 1937).
[6]Ibid., 171 (entry of March, 1940).

cal realm seriously and thoroughly in his endeavor to discern a way of coping affirmatively with the condition of man in our time. As he remarked to himself several years after writing the above-quoted entries in his journal: ". . . modern man is obliged to be concerned with politics. I am concerned with it, in spite of myself and because, through my defects rather than through my virtues, I have never been able to refuse any of the obligations I encountered." [7]

Camus believed that the first duty of the true rebel in politics— one may call it, without exaggeration, his "categorical imperative"—is steadfastly to refuse to accept or collaborate with nihilism, either in thought or in practice. We have already considered in some detail Camus's analysis and criticisms of what he termed "revolutionary nihilism," and at this point it seems appropriate to elaborate his views on the defects of contemporary non-totalitarian society, which he saw as afflicted all too commonly with the disease of "bourgeois nihilism." Although, unlike Jean-Paul Sartre, Camus did not react in a violent and totally negative manner to middle-class values and institutions, he was a persistent critic of the society within which he lived and worked.

In this context, it is very likely that some remarks by Jean-Baptiste Clamence, the equivocal monologuist of *The Fall,* represent the author's own point of view:

"Haven't you noticed that our society is organized for . . . liquidation? You have heard, of course, of those tiny fish in the rivers of Brazil that attack the unwary swimmer by thousands and with swift little nibbles clean him up in a few minutes, leaving only an immaculate skeleton? Well, that's what their organization is. 'Do you want a good clean life? Like everybody else?' You say yes, of course. How can one say no? 'O.K. You'll be cleaned up. Here's a job, a family, and organized leisure activities.' And the little teeth attack the flesh, right down to the bone. But I am unjust. I shouldn't say *their* organization. It is *ours,* after all: it's a question of which will clean up the other." [8]

[7]*Notebooks, 1942–1951,* p. 215 (entry of September, 1948).
[8]*The Fall,* 7–8.

Camus was no enemy of work and family; in fact these concrete human realities were for him basic to any hope for a decent social order. But he was convinced that, within bourgeois society as it presently operates, there can be no "good clean life" and that unquestioning conformity to its mores in effect becomes nihilistic acquiescence in the injustices and spiritual and legal murder sanctioned in Western countries which pride themselves on their antitotalitarianism.

Bourgeois society supports and rewards a multitude of parasites—*les privilégiés*—who "take three meals a day all their lives, have their fortunes tucked away in safe securities, but who scurry home when there is unrest in the streets." [9] These privileged people care little or nothing for humanity and justice. Their overweening desire to maintain the unjust bourgeois social order from which they profit renders them indifferent to its victims; they are covert allies of the plague: "This is precisely what I cannot excuse in our present-day political order: it is a machine for creating human despair." [10]

Furthermore, Camus was convinced that non-Marxist society rests upon ideological foundations that derive in part from the same sources as those of Marxism. As has been elaborated, Camus believed that a secularized version of Christianity, characterized by a conviction that man has an unlimited right and obligation to manipulate nature—including human nature—in his efforts to make what he calls progress, undergirds both totalitarian socialist and Western societies: "The Marxist and capitalist ideologies, both based upon the idea of progress, both convinced that the application of their principles must inevitably lead to social equilibrium, are utopian. . . . They are costing us quite dearly." [11]

Basic to Camus's dissatisfaction with bourgeois society, which he viewed as riddled with gross injustices, was his revulsion

[9] *Actuelles*, 54.
[10] *Ibid.*, 249.
[11] *Ibid.*, 148.

against what he considered the ultimate injustice—the death penalty. Passionately in love with and affirming life and the joys it can yield as man's *summum bonum,* Camus was implacably opposed to men's taking the side of death. Thus one of the specific political "causes" with which he identified himself was the abolition of capital punishment. This problem haunted Camus's thinking for many years. His first novel, *The Stranger,* concerns a man condemned to death for abstract reasons completely alien to the reality of the experience in which he had inadvertently killed another man. In *The Plague,* Jean Tarrou eloquently expresses Camus's own horror at the premeditated murder represented both by condemning men to death within the bourgeois legal system and by the political executions of revolutionary organizations. Such practices in any society contribute to the "plague-strickenness" of all its members.

Late in his unexpectedly shortened career, Camus wrote a long essay in which he subjected capital punishment in France to rigorous analysis and vigorous condemnation.[12] This essay is, I believe, one of the best of the innumerable writings on this much-disputed subject which have appeared within recent years. And further, in one of its aspects the essay makes apparent the practical applicability of Camus's political philosophy.

He begins, as befits an existential thinker, by recounting a vivid personal memory. As a boy, Camus had been told by his mother of a shattering experience his father had once undergone. A man had committed an infamous murder, and everyone in town, including the elder Camus, had agreed that he undoubtedly deserved the decapitation by guillotine to which the court had condemned him. Out of curiosity M. Camus had attended the public execution; upon returning home afterward he had said nothing about it to his wife but had been violently ill all night. Camus's father came to see, as his son expressed it many years later, that no matter what the offense which provokes it, the

[12]Albert Camus "Réflexions sur la guillotine," in Albert Camus and Arthur Koestler, *Réflexions sur la peine capitale* (Paris: Calmann-Levy, 1957).

death penalty "is no less revolting than the crime and that this new murder, far from compensating for the damage done to the body of society, adds a new defilement to the first one." [13]

Camus points out that no one in France dares to speak of an execution in coldly factual terms. The condemned man always "pays a debt to society" or "receives his just punishment"; newspaper reports never describe specifically what happens when a man's head is chopped off. Camus asserts that if these unbearably hideous facts were thoroughly publicized, people would rise up in spontaneous disgust and demand that the death penalty be abolished.

He firmly declares that society has no right to retain such a practice: "Responsibilities must be established by society on a reasonable and effective scale. But a law has its final justification in the good that it does or does not accomplish for society." [14] From this premise it follows that his first argument against capital punishment is based upon the utilitarian ground that the death penalty in reality produces no social good whatsoever. Partisans of capital punishment base their case primarily on the contention that the supreme penalty serves as a deterrent to stay the hand of potential murderers. Camus skillfully demolishes this argument. He shows that society does not really believe in the exemplary character of executions; they take place in private and are reported only in journalistic clichés. If the official representatives of the people sincerely believed that putting a criminal to death actually deterred would-be killers, executions would be held in public and would even be televised: "Indeed one must kill in public or admit that he does not consider himself authorized to kill." [15]

In the second place, it has never been proved that the existence of the death penalty has prevented a single murder, while it is certainly apparent that capital punishment has brought

[13]*Ibid.,* 126.
[14]*Ibid.,* 128.
[15]*Ibid.,* 137.

death to men. Camus points out that few murders are premeditated; most are committed in the heat of violent passion, when the murderer is far from conscious reflection on the penalty his act may incur.

Finally, the deterrence argument is countered by the possibility that capital punishment in some cases may serve as an example with incalculably horrible consequences. Camus claims that psychologists have discovered that at least some people possess so strong a death instinct that the possibility of being executed may actually impel them to commit murder.

Having shown that the principal argument advanced in support of capital punishment is riddled with fallacies, Camus declares that the real inspiration for retaining the death penalty is an irrational desire for revenge. It is the primitive *lex talionis*— "an eye for an eye and a tooth for a tooth"—that motivates a people to demand the life of one who has breached its basic law. Camus viewed this attitude as subrational and maintained that its embodiment in legal codes is evidence of cultural backwardness; law should transcend and discipline brute nature rather than conform to its imperatives. He argues further that capital punishment even exceeds the limits of simple vengeance.

Execution of a murderer is not strictly equivalent retaliation for the crime he has committed, especially in the most common cases which do not involve premeditated murder. For capital punishment is always coldly premeditated killing and thus is freighted with serious moral consequences that transcend the isolated act of taking a man's life. The condemned man must live for months, or even years, in a state of degrading bodily terror that reduces him to the subhuman condition of a disposable object. In few cases must the victims of murderers endure such excruciating fear before they are killed. Furthermore, a man's execution brings upon his family a lifetime of disgrace, even though they may well be wholly innocent of complicity in his criminal act. Even then, if execution is considered as just revenge, it cannot be justified; the condemned man receives a much more horrible punishment than simply the loss of life which his victim suffered.

Consistent with his fundamental philosophic and moral premises, Camus's principal objection to the death penalty was its totality and irreparability. It exceeds the limits which ought to be respected by a creature whose conditon is inescapably marked by finitude, ignorance, and fallibility. No one knows enough or is pure enough to justify his making an ultimate claim upon the life of another man. Any society which claims the right to put murderers to death is itself responsible to some degree for the existence of criminal activity. Bourgeois societies have not eradicated slums and degrading poverty, though it is well known that these conditions are prolific breeders of crime. In France the government itself, by subsidizing the wine industry, incurs partial responsibility for a high rate of alcoholism and for the existence of a host of bistros; these frequently serve as catalytic elements in unpremeditated crimes of passion.

Camus is not arguing that individuals bear no responsibility for illegal acts; he insists that everyone must be held responsible for behavior which harmfully affects others if social cohesion is to be maintained at all. But he could not see how it is possible to deny that no one is *totally* responsible for criminal behavior and, therefore, that *total* punishment cannot be justified: "The death penalty, which is satisfactory neither as an example nor as an instrument of distributive justice, usurps in addition an exorbitant privilege in claiming the right to punish guilt that is always relative with a definitive and irreparable punishment." [16]

Camus maintained that justice must become modest if it is to be just at all. The finality of the death penalty implies a pretentious claim that society is omnipotent and its legal system omniscient. But we know that "justice" has erred in some specific cases, and even if a man is guilty beyond all doubt we have no assurance that he is not potentially a penitent, redeemable human being: "If justice is known to be fallible, would

[16]*Ibid.*, 158.

it not be fitting for it to show a certain modesty, to allow in its sentences for a margin of error great enough so that inevitable mistakes may be undone?" [17] All men make mistakes of judgment and cannot avoid sometimes coming to false conclusions; in fact this common propensity is one of the inescapable elements of solidarity in the human condition. True justice must take account of this solidarity and cannot be divorced from an appropriate degree of modesty.

Camus did not mean to encourage a frivolous indulgence that fails to consider the rights of victims, but sought in this context as in others to enable us to perceive the nature and condition that we share with all other men. He proposed to abolish not all punishment for crime but only the ultimate penalty, the totality of which does not accord with man's finitude and imperfection. Sparing a murderer's life makes it at least possible for even the most hideous criminal to accomplish some good which may partially offset the evil for which he is responsible. Capital punishment is simply inconsonant with Camus's vision of the human condition: "Capital judgment breaks up the only undeniable human solidarity, solidarity against death; and it cannot be legitimized except by virtue of a truth or a principle which is located beyond men." [18]

Such principles and claims to absolute truth were accepted unquestioningly during the centuries of churchly domination of Western societies. Belief in an after-life could justify capital punishment; judges and executioners who possessed this faith did not consider their acts final. Ultimate judgment was the prerogative of a supernatural deity. But this view is simply irrelevant to conditions in the secularized society of our times. Today an agnostic or atheistic judge places himself on the throne of the god he has disavowed when he pronounces a sentence which he believes to be final; in effect the judge kills the condemned man because their forbears believed in life after death.

[17]*Ibid.,* 164.
[18]*Ibid.,* 169.

Reiterating a part of the argument of *The Rebel,* but applying it more specifically in this instance to bourgeois society, Camus asserts that secularized societies retain capital punishment because society itself has been inflated into the end and exhaustive purpose of human existence. We no longer seek to maintain an official belief in an after-life, but we have merely replaced the priest with the bureaucrat as judge and executioner. The state has become the most dangerous and least justifiable killer—most obviously in totalitarian societies but also in all which retain capital punishment. The most serious problem for society is no longer defense against the antisocial individual but warding off the secularized religious pretensions of the state.

To cope with this grave danger, Camus proposes a course of action that would not only spare the lives of murderers but would symbolize a subordination of corporate ends and institutions to enduring human values: "To prohibit putting men to death would proclaim publicly that society and the State are not absolute values and that nothing authorizes them to legislate definitively or to produce the irreparable." [19] In our present situation it is essential to demonstrate that the person is superior in worth to the institutionalized abstraction of the state. Specifically, prohibition of the death penalty should be the first article in the legal code of a United Europe. This provision would be the first—and most important—step toward the creation of a moderate, reasonable, genuinely human society: "Man in this century is asking for laws and institutions of convalescence which will restrain him without crushing him, guide him without annihilating him. Thrown into the unbridled dynamism of history, he naturally requires a constitution and laws to establish equilibrium. In sum, he needs a reasonable society and not the anarchy into which his own pride and the immodest powers of the State have plunged him." [20]

Clearly, Camus's opposition to capital punishment derived

[19]*Ibid.,* 175.
[20]*Ibid.,* 177.

from his revolt against the forces of death. He believed that men cannot justify intentionally shattering the complicity that binds them to one another as sharers in a common fate. Life itself is the ultimate good; to sustain and enhance it are the primordial imperatives born of the rebel's experience. Camus found his own society guilty of the totalitarian fault of illegitimately claiming sufficient wisdom and virtue to justify negating human life. He steadfastly maintained that the first requirement of a society which will no longer create despair in men's hearts is the restriction of justice to the this-worldly modesty which results from genuine awareness of and responsiveness to the limitations and potentialities of the human condition.

It is thus quite apparent that although Camus was a rigorous and unsparing opponent of totalitarian socialism, he was almost equally critical of the bourgeois capitalist social order. As one commentator has remarked, "For Camus, orthodox humanism as it is expressed in conventional middle-class morality is so definitely dead and discredited that it is no longer necessary to satirise or attack it." [21] Camus saw the task of true rebellion as one of finding a middle way between the murderous pretensions of historical nihilism and the smug, revolt-denying pretentiousness of bourgeois nihilism.

This task brought him up against one of the most difficult moral puzzles of twentieth-century politics: how and when can violence, up to and including the killing of one's opponents, be justified as political tactics? Does true revolt imply an absolute prohibition against the taking of human life, or must "progressive" revolutionary movements be exempted from such an apparently crippling limitation? Camus made one of the few sustained efforts to wrestle with this problem as a *moral* issue. Of course, one might make a strong case for the view that moral considerations seem irrelevant to those who have been responsible for the revolutions, pseudo-revolutions, counterrevolutions, and bloody coups d'état which have continuously marked the un-

[21]Thody, *Albert Camus, 1913–1960*, p. 120.

folding of contemporary history. But to accept this conclusion, either resignedly or with satisfaction, is to admit that in practice might makes right and that man is only a hapless pawn of transcendently powerful social forces, with which he can ally himself or by which he can passively allow himself to be crushed. Camus could not agree with these conclusions. He strongly believed that it was precisely the failure of revolutionaries to take into account the moral imperatives and implications of the experience of revolt that made the history of men in our time appear to be a constant clashing of seemingly uncontrollable, irreconcilable, and pitiless opposing forces. Radical politics cannot deny or ignore the relevance of moral considerations without lapsing into ruthless inhumanity.

Camus's effort to grapple with this crucial but almost impenetrable problem of the relationship between moral judgment and political means represents, I believe, one of his most important but least understood contributions to political thought in our time. The significance and difficulty of the problem in his thinking sprang initially from his inability to accept any of the standard short-cut "solutions" usually presented as definitive answers to the question of when violent means are justifiable in politics. Despite his profound attachment to and respect for human life, Camus was not a pacifist. In his youth he was attracted to pacifism, but later on he could not help considering this position to be at best dangerously close to irresponsible moralism which is impotent to remedy the injustices of political and social tyranny.[22] At the other extreme, it is quite obvious that he could not excuse political violence simply because its perpetrators claimed to be riding the crest of the historically inevitable "wave of the future." He found himself more sympathetic toward, though not completely satisfied with, a third perspective: the constitutional

---

[22]In a letter written in 1950, Camus confessed: "I began the war of 1939 as a pacifist and I finished it as a résistant. That inconsistency . . . has rendered me more modest." "Les Vraies Tâches," *Cahiers des saisons*, No. 20 (1960), 616 (quoted in Parker, *Albert Camus: The Artist in the Arena,* 68).

democrat's view that the political system should allow for peaceful and orderly social change, even radical innovations if accomplished by legal means, and that within this type of constitutional order violence is both unnecessary and illegitimate. The problem with this position is that such a reasonable and effective democratic system is seldom found in the real world. This solution has no relevance to circumstances in which the existing regime is oppressive and despotic. What then can legitimately be done?

It was only with great difficulty and after an honestly admitted change of opinion that Camus arrived at his final position on this matter. He first spoke out publicly on it late in 1944 in editorials for the formerly clandestine newspaper *Combat,* which, after the liberation of Paris from the German army, had become the leading spokesman for the left-wing elements of the wartime Resistance movement. This very loosely defined group—composed of socialists, communists, and a number of radical Christian Democrats—espoused the slogan, "De la Résistance à la Révolution," and sought to produce a thoroughgoing economic and political restructuring of French society. A common expectation at the time was that this goal could be attained on the impetus for radical reform built up during the war years by the collaboration of leftist forces and by general resentment against the oppressiveness of the Nazis and the reactionary Vichy regime. To many of the Left it seemed that they need only remain resolute and act determinedly to produce a genuine social revolution in postwar France.

Soon a concrete issue, which was viewed as a test of that determination, came to the fore: what kind of punishment should be meted out to the wartime collaborators, many of whom had not only profited materially from their activities but had actively aided Nazi terrorism? Camus editorialized on this question:

At the extremity of doubt there must be resolution. We are well aware that the day the first death sentence is executed in Paris we will feel repugnance. But we must think then of so many other death sentences that struck innocent men, of beloved faces lying in the dust and of hands that we loved to grasp. When we are tempted to prefer the generous sacrifices of war to the black chores of justice, we shall need our memories of the dead and the unbearable recollection of those of us whom torture turned into traitors. Hard as it may be, we will know then that there are impossible pardons and necessary revolutions.[23]

We see expressed here an instinctive repugnance toward the death penalty, which had already been made apparent in *The Stranger*. But we perceive also in this editorial the implacable sternness of the dedicated revolutionary, a role in which Camus could scarcely rest comfortably for any extended period. But at this time he verbally played the part to the hilt, even declaring that France needed another Saint-Just—the terrorist whom, in *The Rebel*, he was to label a traitor to true revolt. Camus's editorials on this issue caused him to become embroiled in an extended public dispute with the eminent French Catholic writer François Mauriac, who opposed the death penalty for traitors and collaborators on grounds of the fallibility of human justice.

Although Camus opposed Mauriac's argument in late 1944 and early 1945, he apparently became steadily less certain that his position was sound. And in late 1945 Camus addressed this note to himself: "I am not made for politics because I am incapable of wanting or accepting the death of the adversary." [24] About this same time Camus's support was solicited by a few socialists seeking to draw up an appeal for peace and the creation of a neutral and socialist Europe. The document was finally completed and published. But when the group, which included several other partyless intellectuals of the Left, such as Sartre and Simone de Beauvoir, attempted to move on to the discussion of specifics, Camus brought up the problem of the death penalty. He demanded that the group propose as a political measure the abolition of capital punishment. Others—including Sartre and his close companion—opposed Camus, contending that the death penalty

[23]*Combat*, October 21, 1944, p. 1 (quoted in Parker, *Albert Camus: The Artist in the Arena*, 83).
[24]*Notebooks, 1942–1951*, p. 119 (entry of November, 1945).

could be justified only as a political measure. The group then broke up.[25]

In 1948, Camus admitted that in taking the view that had aroused Mauriac's opposition he had been caught up in then prevalent passions and his judgment had been clouded by the poignant memory of several assassinated friends—that, to put it bluntly, he had been wrong and Mauriac right on the question of executing collaborators. In fact, "by November 1946, two years before he admitted that Mauriac was right, Camus had decided that there was no truth in the name of which he would ever again demand the life of another human being." [26] This conclusion led in turn to his principled opposition to the death penalty.

Camus ultimately came to see in the lives of the "just assassins," the Russian Social Revolutionary terrorists of 1905 whom he portrayed in *Les Justes* and praised in *The Rebel*, the paradigm of legitimate political violence. In particular, he admired the actions and attitude of the poet Kaliayev, who he believed epitomized the true greatness of these unhappy rebels. Kaliayev refused to carry out an assassination attempt which would have brought death to innocent children. And when, after a second and successful effort to kill the archduke, he was apprehended by the Tsarist authorities, he not only refused to betray his comrades in order to save his own life, but declared that his execution would constitute just repayment for the life he had taken. "A life for a life" is the rebel terrorist's moral rule.

The problem is how to act out revolt on behalf of life. This overriding purpose seems per se to make killing inexcusable. But in the situation which the just assassins confronted, political murder appeared inescapably necessary. "Mediocre minds," Camus says, can get around this terrible question by ignoring one of the terms of the dilemma. On the one hand, the problem can be avoided by condemning all direct violence in the name of formal principles, but this means giving implicit sanction to "that diffuse

[25]This incident is recounted in Beauvoir, *Force of Circumstance*, 138–39.
[26]Parker, *Albert Camus: The Artist in the Arena*, 95.

form of violence" represented by existing economic and political oppression; we confront again the trap of "bourgeois nihilism." On the other hand, "revolutionary nihilists" console themselves with the homily that eggs must be broken to make an omelet, and "add murder to murder, to the point of making of history nothing but a continuous violation of everything in man which protests against injustice." [27]

There is no entirely satisfactory solution to the dilemma, but the only morally respectable route is to kill only in the most extreme circumstances, to resort to this ultimate form of violence as sparingly as possible in the quest for a more nearly just social order—and to go this far only if one is genuinely willing to pay with his own life for the killing in which he has participated: "He who kills is guilty only if he consents to go on living or if, to remain alive, he betrays his comrades. To die, on the other hand, cancels out both the guilt and the crime itself." [28] The context in which these remarks appear renders their meaning somewhat ambiguous. It is not entirely clear whether Camus is here attempting primarily to interpret the attitude of the tormented terrorist, which I believe to be the case, or is declaring as his own belief that political assassination can be justified only if the killer is actually executed or commits suicide.

The latter interpretation has produced a number of criticisms of Camus's ideas on the limits of political violence. For instance, Philip Thody writes: "To recommend that all conscientious rebels commit suicide after they have been obliged to kill in the service of the revolution is rather an impractical suggestion. No political organisation fighting against a tyranny could possibly succeed if its leaders follow Kaliayev's example." [29] And George Kateb, who has attempted to revive utopian political thought, presents a similar but more extended criticism of Camus's "life for a life" morality. He maintains that Camus's viewpoint in fact, though

[27] *The Rebel,* 169.
[28] *Ibid.,* 171.
[29] Thody, *Albert Camus, 1913–1960,* p. 127.

unwittingly, amounts to defense of a bloody doctrine—the stain of blood can be erased only with more blood. This seems inconsistent with Camus's own attack on the retributory motivation for capital punishment, which leads society to claim the right to take a murderer's life in exchange for the life of his victim. In response to this aspect of the argument, one should note that Camus criticized the retributive character of the death penalty principally, though not exclusively, because capital punishment exceeds the boundaries of *just* retribution; often the victim of capital punishment is made to suffer much more than has his victim. But the main thrust of this argument against Camus is that his principle renders effective revolutionary action impossible; an attempt to comply with his prescription would mean that the revolutionary forces would be constantly losing their numbers, to the point of final futility. "The perpetuation of the established order would seem to be guaranteed: rebellion whether for utopian purposes, or for something less, is to take its moral superiority as compensation enough for its inevitable failure." [30] Yet a third critic interprets Camus's principle as meaning that the rebel assassin must commit suicide in order to "remove the contradiction" created by his having killed in the name of revolt that takes the side of life against death.[31]

These criticisms are just, insofar as Camus's presentation of the "life for a life" principle is ambiguous. But ultimately they merely point up the difference in premises and purposes between the critics and Camus. In *The Rebel,* Camus is indeed ambiguous on the question of whether the rebel assassin must actually be executed or kill himself in order literally to pay for the life he has taken. I believe, however, that it is entirely possible to interpret his presentation as meaning that bloodshed does not necessarily require the shedding of further blood in retribution, but only a genuine recognition on the assassin's part that if

[30]George Kateb, *Utopia and Its Enemies* (New York: Free Press of Glencoe, 1963), 38–40.
[31]Herbert Hochberg, "Albert Camus and the Ethic of Absurdity," *Ethics,* LXXV (January, 1965), 100–101.

he must kill, he can do so only to further the chances for realizing
a relatively more just social order—and that if he is to be a
just man he must have a genuine willingness to sacrifice his own
life if necessary and recognize that it is intrinsically worth no
more than the life of any other human being. In other words, he
cannot justify killing on a wholesale basis in the name of abstractions that are supposed to become concrete reality in a remote future. Adherence to the "life for a life" principle is the
most efficacious way of keeping revolt on behalf of life-enhanc-
ing justice true to itself and preventing it from degenerating into
massively death-dealing revolutionary nihilism. It should be recalled that the real conflict in Camus's play is between the true
rebel, Kaliayev, and Stepan, an obvious prototype of the ruthless Bolsheviks who were ultimately to seize control of the anti-
Tsarist forces in Russia.

Further support for this interpretation is found in an entry
from Camus's journal: "The great purity of the terrorist of the
Kaliayev type is that for him murder coincides with suicide. . . .
A life is paid for by a life. The reasoning is false, but respectable. (A life taken is not worth a life given.) Today, murder by
proxy. No one pays." [32] Note especially in this passage Camus's
characterization of Kaliayev's reasoning as "false." The critics
who have interpreted the "life for a life" principle as *requiring*
the rebel assassin's suicide have overlooked Camus's explicit
repudiation of suicide in *The Myth of Sisyphus,* a conclusion
about which he never changed his mind.

These considerations lead me to conclude that Camus did not
mean that every rebel whose felt duty leads him to kill must
necessarily suffer execution or commit suicide; rather, by being
willing, if he must, to die for what he has done, "the revolutionary will be inclined to resort to violence only when no other
alternative is possible, and then only as an extraordinary measure,
the justification for which ends the moment a *relatively* just order
is established or reestablished." [33]

[32]*Notebooks, 1942–1951,* p. 156 (entry of 1947).
[33]Parker, *Albert Camus: The Artist in the Arena,* 132.

The most penetrating interpreter of Camus's ethics has cogently summed up the central meaning of the "life for a life" principle: "Camus never denied that in certain exceptional cases, the use of violence might be a weapon, but he always refused to accept that it might become a policy. A simple nuance perhaps, but for millions of human beings, one which is capital in importance."[34] This takes us to the heart of the differences in intent and premises between Camus and the critics of his views on political violence. These dissimilarities are particularly obvious in the case of Kateb, who seeks to defend the goal of creating a utopian society, an aim which Camus not only does not share but of which he is an uncompromising critic. Furthermore, Kateb maintains that a policy of revolutionary violence, though undoubtedly bloody in its immediate effects, is intended ultimately to produce a social order in which violence and killing will no longer exist. It is difficult to see any differences between this argument and Stepan's position in *The Just Assassins,* or the "end justifies the means" rationalizations presented in great profusion on behalf of the policies of Lenin and Stalin. What is most intriguing—and refreshing—about Kateb's argument is his own admission, ultimately, that as a matter of fact we have no way of knowing with any high degree of probability, much less with certainty, that the outcome of massive, violent revolution in the name of utopia will be an ideal social order in which oppression and killing will never reappear.[35] In short, utopian ends cannot justify means that involve violence and killing as policies, because we cannot know whether those ends will be realized. That, of course, was precisely Camus's point; Kateb's concurrence in it destroys the very basis of his principal criticism of Camus's attempt to establish a moral rule applicable to violent political means.

There can be no doubt that Camus's attitude toward political violence was, in the final analysis, profoundly skeptical, even es-

[34]Doubrovsky, "The Ethics of Albert Camus," 82.
[35]*See* Kateb, *Utopia and Its Enemies,* 50–51, 66–67.

sentially antagonistic. The best example of his position is the stance he assumed in relation to the Algerian war, which broke out in 1954 and did not end until two years after his death. In a sense, this can be viewed as a crucial test case of Camus's existential political morality. For Camus never ceased thinking of himself as simultaneously an Algerian and a Frenchman. The impact made upon him by his upbringing in the brilliant sunlight of North Africa has been made evident repeatedly, and that undiluted natural light always remained for him the primary symbol of lucidity, of life confronted openly and concretely in the present. It is not at all surprising, then, that he was mercilessly torn and tormented by a conflict on his native soil that became on both sides one of the bloodiest and most ruthless colonial wars of modern times.

In the 1930's Camus was among the first Frenchmen to call attention to the misery and oppression imposed upon the Algerian Arab population by French governmental administrators, and shortly after the Second World War he wrote extensive journalistic reports on an essentially unchanged situation which he then predicted would lead to violent revolt unless strenuous corrective measures were soon undertaken. His warning was not heeded, and his prediction came true. Very soon the war began, with virtually no limits on the tactics employed. Cruel torture of prisoners and suspects, massive reprisals against whole groups and villages, and creation of virtual concentration camps were resorted to by the French army. The Algerian rebels also used torture, systematically murdered both French civilians and Arab civilians suspected of friendship with the French, and in effect declared total war on the more than one million Algerian Frenchmen.

These measures Camus simply could not condone. No matter what the degree of "right" and "wrong" in the aims of the Algerian rebels and of the French government, tactics on both sides exceeded the boundaries of legitimacy. On the substantive question of which party to the conflict was "in the right," Camus took the position that neither the F.L.N. (*Fédération pour la Libération Nationale*) partisans who sought total independence for Algeria nor the French forces who aimed at keeping Algeria totally integrated with France—in effect perpetuating French domination of the Arab population—stood for a position that would ultimately benefit to the greatest possible degree all the people of Algeria.

He explained his own proposals for Algeria most clearly and succinctly in a letter to a British journal in which he attempted to reply to a correspondent's demand that he speak out on French repression of the Algerian rebels as clearly and strongly as he had denounced the Soviets' crushing of the Hungarian revolt. Camus responded that he had indeed made quite specific proposals for coping with the Algerian crisis: proclamation of the end of colonial status for Algeria, a round-table conference held without preconditions and in which representatives of all Algerian parties and groups would be included, and exploration of the possibility of an autonomous, federally structured Algeria as the best hope for safeguarding the liberties of both Arab and French Algerians. He further explained that as a Frenchman he could not join the ranks of the Arab guerrillas and as an Algerian Frenchman he could not approve a terrorism which struck even more Arab civilians than French. "One cannot ask me to protest against a particular repression, which I have done, and to justify a particular terrorism, which I shall never do." He concluded by denying that the Hungarian and Algerian situations were in any meaningful sense analogous. To view them in the same light required overlooking a significant historical fact: "There was not in Hungary, installed for more than a century, more than a million Russians (of whom 80% are ordinary folk) whose lives, whose rights (and not merely privileges) the Hungarian revolution menaced." The million Algerians of French descent, most of them born in North Africa, could not be ignored by anyone concerned for a humanly beneficial settlement of the conflict. "The Hungarian problem is simple: the Hungarians must be

given back their liberty. The Algerian problem is different:
there it is necessary to assure the liberties of the two peoples
of the country." [36]

One may well raise the question whether Camus would have
been so vehemently critical of the means employed by the Algerian rebels if he had been wholeheartedly in agreement with
the end which they sought to attain. But one should note that
he did sympathize completely with the Algerian Arabs' revolt
against French oppression. Furthermore, he considered any failure to take into realistic account the fate of the hundreds of
thousands of French Algerians deeply rooted in the country to
be a betrayal in principle of efforts to find a humane solution
to an inhumane conflict—in other words, as nihilistic political
romanticism of the most irresponsible variety.

This viewpoint involved Camus once more in a direct clash
with his former friends of the French intellectual Left. Sartre
viewed the Algerian conflict as purely an anticolonial struggle in
which the F.L.N. militants represented the tortuous but glorious
march of history toward socialism and freedom; their use of extreme violence was both comprehensible and justified. It was
nothing but a long-suppressed outburst in response to the systematic and daily economic, social, and political oppression that the
French in Algeria had inflicted upon the Arab population for
more than a century. In his terms, the rebels' violence was "nothing else but the violence of the colonial; there was never any
other violence." [37] The practical implications of this point of view
were spelled out by Sartre's longtime companion: "Partly out of
caution, but also with virtuous sincerity, most people began their
denunciations of the use of torture and machine-gunnings by saying: 'Of course we realize that the other side is guilty of terrible

[36]Letter from Camus in *Encounter,* VIII (June, 1957), 68.
[37]Jean-Paul Sartre, *Critique de la raison dialectique, précédé de question
de méthode,* Vol. I, *Théorie des ensembles pratiques* (Paris: Gallimard,
1960), 687 (quoted in Desan, *The Marxism of Jean-Paul Sartre,* 232).

excesses.' What excesses? The word had no meaning when applied to either side." [38]

From Camus's perspective, such a viewpoint reduces men to will-less role-players on a stage dominated by brutal events; it makes them slaves of a "history" that has become an abstract force wholly beyond direction by man's exercise of his capacity for moral choice. Camus could not help considering this interpretation of violence in Algeria as yet another instance of that curious antihuman form of submissiveness that has been strangely attractive to the contemporary intellectual Left in France (and which Camus had relentlessly satirized in *The Fall*). He responded to the Sartrean view of atrocities in Algeria by observing:

> People are too readily resigned to fatality. They are too ready to believe that, after all, nothing but bloodshed makes history progress and that the stronger always progresses at the expense of the weaker. Such fatality exists perhaps. But man's task is not to accept it or to bow to its laws. . . . The task of men of culture and faith, in any case, is not to desert historical struggles nor to serve the cruel and inhuman elements in those struggles. It is rather to remain what they are, to help man against what is oppressing him, to favor freedom against the fatalities that close in upon it.[39]

Camus simply could not agree that moral judgment and choice are wholly irrelevant to political conflict, even to the Algerian struggle in which intensely passionate hatreds and fearfully defended vested interests seemed to render impotent any effort to limit the tactics resorted to by either side. Camus was severely criticized for directing his negative comments principally toward the Algerian rebels, but this criticism overlooks his frequent condemnations of the use of inhuman means by the French army and the condoning of such acts by the political Right. He was acutely conscious that his arduous effort to point out and adhere to the narrow path of humanity in the midst of violently clashing

---

[38]Beauvoir, *Force of Circumstance,* 341.
[39]*Resistance, Rebellion, and Death,* 141.

forces was little understood and even less popular. He saw his viewpoint on Algeria as a case of "taking one's stand in the no man's land between two armies and preaching amid the bullets that war is a deception and that bloodshed, if it sometimes makes history progress, makes it progress toward even greater barbarism and misery." Although he realized that an effort to bring moral force to bear upon such conditions might well turn into practical futility, he felt any other course of action to be personally untenable: "If anyone dares to put his whole heart and all his suffering into such a cry, he will hear in reply nothing but laughter and a louder clash of arms. And yet we must cry it aloud. . . ." [40]

And cry aloud he did. Simone de Beauvoir's remark that she was disgusted by Camus's refusal to denounce torture in Algeria [41] seems to border on willful perversity, in light of Camus's published observations on the steadily deteriorating Algerian situation in 1958. In the preface to his collected essays on Algeria, he declared: "The truth, alas, is that a part of French opinion vaguely holds that the Arabs have in a way earned the right to slaughter and mutilate while another part is willing to justify in a way all excesses. . . . But that is a casuistry of blood. . . ." The Right had failed by not supporting timely reforms in Algeria and by not attempting to persuade its members that "certain forms of behavior"—such, apparently, as torture and bloody reprisals against civilian communities—are "discreditable." But the Left had erred also in not seeking to convince the rebels that "certain methods were essentially base." Tragically, the Right had usually approved, in the name of French honor, what was most dishonorable, and the Left, claiming to speak for justice, had often excused horrifying acts of injustice. "It seems as if metropolitan France was unable to think of any policies other than those which consisted in saying to the French in Algeria: 'Go ahead and die; that's what you deserve' or else 'Kill them; that's what they deserve.' " Both Right and Left, though fierce antagonists, had fallen

[40]*Ibid.,* 128.
[41]Beauvoir, *Force of Circumstance,* 383.

victim to "a single abdication, for the question is not how to die separately but rather how to live together." [42]

Camus sought persistently to interpret and comment upon events in the Algerian conflict from the distinctive standpoint of his understanding of true rebellion. It is obvious from this point of view that the terrorism of the Right and of the French army was unjustifiable, as had been the prolonged oppression of the Arab population in Algeria. His more controversial claim—at least in the eyes of the French intellectual Leftists—was that the F.L.N. militants, in carrying out their revolt, had gone far beyond the boundaries respected by the genuine rebel. One aspect of this was their "dream of eradicating the existence of the French in Algeria; to deny the presence of a million Frenchmen, in Camus's eyes . . . exceed[s] the limits of justifiable rebellion and bring[s] down suffering upon everyone." [43]

In addition, Camus made quite clear his belief that the F.L.N. had acted unfaithfully to true rebellion in its massive and almost indiscriminate terrorism directed against both French and Arab civilians:

Such terrorism is a crime that can be neither excused nor allowed to develop. Under the form it has assumed, no revolutionary movement has ever accepted it, and the Russian terrorists of 1905, for instance, would have died (they proved this statement) rather than stoop to it. It would be impossible to transform an awareness of the injustices imposed on the Arab population into a systematic indulgence toward those who indiscriminately slaughter Arab and French civilians without regard for age or sex.[44]

In an effort to place some limits on the violent tactics employed by both sides in the Algerian conflict, Camus took the lead in organizing an effort to bring about a civilian truce in the midst of the war. He hoped to persuade the leaders of the F.L.N. and

[42]*Resistance, Rebellion, and Death,* 116–17.
[43]Roger Quilliot, "Albert Camus's Algeria," trans. Emmett Parker, in Brée (ed.), *Camus: A Collection of Critical Essays,* 44.
[44]*Resistance, Rebellion, and Death,* 115.

the French authorities simultaneously to commit themselves in public to respect and protect the civilian population for the duration of the armed conflict. "Whatever the ancient and deep origins of the Algerian tragedy, one fact remains: no cause justifies the death of the innocent. . . . even if our present initiative saved but one innocent life, it would be justified." [45] But this project succeeded only in bringing down upon Camus the hostility of Right and Left, of *colons* and sympathizers with the F.L.N.

Typical of Leftist reaction was Simone de Beauvoir's biting statement that "Camus' language had never sounded hollower than when he demanded pity for the civilians." [46] In her view the conflict was between two civilian communities, the European colonists and the Arabs. The former were the real enemy of the latter, and the army was only the colonists' tool of suppression. But surely this is an attempt to package enormously complicated circumstances neatly in bundles labeled with such sloganeering political abstractions as "colonial" and "anti-imperialist." Camus persistently maintained that this approach could only distort and render even less ameliorable a condition that could be comprehended only in its complex uniqueness. To treat the million European Algerians, the majority of whom were natives of North Africa, as the equivalent of a ruthless, exploiting band of conquistadors was to propagate a distortion of the truth in order to justify the torture and slaughter of innumerable victims, most of them at least relatively innocent.

It may well be that one reason Camus did not engage constantly in denouncing particular French army atrocities in Algeria was a fear of bringing upon his mother, brother, and many close friends in Algiers savage reprisals by *colon* terrorists.[47] But his views on the Algerian tragedy reveal both integrity and consistency as expressions of his effort to defend his understanding of true rebellion against the threat of nihilism which he

[45]*Ibid.*, 134–35.
[46]Beauvoir, *Force of Circumstance*, 341.
[47]This view is expressed by Thody, in *Albert Camus, 1913–1960*, p. 3.

perceived to be emanating from almost every political quarter: "There are those who pass without transition from a speech on the principles of honor or of fraternity to a worship of the accomplished fact or of the cruelest faction. I continue to believe, however, in the case of Algeria as in all other cases, that such aberrations on the part of the right as well as on the part of the left point up clearly the nihilism of our time." [48]

Camus's distinctive stance in regard to the Algerian conflict comprised an insistence upon the relevance of moral judgment to even the most violent of political means and efforts—however unsuccessful—to lessen the inhumanity of the tactics resorted to by combatants on both sides. His reaction to this particular crisis epitomized almost perfectly his approach to the larger issue of the proper relationship between political ends and the means employed to attain them: "Does the end justify the means? That is possible. But what will justify the end? To that question, which historical thought leaves pending, rebellion replies: the means." [49] Inhumanly excessive, unjust, and indiscriminately terroristic means can in no sense be guaranteed to produce humane, just, and pacific ends, whereas such means in themselves unjustifiably violate the rebel's existential choice for life against the forces of death and oppression.

Actually Camus's position seems to represent a marked, if inchoate, uneasiness about basing political thought and activity upon ends-means premises. Both the scope and the limits of his dissatisfaction may be clarified by comparing his position on this point with Hannah Arendt's critique of ends-means political categorization. She maintains that the primordial, distinctively human meaning of political action is free, spontaneous, responsive activity that springs from man's unique capacity for communication through intelligible speech. Her prototype of political activity in this sense is the pre-socratic Athenian *polis*. There men revealed themselves in the political order, disclosing their

[48]Quoted in Quilliot, "Albert Camus's Algeria," 44.
[49]*The Rebel*, 292.

individual distinctiveness through the initiatives they took in the course of common deliberation, and sought to immortalize themselves by uttering memorable words and performing great deeds. The political realm was an end in itself; its sole "purpose" was to serve as an arena for humanly significant speaking and acting.[50]

But Socrates and, pre-eminently, his disciple Plato introduced ends-means categories into political thought. For Plato the true statesman is not simply one who acts and speaks politically in order to reveal himself; he is rather a deliberate architect of the political order who seeks to apply to it criteria which are external to politics. To Plato this meant consciously molding the order of the *polis* to attain the end of creating a collective order in conformity with the absolute ideas of beauty, truth, and justice. In the context of the significance and problematic character of ends-means political categorization, the enduring element in Plato's thought is the distinction he made between politics as a means and political ends which it is the wise and good man's duty to seek to attain. So long as a capacity for contemplation and reason were considered man's highest faculties, however, there prevailed a general belief in the existence of transcendent criteria which limited the choice both of earthly ends and of political means that might be legitimately employed to transform those ends into mundane reality.

But in the modern age the conception of man as a rational animal in the classical-Thomistic sense has been steadily displaced by a view that man is defined essentially as a creature who makes things (*homo faber*) and/or whose essence is identified with the labor he performs to sustain his physical existence (*animal laborans*). The social impact of technological achievement; the intellectual influence of self-consciously created, mathematically precise science; and the philosophical force of perspectives such as those of Descartes and Marx have combined to produce the widespread conception of the public sphere as an

[50]Arendt, *The Human Condition*, 156–59.

arena in which men seek to remake an entire society in conformity with consciously predetermined ends. This view has particularly characterized partisans of modern revolutions, "all of
which—with the exception of the American Revolution—show
the same combination of the old Roman enthusiasm for the
foundation of a new body politic with the glorification of violence as the only means for 'making' it." [51]

With the decay of belief in transcendent limitations on human behavior, the conviction that all efficient means are per-
missible in pursuance of desired ends has produced murderous
consequences in political practice. The hope for ameliorating this
tragic condition lies not in revival of belief in natural law or
in regulative divine will, but rather in ceasing to think in ends-
means categories in the political sphere: "As long as we believe
that we deal with ends and means in the political realm, we
shall not be able to prevent anybody's using all means to pursue
recognized ends." [52]

Certainly Hannah Arendt has pointed out sharply and critical-
ly the dangers always latent in conceiving of political ideas and
activity within an ends-means framework; in this respect her
analysis powerfully reinforces that of Camus. But Camus's proposed manner of coping with this situation seems to me to be
more realistic than hers. It seems hopelessly utopian in the
present age to desire the elimination from our very consciousness of ends-means thinking about public affairs. Our ubiquitous
technology can scarcely be managed at all, much less in any
manner that is beneficial, without a great deal of politically relevant self-conscious planning and coordination for the sake of
desired ends. Camus's more modest proposal that we devote as
much attention, in the sense of critical and moral judgment, to
political means as to social goals may also represent an un-
heeded cry in the wilderness. But it seems to be perhaps the
only feasible alternative to simple submission to blind "social

[51]*Ibid.*, 204.
[52]*Ibid.*, 205.

forces" or to "historical inevitability." This submission Camus could never accede to or defend.

In the final analysis, Camus was extremely skeptical about violent revolution as a means for beneficent social change in the contemporary world. "He never denied that in extreme cases a revolution might be justified, but the ethical conduct he was to demand of the revolutionist . . . was so stringent as to make revolution in our time nearly impossible." [53] His conviction that modern "historical rebellion" on any sizable scale has inevitably turned into "revolutionary nihilism" points clearly to the conclusion which he stated explicitly in his journal: "One must declare that one is not a revolutionary—but more modestly a reformer. An uncompromising theory of reform. Finally, and taking everything into consideration, one may call oneself a rebel." [54] There is no political hope for man in massive violence; hence the true rebel must conscientiously evade its lures in his unbending quest to make of justice, liberty, and happiness present realities, not merely components of a futuristic vision.

It is obvious that Camus's intense concern for justice and liberty, and to some degree the meaning which these terms had for him, make this aspect of his thought akin to humanistic liberalism. However, before exploring more fully his ideas on the meanings of and relationships between liberty and justice, we should note also a fundamental difference between Camus's perspective and the views of such bellwethers of the liberal tradition as Jeremy Bentham and John Stuart Mill. A perceptive commentator has pointed out that the utilitarian liberals conceived of men as discrete maximizers of pleasure (or happiness) and minimizers of pain; implicitly each individual then must view others simply as instruments in his pursuit of private fulfillment: ". . . other persons are obstacles to be overcome or resources to be exploited—always means, that is to say, and never ends in themselves." Though Mill recognized that men

---

[53]Parker, *Albert Camus: The Artist in the Arena*, p. 95.
[54]*Notebooks, 1942–1951*, p. 214 (entry of September, 1948).

may pursue ends higher than mere pleasurable sensations, he continued to view society as composed of a series of independent centers of consciousness, each seeking self-gratification "and confronting the others as beings standing-over-against the self, which is to say, as *objects*. The condition of the individual in such a state of affairs is what a different tradition of social philosophy would call 'alienation.' " [55]

Camus, as we have seen, in contrast came to believe in the utter inadequacy of such an individualistic view of man. Man indeed seeks happiness, but he cannot find it through the devices of egoistic calculation. Camus's belief in the potentiality—and at times the reality—of present, open, existential inter-human relatedness represents a very different standpoint from that of liberal utilitarianism. In a real sense persons are ends in themselves, and we discover in dialogical communion that our meaningful happiness is bound up with concern for that which enhances the lives of everyone. An understanding of this difference is essential to grasping the significance of liberty in Camus's political thought.

Camus regarded liberty as a most important value under heavy siege from prevalent tendencies within the contemporary world, above all from a concern to realize absolute justice at any price—including the suppression of existing liberties. Shortly after the Second World War he indicated a fear that freedom of expression—the aspect of liberty which he valued most highly—especially was endangered: "I am quite aware that this concern is not the primary one of a very large number of Europeans because justice alone can give them the material minimum they need and rightly or wrongly they would gladly sacrifice liberty to that elementary justice." [56] Not only great numbers of ordinary men but a host of intellectuals were decreasingly concerned about liberty; in fact the intellectuals tended

[55]Robert Paul Wolff, "Beyond Tolerance," in Robert Paul Wolff, Barrington Moore, Jr., and Herbert Marcuse, *A Critique of Pure Tolerance* (Boston: Beacon Press, 1965), 28–29.
[56]*Notebooks, 1942–1951*, pp. 109–10 (entry of September, 1945).

to consider the existing democratic freedom as an obstacle in the path of man's progress toward a future condition of "true liberty" for everyone: "Such solemn stupidities were uttered because for a hundred years a society of merchants made an exclusive and unilateral use of liberty, looking upon it as a right rather than as a duty, and did not fear to use an ideal liberty . . . to justify a very real oppression." [57] A liberty which, in practice, had largely meant freedom for the bourgeoisie to exploit and dominate the working class had unfortunately turned those who sought justice for the nonbourgeois elements of society against the very principles of political and intellectual liberty.

Liberty must not be identified with *laissez-faire*, which in practice means that the stronger social and economic forces enjoy unlimited privileges at the expense of the weaker: "Fundamentally, freedom is not made up of privileges; above all it is composed of duties." [58] The basic duty required by liberty is to work for the attainment of a common justice, which means happiness and the end of humiliation for all men; but intrinsic to this humanly just order of happiness is the central value of liberty, which Camus understood pre-eminently as untrammeled and open communication. Justice interpreted as equitable distribution of material possessions and rewards is extremely significant for the true rebel. But he will not consider it an absolute end the attainment of which justifies the use of any and all means, including the suppression of liberty. In our finitude and fallibility we have no way of guaranteeing that absolute distributive justice can or will ever be fully realized, and tragic experience has demonstrated that those who claim to be historical agents of such a perfect justice have continually inflicted new humiliations, injustices, and oppression upon those whose lives have fallen within the ambit of their power: "Liberty is the way, and the only way, of perfectibility. Without liberty heavy industry can be perfected,

---

[57]*Resistance, Rebellion, and Death*, 254.
[58]Albert Camus, *Actuelles II: Chroniques, 1948–1953* (Paris: Gallimard, 1953), 170.

but not justice or truth. . . . After twenty years of our harsh history, during which I have tried to accept every experience it offered, liberty ultimately seems to me, for societies and for individuals, for labor and for culture, the supreme good that governs all the others." [59]

If a choice must be made between a plan or ideology which promises ideal distributive justice, and liberty, Camus clearly indicates that he will side with liberty: "For even if justice is not realized, liberty maintains the power of protest against injustice and keeps communication open." But, despite the difficulty and tension involved in the requirement, the true rebel must clear-sightedly insist simultaneously upon the necessity of justice: "Once this is established, there is a justice likewise, though quite different, in laying the foundation of the only constant value in the history of men, who have never really died except for liberty." [60] This view is consistent with Camus's presentation of the prototypical slave-rebel's experience; he revolts against suppression of his freedom to be genuinely human. And it is no distortion to interpret the whole tradition of modern socialist thought, including the ideas of Marx, as, at least in its original impulse, revolt on behalf of human liberty against the distinctive types of social and economic oppression which typify the age of industrialism.

Justice demands liberty, not new forms of oppression under masters who promise material abundance for all or "true liberty-in-the-long-run." "It is essential to know that, without liberty, we shall achieve nothing and that we shall lose both future justice and ancient beauty. Liberty alone draws men from their isolation; but slavery dominates a crowd of solitudes." [61] The supreme value of liberty is that it nurtures the meaningfulness discerned in the experience of revolt—the vision of human solidarity in complicity against death. Injustice in the form of oppression "is bad for the

[59]*Resistance, Rebellion, and Death,* 248.
[60]*Notebooks, 1942–1951,* pp. 104–105 (entry of July, 1945).
[61]*Resistance, Rebellion, and Death,* 269.

rebel, . . . not because it contradicts an eternal idea of justice, but because it perpetuates the silent hostility that separates the oppressor from the oppressed. It kills the small part of existence that can be realized on this earth through the mutual understanding of men." [62]

Hence the value of free speech was staunchly defended by Camus, not primarily, as John Stuart Mill defended it, because its protection enables us to verify an increasing quantity of propositional truth,[63] but because freedom of expression enables men to come to awareness of their common destiny and act in accordance with their essential solidarity. Like Mill, however, Camus sees that genuinely free expression necessitates recognizing the equal right of our opponents to speak or print that with which we disagree: "Liberty is the ability to defend what I do not think, even in a regime or a world that I approve. It is the ability to admit that the adversary is right." [64] Camus desired the creation of what he termed a *civilisation du dialogue* in order that the mutuality of the human condition might be affirmed and coped with in the most genuinely human way possible. The essential point of free expression for Camus, then, is to make possible the realization of life as dialogical communion.

The unprovability and practical murderousness of claims to absolute justice, coupled with the need for maintaining freedom of expression, make it necessary that we accept proximate distributive justice as the only substantive social goal of true rebellion: "Revolt. If man fails in reconciling justice and liberty, then he fails in everything. . . . No, if he accepts approximation." [65] This is a hard lesson for men today, but learning it is our only hope for sustaining and enhancing the supreme value of genuinely human life: "Mania for virtue that shakes this age. Turning its back on skepticism which is in part humility, humanity strives to

[62]*The Rebel*, 283.
[63]*See* Maurice Cowling, *Mill and Liberalism* (Cambridge: Cambridge University Press, 1963), Chap. 2.
[64]*Notebooks, 1942–1951*, p. 105 (entry of July, 1945).
[65]*Ibid.*, 119 (entry of November, 1945).

find a truth. It will relax when society has found an error that is livable." [66] But this relaxation must not lead to resigned acquiescence in continued injustices; the true rebel continues to live in creative tension between his belief in the ultimate value of life and his rejection of those forces which debase and humiliate the lives of men: "Vigny (correspondence): 'The social order is always bad; from time to time it is merely bearable. From the bad to the bearable, the dispute is not worth a drop of blood.' No, the bearable deserves, if not blood, at least the effort of a whole lifetime." [67] Liberty must not be suppressed, for it is essential to meaningful human existence, yet the true rebel must persist in a lucid awareness of his responsibility, within man's corporate life, for "finding proximate solutions for insoluble problems." [68]

In this spirit Camus became an unyielding partisan of liberal constitutional democracy. He was well aware of the shortcomings, in practice, of democratic systems—particularly their frequent tendency to show insufficient vigor in the correction of social and economic injustices. However, like Winston Churchill, he nevertheless concluded: "Perhaps there is no good type of political regime, but democracy is assuredly the least bad one." [69] As a very young man, Camus recognized the impossibility in the modern world of democracy as direct popular sovereignty. He pointed out that in ancient Athens such a system was possible because a slave population did most of the work, allowing citizens time to devote much attention to political affairs. "Once slavery is abolished, everyone has to work. And it is when the European has reached the furthest extreme of proletarianization that the idea of popular sovereignty is at its strongest: the two things cannot be combined." [70]

Our only realistic hope for free institutions which will protect

---

[66]*Ibid.,* 197 (entry of July, 1948).
[67]*Ibid.,* 172 (entry of 1947).
[68]Reinhold Niebuhr, *The Children of Light and the Children of Darkness* (New York: Charles Scribner's Sons, 1944), 118.
[69]*Actuelles,* 124.
[70]*Notebooks, 1935–1942,* p. 204 (entry of October, 1941).

and nurture freedom of expression is a regime that permits the existence of more than one political party. The essential mark of a totalitarian system, whether of the Right or of the Left, is a single party with a vested interest in preventing the development of that liberty which would threaten its monopoly. Only a political system which incorporates into its structure a plurality of parties deserves our critical but active support, for "it alone allows one to denounce, hence to correct, injustice and crime. It alone today allows one to denounce torture, disgraceful torture, as contemptible in Algiers as in Budapest." [71]

A singular virtue of political democracy for Camus, as for all liberal democrats, was that its plurality of parties and its protection of freedom of expression establish institutionalized barriers against the abuse of governmental power. The sad experience of our times points up anew the continuing relevance of the liberal's conviction that "nowhere in the world has there been a party or a man with absolute power who did not use it absolutely." [72] This conviction reinforced Camus's determination to defend democratic liberties which have already been obtained against the totalitarians' claim that these represent only the negation of "true" freedom. Existing liberties—"all that remains with us from the great revolutionary conquests of the last two centuries"—must be viewed as halting steps along the road toward a greater degree of liberation, not as roadblocks to perfection. "If one agrees to suppress them, he will not thereby advance. On the contrary, this means retreat; . . . and one day it will again be necessary to travel the road toward liberty, but this new effort will once more be accomplished only through the sweat and blood of men." [73]

Camus's commitment to liberal democracy and to the pursuit of relatively just ends within its framework was exemplified in his stance toward the French national election of January, 1956. Although he did not then, or ever, assume membership in any

[71]*Resistance, Rebellion, and Death,* 161.
[72]*Ibid.*
[73]*Actuelles II,* 166–67.

political party, he indicated strong support for the effort of Pierre Mendès-France to revitalize the liberal left. In an article in *L'Express,* he justified backing Mendès-France's *Front Républicain.* "Unable to condone the 'social immobility that upholds the privileges of wealth,' or 'the refusal to accept reforms on the pretext that they compromise the possibility of revolution,' Camus preferred the middle ground of progressive reform. . . ." [74]

Incapable of ever being a self-righteous and jingoistic partisan of the "free world," Camus yet concluded that in the context of our times the true rebel must endorse Western democracy, while simultaneously seeking its amelioration:

> The defects of the West are innumerable, its crimes and errors very real. But in the end, let's not forget that we are the only ones to have the possibility of improvement and emancipation that lies in free genius. Let's not forget that when totalitarian society, by its very principles, forces the friend to denounce his friend, Western society, despite its wanderings from the path of virtue, always produces a race of men who uphold honor in life—I mean men who stretch out their hands even to their enemy to save him from suffering or death. [75]

Purporting to derive from the experience of rebellion principles such as moderation in politics, the relativity of ends, and the inviolability of just means and procedures, Camus sought to bridge the theoretical and practical gap between the European revolutionary tradition and liberal constitutional democracy that can effectively cope with social and economic injustice. He presented himself not only as a determined foe of political messianism but as a relentless critic of bourgeois regimes which indicate little concern for the attainment of that proximate justice for which free men can reasonably hope.

As in the realm of ethics, so also in the sphere of political institutions and values, Camus arrived at conclusions markedly similar to those of humanistic liberalism—though his point of

---

[74] Parker, *Albert Camus: The Artist in the Arena,* 154.
[75] *Resistance, Rebellion, and Death,* 163.

departure differed radically from the presuppositions of the pre-
eminent liberal political thinkers (Locke, Jefferson, and Mill
would have been most reluctant, to say the least, to take seriously a "philosophy of the absurd"). But Camus spoke to a situation
in which despair and spiritual chaos were ubiquitous realities,
and out of an existential knowledge that derived from the
harsh experiences and dashed hopes brought on by the German
occupation of France and by irrefutable postwar revelations of
Stalinist terrorism. Yet, refusing to give up all hope for the human
condition, "Camus would seem to have created (possibly in his
own despite) what has been wanted so urgently and so long but
has been so infrequently produced, a sustained and reasoned
apology for Liberalism." [76]

Camus's political concern was not by any means restricted to
a defense of free institutions and an insistence on limiting governmental power; he also showed considerable interest in the
substance of social and economic policies. Poverty he certainly
viewed as an indignity to be combated, but here again it must be
remembered that not only material security but genuine freedom is sought by men who are economic outcasts: "The oppressed do not want simply to be liberated from their hunger;
they also desire to be freed from their masters." [77]

Camus was vitally concerned with the condition of the working class, and one observer has declared that "the contemporary
writer who is most successful in touching a popular public and
who is in fact closest to the militant workers is none other
than . . . Albert Camus." [78] After the public announcement, in
the autumn of 1957, that Camus had been awarded the Nobel
Prize for Literature, the book bindery workers' union of Paris
sent him a congratulatory letter and invited him to speak before
a meeting of their group. This incident, which culminated in his
pleased compliance with their request, was indicative of Camus's

[76]Leon Roth, "A Contemporary Moralist: Albert Camus," *Philosophy,*
XXX (October, 1955), 302.
[77]*Actuelles II,* 168.
[78]Aubery, "Albert Camus et la classe ouvrière," 14.

close kinship with the French working class. Camus never forgot his humble origins or the years he spent in a variety of ordinary jobs. The highly class-conscious French workers appreciated his obstinate refusal to succumb, despite his worldly success, to the temptations of bourgeois standards and attitudes. Furthermore, though possessed of considerable learning and keen intelligence, he wrote in a simple language which the man of little education could understand. As a result, "before becoming an object of scholarly study Camus's work was for many workers . . . a comfort and an invitation to reflect upon our times." [79] Shortly after coming to metropolitan France, Camus noted his own affinity for working-class people: "French workmen—the only ones among whom I feel at home, whom I want to know and to 'live' among. They are like me." [80]

Camus's own work experience and his consequent appreciation of both the joys and the pain of the workingman's life helped reinforce his fidelity to the concrete realities of human existence. For instance, at one point in *The Plague* Dr. Rieux, greatly preoccupied, walks down a street in Oran: "The brief, intermittent sibilance of a machine-saw came from a near-by workshop. Rieux pulled himself together. There lay certitude; there, in the daily round. All the rest hung on mere threads and trivial contingencies; you couldn't waste your time on it. The thing was to do your job as it should be done." [81] "Doing one's job" implied for Camus an intrinsic dignity that work should possess but which he thought had been largely destroyed by the pressures of the productive imperative in contemporary industrial society.

Camus did not claim to present any definitive solution for the meaninglessness of industrial labor organized on the assumption that each worker is a replaceable cog in a giant machine. Even if the worker is guaranteed a certain degree of job security, the

---

[79]*Ibid.*, 15.
[80]*Notebooks, 1942–1951*, p. 23 (entry of March, 1942).
[81]*The Plague*, 38.

routinized task which he performs, usually but a minute division
of the production process, is often so boring that his efforts
take on the deadening cast of "alienated labor"—a phenomenon
that has concerned social theorists at least since Marx. Camus
declares: "Industrial society will open the way to a new civilization only by restoring to the worker the dignity of a creator;
in other words, by making him apply his interest and his intelligence as much to the work itself as to what it produces." [82]

But how is "alienated labor" to be transformed into creative
work? Camus really does not answer this question in any very
detailed way. Virtually his only response is a favorable estima-
tion of syndicalism, but even on this point it is not entirely clear
whether he is speaking simply of tight-knit union organization or
of workers' participation in the control and management of industrial enterprises. At the very least he intends to endorse the
former interpretation, holding that there should exist within every
industrial enterprise "a core of active and able syndicalists, capable of seeing that social regulations are observed, and also capable
of conducting competently and authoritatively the negotiation of
collective contracts." [83]

But it also seems legitimate to interpret his endorsement of
syndicalism as encompassing the latter meaning, that is, workers'
control and management in a democratically organized industrial community. What he admires is not so much an abstract
theory of syndicalism—such as, for example, Georges Sorel's—
as the practice of syndicalism, however limited its success may
have been. In fact, he viewed syndicalism as in part a protest
against abstraction on behalf of real life-in-communion: "*Communication. A hindrance for man because he cannot go beyond
the circle of people he knows. Beyond, he makes an abstraction of them. Man *must live* in the circle of flesh." [84]

Camus declared that although syndicalist socialism is usually

[82]*The Rebel,* 273.
[83]Aubery, "Albert Camus et la classe ouvrière," 17.
[84]*Notebooks, 1942–1951,* p. 103 (entry of September, 1944).

considered an historical failure, both politically and economically, the syndicalist movement in reality helped greatly to improve the condition of French workers; in particular it was instrumental in gradually cutting the duration of the working day from sixteen to eight hours. It was the "ideological empire" of "German" (Marxist) socialism that sabotaged syndicalism. The history of the First International is a record of unceasing struggle between German politico-revolutionary socialism and the libertarian syndicalism of France, Spain, and Italy—a fateful instance of the long-standing conflict between the "German" spirit of totality and the "Mediterranean" spirit of *mesure* of which the ancient Greeks were the prototypical defenders.

Camus contended that syndicalism is more humanly realistic than ideological, totalist socialism; the former deals with mundane reality as it appears to the clear-sighted and compassionate man, while the latter imposes an alien framework of abstractions upon unyielding facts. Syndicalism is therefore a consistent socioeconomic form of true rebellion, which deals with life as it is and seeks to enhance it; for syndicalism "relies primarily on the most concrete realities—on occupation, on the village, where the living heart of things and of men is to be found. Politics, to satisfy the demands of rebellion, must submit to the eternal verities." [85]

In accord with these views, Camus proposed, at the end of the Second World War, the formulation of a "new social contract" which would establish within the nation a large number of "communities of work" bound to each other by a series of reciprocal cooperative compacts.[86] Although he engaged in no extended effort to make this proposal an accomplished reality, he did continue to endorse syndicalism, particularly as concretely expressed in the labor movement. In 1955 he responded to an interviewer's question about his political beliefs and activities by

[85]*The Rebel*, 298.
[86]*Actuelles*, 172–73. For a description of the "communities of work" movement in postwar Europe, see Claire Huchet Bishop, *All Things Common* (New York: Harper & Bros., 1950).

declaring: "My choice . . . would at least be never to sit on a judge's bench, or beneath it, like so many of our philosophers. Aside from that, there is no dearth of opportunities for action, in the relative. Trade-unionism is today the first, and the most fruitful among them." [87]

Obviously Camus's effort to revive interest in syndicalism does not help us very far along the road toward coping in an ameliorative way with the social and economic problems of industrial society. He does not deal with the many complicated problems raised by the very fact of large-scale industrialism, such as the necessity for technically competent and far-sighted management—even though he recognized the danger that power might gravitate steadily into the hands of an irresponsible technocracy. In commenting on a similar advocacy of workers' management and control in the thought of Erich Fromm, John Schaar has suggested a number of particular proposals which anyone concerned, as Camus was, with the problems of labor in an industrial setting might well explore. These include defense of a nonmaterialistic ethic which emphasizes intellectual, aesthetic, and recreational activities rather than economic gain; abolition of economic goods and services which we could do without; unyielding criticism of the ideology of unlimited consumption; encouragement of all types of individual initiative; reduction in size of enormous cities; thoroughgoing decentralization of production and administration; championing the view that each worker, or a small group at most, should make a whole product, even if this is less "efficient" than mass assembly-line production; defense of the workers' right to set the pace and tempo of their own work; rapid automation of all necessary jobs which are tedious and unchallenging; and systematic application of the principles that each man shall do the job he likes best and that each man shall be paid well enough so that he can leave his present job and train himself for another that he prefers. "Such measures as these seem to be implied in any

[87]"The Artist and His Time," 207.

serious intention to give meaning and dignity to work. At least, they get at the problem in a way that the slogan of co-management and workers' participation never can." [88]

It is apparent that such an effort would require extensive social planning, in effect some form of socialist organization, even to begin to be carried out. Relevant at this point is Michael Harrington's effort to make a convincing case for revival of the socialist tradition, in a form that takes realistic account of the constructive potentialities latent in the present condition of the economy and society of the United States. Harrington maintains that domination of contemporary economies by large corporations, plus the steady advance of automation and cybernation (automated processes controlled by computers) in industry, presents us with the prospect of a privately controlled collectivist system in which human workers will become increasingly superfluous. But these developments also make possible a publicly controlled collectivism in which work can be redefined so that men are freed from drudgery to spend their lives in meaningful human activity. The socialist dream of freedom from economic want and exploitation is now, he claims, a realistic possibility.

Specifically, Harrington calls, for example, for defining work in order to include and emphasize lifelong education, provision of and participation in meaningful leisure and cultural activities, the efforts necessary for supplying decent housing for all citizens, and a greatly expanded emphasis on provision of human services to human beings. Such measures would require a thoroughgoing commitment to social planning, but, he points out, corporations have long been engaged in sophisticated planning operations for their own purposes, and government has developed planning for defense on a scale massive enough to demonstrate the feasibility of planning to meet all our social needs.

Like Camus, Harrington insists upon the necessity for democratic procedures in effecting the programs for which he calls.

[88]John H. Schaar, *Escape from Authority: The Perspectives of Erich Fromm* (New York: Basic Books, 1961), 274–75.

Not only should workers have a voice in the management of the enterprises in which they are employed, but techniques should be developed for presenting meaningful policy alternatives in specific planning areas to the democratic electorate.[89]

A democratic socialism of this type is, I believe, thoroughly in accordance with Camus's politics of fidelity to rebellion. The similarity of perspectives is particularly evident in Harrington's outright dismissal of all claims to the historical inevitability of socialism—"History can no longer be blamed; it is man who is in doubt"—and of violent revolution—"an apocalyptic day on which history literally makes it[s] leap from the realm of necessity into that of freedom"—as the means for the attainment of socialism.[90]

Camus was an avowed partisan of socialism, which, he claimed, in its true form "refuses equally both falsehood and weakness. It . . . is convinced that man's fate is always in his hands. It does not believe in absolute and infallible doctrines, but in the stubborn, difficult, and untiring amelioration of the human condition." [91] Like Harrington, he was a socialist without a grand crypto-religious ideology premised on a claim to total comprehension of the direction of history and devoted to apocalyptic utopianism. He contended that "social justice can very well be achieved without an ingenious philosophy. It requires several truths of good sense and such simple things as clearsightedness, energy, and impartiality." [92]

In rebellion, then, Camus not only found a rationale for rejecting and resisting the political ideas and programs of men who have succumbed to the temptation to play god in relation to their fellow men; he also discovered hope for a political order cut to man's measure and respectful of the limits disclosed to the rebel within the heart of his experience of revolt. An exis-

[89]For a full discussion of these proposals, see Harrington, *The Accidental Century*, especially Chaps. 8 and 9.
[90]*Ibid.*, 296.
[91]*Actuelles*, 65–66.
[92]*Ibid.*, 63.

tential awareness of human solidarity and an intense desire to exalt and enhance human life impel the true rebel to advance even in the face of apparent historical disaster—because he is keenly cognizant of and responsive to what it means to be a man. "I have always thought that if the man who has hope for the human condition is a fool, he who gives up all hope is a coward." [93]

[93]*Ibid.*, 179.

VI
Beyond Nihilism

Au plus noir de notre nihilisme, j'ai cherché seulement des raisons de dépasser ce nihilisme.   ALBERT CAMUS, "L'Enigme"

Perhaps the central problem of political philosophy today is the validation of moral norms. It is extremely difficult to envisage the emergence in our time of a universally accepted "solution" to this great quandary, which is endemic to a culture characterized by value pluralism and dominated by the scientific ethos. Nevertheless, valuation seems to be an enterprise with which we are unable to cease concerning ourselves, despite a lurking suspicion—even a fear—inspired by logical positivism that value statements are inherently and inescapably noncognitive. By now it should be apparent that Camus grappled mightily with this exasperating problem, particularly in respect to the nature, status, and place of moral judgments in politics. He believed that the collective tragedies of the twentieth century occurred in large measure because of ideologies which, rather than surpassing nihilism, embraced it in what proved to be a death grip—in the form of allegiance either to nothing but brute force or to a distant future condition of historical perfection. It would be easy, of course, to assert that Camus's fervent wish to escape the horrors of nihilism was father to his thought that moral standards can be established, but such a conclusion, I believe, would seriously underestimate both his effort and his achievement.

Some of the reasons the specter of nihilism haunts contemporary Western civilization have already been discussed, but an additional element in our situation should also be pointed out. This is that self-consciousness of the "will for truth" which Nietzsche most clearly elucidated. We cannot—or at least do not—take for granted a traditional morality by which we unreflectively conduct our lives. Ironically, even significant contemporary efforts to defend traditionalism are the products of highly self-conscious analysis.

For example, the articulate conservative political philosopher Michael Oakeshott does not advocate a simple allegiance to tradition; in fact, he has little liking for what he considers the dominant intellectual mood of Western culture for the past three centuries. He calls this perspective "rationalism" and believes its effects have been largely destructive of order and stability.[1] The rationalist believes that the only kind of valid knowledge is precise and technical; he takes account of human experience only in order to condense and convert it into a formula—in politics, an ideology. In so doing he neglects—whether or not he consciously denies its validity—practical, traditional knowledge, which cannot be converted into a neat formula but can be acquired only through practice, by doing things in an established customary manner. Beginning with Francis Bacon's assumption that it is possible to formulate an exact technique for the discovery of knowledge and with Descartes's similar quest for precise and certain knowledge through an allegedly infallible method, technique has acquired sovereignty through the efforts of men of lesser intellect than that of these two great progenitors of modern rationalism. And the rationalist mood, which sees government as a device to solve problems, has come

---

[1]*See* Michael Oakeshott, "Rationalism in Politics," in Michael Oakeshott, *Rationalism in Politics and Other Essays* (London: Methuen & Co., 1962).

to dominate modern political thought and practice because it perfectly fitted the need for guidebooks or "recipes" of the new classes which have steadily acquired social and political power during the last two centuries.

These developments have led to a misconception of the relation of moral ideals to politics: they are treated as abstractions by which the attainments of political technique are evaluated. But, Oakeshott maintains, in themselves "moral ideals are a sediment; they have significance only so long as they are suspended in a religious or social tradition, so long as they belong to a religious or a social life." [2] And rationalists have so long been at work draining away what they considered to be the irrational and worthless elements in the "liquid" in which moral ideals were suspended that the latter have come to appear increasingly as abstract irrelevancies, powerless to restrain our desires and channel our energies into the maintenance of social order.

There are significant similarities between Oakeshott's position and Camus's. Both have protested strongly against abstract morality as a root cause of nihilism and of ideological politics. And, significantly, neither looks to the ancient natural law tradition or to theological sources for a recovery and revival of genuine morality in politics. Furthermore, both appeal to human experience in seeking to validate a moral stance. But on this latter point the similarity is less genuine than it might appear at first glance. Whereas Camus speaks of experience primarily in an existential and phenomenological sense, Oakeshott means by experience simply long-established patterns of behavior. Somewhat strangely, Oakeshott fastens upon a condition produced by the rationalism he deplores as the source of a meaningful political morality for our time, namely: "Human beings impelled by an acquired love of making choices for themselves." [3] He asserts that we need no metaphysical or theological props for collective morality, only a

[2] *Ibid.*, 36.
[3] Michael Oakeshott, "On Being Conservative," in Oakeshott, *Rationalism in Politics and Other Essays*, 185.

socially established respect for individual autonomy. Government should not be thought of as a social problem-solver, but as the source and custodian of general rules for the authoritative arbitration of the conflicts which often arise among men seeking to conduct their lives as they see fit. "In short, the intimations of government are to be found in ritual, not in religion or philosophy; in the enjoyment of orderly and peaceable behavior, not in the search for truth or perfection." [4] Once it could be firmly established that the sole purpose of government is to maintain peace and order, this criterion of political morality would presumably suffice for a society composed of men whose individual value perspectives are otherwise widely divergent.

At first glance, Oakeshott seems to have proposed a realistically minimal consensus on political principles, which not only takes into account the lack of substantive agreement on a moral perspective in contemporary society but makes this very disagreement—which encompasses even skepticism and nihilism—the basic premise of his conservative view of government. But closer examination reveals some difficulties in his approach. Granted, the fundamental purpose of government is to arbitrate social conflicts so as to maintain peace and order. However, what criteria ought to be employed in making and enforcing laws which effect authoritative arbitration? Apparently the only criterion is the maintenance of social peace—at any price. But this view entangles Oakeshott in the moral and practical dilemmas which inexorably confront any advocate of an essentially laissez-faire concept of government.

It appears impossible to reconcile his two fundamental premises—preservation of individual freedom and government severely limited in powers and functions. Or, at best, reconciliation of these premises is possible only if one completely identifies liberty with freedom from arbitrary and tyrannical governmental power. But surely such a view scarcely begins to exhaust the meaning of individual autonomy. One need not agree wholly with Marx's

[4] *Ibid.,* 188.

analysis of capitalist society to recognize the truth in his view that great inequalities of economic power can nullify the freedom of workers and the poor, no matter what formal guarantees may be provided to each citizen by law or constitution. Anatole France's famous remark about the poor man's equal right with the rich to sleep under the bridges of Paris makes this point in an ironic and unforgettable way. In effect, Oakeshott's view implicitly equates the capitalist's freedom to exploit labor with the worker's "freedom" to submit—or to starve. It seems more than a little likely that in such a system freedom in any meaningful sense for the great majority of citizens would ordinarily give way to the demands of simple peace and order. If freedom were guaranteed in the form of a universal and meaningful right to vote, it is difficult to see how the majority could be induced to refrain from electing rulers who would use the powers of government to guarantee workers' rights to organize and bargain collectively and to provide social insurance and welfare policies in order to protect workers against the hazards of an industrial society—that is, to enlarge their freedom from want and insecurity. But this contradicts Oakeshott's concept of government as a purely neutral umpire that does not take sides in social conflicts. That these developments have in fact occurred in Western constitutional democracies during the late nineteenth and twentieth centuries points up the fancifulness of his point of view, which amounts to a curious reversion to the classical economists' vision of society.

Essentially, Oakeshott is most distressed by self-conscious political morality and desires a traditionalist social order in which questions about the nature of distributive justice and substantive freedom will simply not be asked. In effect, he seeks to transcend the moral impasse of contemporary political philosophy by suppressing explicit questions about moral principles in politics. But it is extremely difficult to see anything more than self-deluding fantasy in his intellectual endeavor. Not only does he settle upon the rationalist ideal of individual freedom of choice as the cornerstone of his perspective, but the effectuation of his desires would require radical innovations in existing political beliefs, policies, and governmental operations—a work of wholesale reconstruction sufficient in magnitude to deter the most optimistic and determined rationalist. And the entire gigantic enterprise would be designed to re-establish permanently a conception and practice of "freedom" such as that exposed and denounced by Camus and countless other political thinkers—a formal liberty which conceals under the cloak of strict legality the social and economic servitude of the weaker to the stronger.

Oakeshott presents a number of incisive arguments against moral abstractionism and against its political accompaniment, ideological thought and action. But his own appeals to experience, and even more so his laissez-faire view of government, appear themselves to be hyper-abstractions in comparison with Camus's existential approach to the situation of contemporary men in their relationships with government and society. For Oakeshott lacks—in fact he views as pernicious—sensitivity to all forms of oppression and the resolute determination to oppose them which is the root impulse of true rebellion. He actually provides no way out of political nihilism but builds his whole system upon it. And the result is the reinforcement of that bourgeois nihilism which Camus denounced as productive of widespread human despair through its fostering of relatively subtle but nonetheless deadening forms of servitude.

The leading present-day conservative political theorist thus fails to grapple realistically with the problems raised by our self-consciousness about the nature and status of political morality, and this failure would seem to indicate the impossibility of escaping that self-consciousness by deliberately suppressing it. The way out of nihilism can only be through heightened moral self-consciousness; at least this was Camus's firm conviction. Somewhat wistfully, he posed these questions in a conversation recorded in his private journal: " 'Don't you believe that we are all responsible for the absence of values? And that if all of us who come from Nietzscheism, from nihilism, or from historical

realism said in public that we were wrong and that there are
moral values and that in the future we shall do the necessary
to establish and illustrate them, don't you believe this would be
the beginning of a hope?' " [5] There is no evidence that he
seriously expected such a joint public confession and proclamation to be made by contemporary intellectuals, but his own
political writings reflect his personal determination to engage
persistently in this demanding enterprise.

Undoubtedly the most formidable intellectual barrier to the
validation of moral norms for politics is a belief generally held
by contemporary social scientists that the proper model for their
inquiries is precise, and if possible quantitative, science, from
which all judgments of value must necessarily be rigorously excluded. Perhaps the most nearly definitive statement of this view
of social "science" has been presented by Arnold Brecht in a
thorough and monumental work.[6] Brecht distinguishes three meanings of the term "science," ranking them according to the degree
of certainty (or "intersubjectively transmissible knowledge") that
each approach can provide. Pre-eminently "scientific" is "knowledge, intersubjectively transmissible *qua* knowledge (*scientia
transmissibilis*)."* Next in line on this cognitive scale is "knowledge, considered such, but not intersubjectively transmissible
qua knowledge (*scientia [sive vera sive putativa] non transmissibilis*)."* And finally there are "mere speculations, not claimed
to be knowledge (*scientia mere speculativa*)."* [7]

Knowledge in the first category, which alone includes the "intersubjectively transmissible," can be acquired—whether in the
natural or in the social sciences—only by a precise "Scientific
Method," which Brecht summarizes in eleven steps: observation,
description, measurement (of what can be measured), tentative
acceptance or nonacceptance as facts of the first three steps, tentative inductive generalization offered as a factual hypothesis,

[5]*Notebooks, 1942–1951,* pp. 145–46 (entry of October, 1946).
[6]Arnold Brecht, *Political Theory: The Foundations of Twentieth-Century
Political Thought* (Princeton: Princeton University Press, 1959).
[7]*Ibid.,* 280.

tentative explanation or theoretical hypothesizing, logical deductive reasoning from tentative hypotheses, testing by further observations, correcting tentative acceptance of previously accepted results as required by new evidence, prediction of future events or conditions, and nonacceptance of all statements not obtained by this method.[8]

"Science" in the second sense consists of private knowledge based on observations and experiences not verifiable according to the steps of "Scientific Method"—for example, personal memories, philosophical intuitions, or alleged religious revelations. Such personal claims to knowledge may or may not be true, Brecht maintains, but they are not knowledge in the fully scientific sense because they cannot invariably be intersubjectively communicated to others. He admits, however, that without a large stock of such *scientia non transmissibilis,* "we could hardly live as human beings, because the stream of *scientia transmissibilis* runs dry in so many vital fields. We live by the individuality of our knowledge." [9]

Finally, "mere speculations, as for example about the nature of God or about life after death, constitute no science in the sense of the two preceding categories, not even the second unless the author regards their results as revealed or intuitive knowledge." Speculations provide knowledge only insofar as they clarify the nature of particular problems or contribute to increasing clarity about the relative probabilities of alternative hypotheses. Thus they frequently play a very significant part in scientific inquiry, but only as auxiliary steps in efforts to acquire knowledge in the first, or fully scientific, sense.[10]

There can be no doubt that although Brecht employs the term "science" in reference to all three types of knowledge, only for that which becomes known through the procedures of "Scientific Method" does he consider the scientist or scholar justified in

[8]*Ibid.,* 28–29.
[9]*Ibid.,* 280.
[10]*Ibid.,* 280–81.

claiming cognitive verifiability. His position on this matter is made clear in his discussion of the relationships between science and valuation. He strongly denies that science can establish the validity of any "dogmatic doctrines regarding justice," because the mere fact that a condition exists or that a doctrine is believed entails no moral imperative to accept it. "Scientific Method" can only tell us what is or what might be, not what ought to be. Logically, an imperative conclusion cannot be derived from indicative premises, and "Scientific Method" is restricted to dealing with indicatives and hypotheticals. Brecht thus calls his viewpoint "Scientific Value Relativism," by which he does not mean that science has demonstrated that "all values are relative," but rather that "Scientific Method" cannot answer the question of what value standards are absolute, or even determine whether such moral absolutes do or do not exist: "The absolute standard of justice . . . cannot be proved or disproved, only believed and taken for granted, or disbelieved and not so taken." [11]

Discernment of moral norms is simply beyond the reach of science and belongs to the spheres of religious revelation, ethical intuition, and philosophical speculation. Science can neither affirm nor deny truth claims presented as putative knowledge acquired by these methods. However, Brecht does maintain that science can, at least in principle, discover factual links between Is and Ought, and as an example he provides "a tentative list of universal and invariant postulates of justice": first, truth, in the sense that all pertinent statements dealing with facts and relations must be objectively true and, subjectively, that a just person must seek to act in accord with what he believes to be true; second, generality—that is, consistent and unarbitrary application of the system of values in question; third, equal treatment of what is considered to be equal within the system; fourth, no restrictions on freedom beyond the requirements of

[11]*Ibid.*

the system; and fifth, respect for the necessities of nature which render certain kinds of action physically impossible.[12]

Brecht places special emphasis upon what he claims is the firmly established factual link between justice and truth: "The intertwining fact in this case is that apparently all human beings *do* feel and think that way, that they are unable to feel and think otherwise, even if they want to, or to imagine, concretely and realistically, that they could feel and think otherwise." [13] Although he maintains that in the strict scientific sense the factual existence of this link can be considered as only an "inductive generalization from observed facts," he appears to be thoroughly convinced of the certainty that this hypothesis will be confirmed by whatever future tests may be employed to examine it. Brecht's "scientific hypothesis" on this point, and even his manner of deriving it, appear strikingly similar to Camus's existentially felt obligation to remain steadfastly faithful to his personal experience and perceptions—that is, to seek to maintain a rigorous personal truthfulness.

I find Brecht's analysis to be quite thorough, honestly and straightforwardly presented, and in most respects convincing. There does seem, however, to be one major difficulty, perhaps even a point of confusion, in his discussion of the meaning of science; this is his assertion that only knowledge attained through the procedures of "Scientific Method" is "intersubjectively transmissible *qua* knowledge." Brecht seems to be restricting that which can be transmitted from one person to another as knowledge to the analytically precise and/or the quantitative. These appear to me as unnecessarily narrow limitations on what we can know and communicate meaningfully to one another. It is true that, unlike the dogmatic positivist, Brecht does not assert that nothing we come to believe to be truthful by means other than the procedures of "Scientific Method" can be claimed

[12]Brecht, *Political Theory*, 395–96.
[13]*Ibid.*, 415.

as knowledge: "It is quite possible, as a rule, to communicate this private knowledge to others by narrating it to them, and we are often driven to do so by an almost irresistible urge." But such personal perceptions of and beliefs about what is true cannot "transmit our own (real or putative) knowledge as knowledge; transmission is limited to the personal report, . . . saying that we believe we have knowledge on such and such a basis." [14]

Whether Brecht intends to or not, his classifications and definitions convey the impression that knowledge acquired in any way other than by the procedures of "Scientific Method" is somewhat less intellectually respectable than are the fruits of scientific investigation. But why should this be the case when, as he admits, our life owes its very humanness to nonscientific knowledge and belief? Perhaps Brecht's honest and admirable modesty about the scope of "Scientific Method" would have been even more adequately formulated if he had declared that only discoveries made by use of this method can be invariably transmitted as precise, unambiguous, and certain knowledge, rather than asserting that strict scientific procedures alone can bring to light that which is transmissible as knowledge. Brecht's formulation does not take into account, for example, the possibility of the dialogical transmission of nonscientifically derived knowledge—as knowledge that is compelling and difficult to evade, even if not incontestable.

Brecht's scrupulous, careful, and undogmatic analysis is symptomatic of the view of many contemporary social scientists that insuperable intellectual barriers foreclose any possibility of linking their commitment to discover "intersubjectively transmissible" knowledge through the procedures of "Scientific Method" with valuation in the social and political sphere which they study. However, a significant effort to forge such a link has been made by Thomas Landon Thorson.[15] Writing from a perspective which

---

[14]*Ibid.,* 280.
[15]Thomas Landon Thorson, *The Logic of Democracy* (New York: Holt, Rinehart and Winston, 1962).

he labels "post-positivist," Thorson is particularly concerned with presenting a rational justification of democracy, but in the process he attacks head on the view that science and valuation are wholly distinct and dissimilar and that the latter activity can consist only of stating rationally undemonstrable preferences. Thus his work has ramifications for the wider problem of validating moral norms in politics.

Profoundly influenced by empiricist and positivist philosophies, Thorson disproves—to his satisfaction, at least—that it is possible to justify democracy by deduction from the premises of any grand metaphysical or theological system, principally because such premises cannot themselves be validated and because, historically, very different political values have been allegedly inferred from very similar philosophical systems. But, he contends, the intellectual unfeasibility of taking this route need not lead us to nihilistic conclusions. Comprehension of the true nature of scientific inquiry can set us on the road at the end of which we shall find a rationally defensible justification of such a fundamental political value as commitment to democracy as the best form of government.

We must first of all understand that justification and proof are not at all identical. Certain proof of a conclusion can be attained only through rigorous logical deduction or, somewhat less securely, by inductive generalization. But proof in this sense does not exhaust the procedures and logic of science. Scientists do not merely gather facts from which hypotheses and theories automatically emerge. Rather, " 'recommending' and 'fact-stating' tend to merge in scientific endeavor, and the fundamental dichotomy that has so often been interjected between the two emerges as in many important respects artificial." [16] In particular, scientists who are seeking to formulate a new explanatory theory in effect recommend that the phenomena in question be regarded in a particular manner. As a rule, this is not the only intelligible way in which the phenomena may be viewed, but every scientific theorist must

[16]*Ibid.*, 107.

simply choose a perspective that appears to him most intellectually satisfying and fruitful. These "recommendations" usually change over a span of time, as new evidence is discovered and new interests come to the fore, but—and this is Thorson's main point— the act of philosophical choice is just as intrinsic to scientific procedure as are empirical investigation, deductive reasoning, and inductive generalization. In fact, he views the whole enterprise of science as founded upon a scientifically unverifiable but nevertheless unarbitrary choice to attempt to discover the nature of empirical reality.

Given this decision by men—or at least by certain men—there follows the necessity of adhering to certain canons of procedure in order to prevent the quest from being self-defeating. "The ignorant, finite, limited man seeks to understand the world. 'How should he do it?'—that is the question." The appropriate response, according to Thorson, is the basic imperative of the scientific enterprise, summed up in Charles Sanders Peirce's injunction: " 'Do not block the way of inquiry.' " [17] This statement is neither a description of empirical fact nor the conclusion of a syllogism; it represents rather "the logic of recommendation." That is, within the context of man's effort to learn the truth about the world and of the human fallibility demonstrated by constant changes in the accepted content of scientific "truth," the only rational way of conducting this quest is to permit free and unfettered scientific inquiry. It is absurd to contend that because one cannot *prove* Peirce's imperative either empirically or deductively it is arbitrary and irrational; "What can 'rationality' possibly mean if it is not rational to assent to the recommendation 'Do not block the way of inquiry'? What could be more clear than that rational justification is not always a matter of proof?" [18]

Thorson attempts to carry over this same type of reasoning into the sphere of political valuation. Taking his cue from Camus's assertion that "the important thing . . . is not . . . to go to the root

[17]*Ibid.*, 119–20.
[18]*Ibid.*, 124.

of things, but, the world being what it is, to know how to live in it," [19] Thorson poses this as the basic question we must confront: " 'The human situation being what it is, what is it rational to do?' We are here; now what do we do? We have a context; what is the best recommendation in this context?" [20] The defining characteristics of the human political context are simply aspects of man's general situation in the world—namely ignorance, fallibility, and finite and limited intellectual capacity. Hence we are incapable of predicting with certitude the results of political decisions or of establishing the ultimate rightness of any political goals. It follows that rule by an elite on the grounds of its claims to infallibility and virtue cannot be rationally justified. "Just because the 'rightness' of a political decision *cannot* be proved— because its consequences . . . cannot be predicted with certitude nor its ultimate ethical supremacy demonstrated—are we obligated to construct a decision-making procedure that will leave the way open for new ideas and social change." The Peirce-like general recommendation that Thorson proposes as the foundation for political philosophy is, then: " 'Do not block the possibility of change with respect to social goals.' " [21] This is no divine or deductively validated imperative; it is merely—but sufficiently— a conclusion of the logic of recommendation that accords with the real human situation in the political realm.

This recommendation entails the maintenance of political freedom for everyone, which requires democratic government—that is, the interdependent elements of popular sovereignty, political equality, individual political rights, and majority rule. Thus a rational justification of democracy and its concomitant political values is possible, and we need not consider such a political value preference either as an arbitrary and indefensible choice or as requiring validation in terms of an elaborate metaphysical or theological system.

[19]*The Rebel,* 4; quoted in *ibid.,* 130.
[20]Thorson, *The Logic of Democracy,* 130.
[21]*Ibid.,* 139.

There are certain obvious similarities between the approaches to valuation of Thorson and of Camus. Both are suspicious of theology and of philosophical systematizing and seek strenuously to avoid any "appeal to the transcendental." Both pose the questions, what is the human condition, and what is it reasonable to do within this context? (One might well note, in passing, that either explicitly or implicitly all political philosophers have raised these questions; Thorson differs from thinkers whom he calls absolutists—such as Plato—not in posing the questions but in the nature of the answers he provides to them.)

However, the differences between the perspectives of Thorson and Camus seem to me much more important than these similarities. Thorson is pre-eminently concerned with accommodating political valuation to the positivistic proclivities of contemporary social science; as a result, he provides us with no standards of normative judgment for the assessment of the diverse social goals the fulfillment of which we are not supposed to block— except, presumably, that such goals should not be incompatible with the maintenance of democracy. Camus, as we have seen however, did not believe that the human condition could be exhaustively or even adequately described as one of fallibility and ignorance, although he never denied the reality and crucial significance of these characteristics of man's situation.

The fundamental difference in philosophic method between these two thinkers can be seen, ironically, in Thorson's effort to identify Camus's position with his own. Thorson sought to claim Camus's authority for his assertion of the lack of any necessity "to go to the root of things" in order to engage in political valuation. However, Thorson omitted certain words from Camus's sentence, which reads in full: "The important thing, therefore, is not, as yet, to go to the root of things, but, the world being what it is, to know how to live in it." [22] The two words, "as yet," were the significant omissions; this sentence appears on the second page of Camus's introduction to The Rebel,

[22]The Rebel, 4.

in which Camus did indeed attempt to go to the human and historical "root of things." Rather than restricting himself to the boundaries of a "post-positivist" philosophy, Camus employed a radically existential philosophical method in an effort to explicate much more fully than does Thorson the nature of the human condition. This accounts for the richness, complexity—and, admittedly, ambiguity—of the former's portrayal of man's situation as opposed to the "scientifically tenable" but highly abstract and denatured character of the latter's.

Camus implicitly maintained that what we learn through existential "knowing" is just as valid for our genuinely human needs and purposes as are the discoveries and theories of empirical science. And in fact the former approach can provide us with a kind of knowledge that the latter can never discern, namely the "awareness of meaning and value" that we can attain only through involvement of our whole beings in dialogical relationships. Maurice Friedman maintains that science investigates man not as a whole but only in selective aspects, and that scientific method is "man's most highly perfected development of the I-It, or subject-object, way of knowing." This method abstracts from the concrete richness of human circumstances and seeks to "reduce the I in so far as possible to the abstract knowing subject and the It in so far as possible to the passive and abstract object of thought." This approach is useful for categorizing men as certain kinds of objects in a world of objects, but not for discovering the human uniqueness of man. Only as a participant in I-Thou relations can one begin to conceive the meaning of man's wholeness and uniqueness: "Only I-Thou sees this wholeness as the whole person in unreserved relation with what is over against him rather than as a sum of parts, some of which are labelled objective . . . and some subjective. . . ." [23]

There are, in the final analysis, a great gulf and an impasse

[23]Maurice Friedman, "Introductory Essay" to Martin Buber, *The Knowledge of Man,* trans. Maurice Friedman and Ronald Gregor Smith (New York: Harper & Row, 1965), 19–20.

between the assumptions about knowledge of positivist or "post-positivist" social science and the existential approach to knowing of Camus. The main point I want to make in this connection is that Camus's perspective deserves recognition and very careful consideration by students of politics and society whose philosophical commitments—either overt or implicit—make them feel uneasy or even guilty about the intrusion of value judgments into their professional work. Perhaps contemporary social science could gain in depth and human significance if those who are caught up in its dominantly positivistic mood could at least subject their presuppositions to critical scrutiny in light of the existential, dialogical approach which holds that man cannot be fully comprehended by objective observation, description, and measurement of his patterns of behavior.

For example, the existential thinker maintains that the logical positivist's reduction of value statements to mere descriptive reports of what the people who utter them desire shrinks "values to objective, descriptive, 'handleable' dimensions for which one claims scientific warrant without personal involvement, decision, and risk." And this reduction distorts the real meaning of valuation—"the ultimate choice of what personal or social way of life is meaningful, what is authentic, what embodies real value"—by ignoring the often painful and chaotic realities of the individual's effort to decide within himself what he should do in response to a particular situation. "The logical positivist tends to use his concern with logic and methodology as a means of escaping from the inundations of actual experience into the high plains of pure abstraction." [24]

The existential thinker distrusts abstractions, because he is intensely and immediately aware that no general categorizations can begin to exhaust the human uniqueness which he knows in his own experience and perceives in every other person as well. The danger of pure subjectivism—which lurks, for example, in the thought of Kierkegaard—is overcome in the dialogical ap-

[24]Friedman, *Problematic Rebel*, 472.

proach common to Camus and Buber, who find meaning ultimately in the sphere "between man and man" and betweeen the person and the world.[25] Particularly significant in Camus's existential valuations are his experienced awareness of the implications for man of finitude and mortality and the dialogically known worth of concrete, particular persons in the here and now. We have noted the normative implications for the political realm which he drew from these lessons of his own experience and sensitivity to human realities.

There is by no means any certainty—nor do I entertain any real hope—that the positivistic social scientist will pay any heed to existential views of man, or, if he does, that he will be inclined to consider them as more than vague, emotive expressions. But it might be instructive to him to come to the realization that his own approach is grounded in an unverifiable and far from self-evident philosophical commitment, and perhaps even to entertain a suspicion that some of those who differ with him about the proper ways of comprehending human reality may be as intelligent and as concerned about discovering truth and avoiding obscurantism as he believes himself to be. Such a minimal awareness might serve to introduce into social science an openness and modesty in regard to methods of investigation and study that could, in the long run, provide us with a fuller knowledge of man than may ever be attained by single-minded insistence upon the sole legitimacy of a hyper-empirical and allegedly objectivistic "Scientific Method." "Humility here means no obscurantism or romantic rebellion against science. It is, rather, the growing awareness by each science of its proper limits and the salutary fear of overstepping them." [26] Even the problem of valuation may appear to us in a new light if we can go beyond the true conclusion that science cannot validate moral norms—

[25]For the distinctions between Kierkegaard's hyper-individualistic existentialism and Buber's dialogical perspective, see the essay, "The Question to the Single One," in Martin Buber, *Between Man and Man* (New York: Macmillan Company, 1965).
[26]Friedman, *Problematic Rebel*, 469.

it was never designed or intended for this purpose—to explore the human implications of existential perception and awareness.

Jacques Barzun has maintained, in a recent provocative book, that our culture is dominated by a scientific ideology which leads us to accept unquestioningly claims to sole legitimacy made on behalf of methods which can deal with our thoughts and experience only from a strictly limited perspective—one which necessarily excludes much of what is essential to meaningful human existence. His critique converges with the existential perspective in pointing to the concentration of science upon the formulation of and quest for explanatory abstractions which are often remote from our experience, perceptions, and common sense. His quarrel is not with the scientific enterprise but with our tendency to commit the "fallacy of misplaced abstraction" (a label Barzun considers more apt than Whitehead's "fallacy of misplaced concreteness") in assuming that only scientific knowledge is genuine and significant knowledge. He sees our problem as one of recovering belief in a multiplicity of sources of human truth, displacing the dangerously narrow "single vision" of science: "The predicament of the age is to regain the high ground where the thoughtful man can be at ease with his repressed intuitions and satisfy through many means his equally many capacities for reason and belief." [27] Barzun is not seeking to promote an unbounded subjectivism or claiming that credence should be given to any and all truth claims that people happen to make. He is simply defending the view that knowledge need not possess the alleged certainty and precision of scientific findings in order to be tenable and give to our lives a richness, coherence, and joyfulness that no unitary approach to truth can ever provide: "Life, which spurs desire and fills the mind, is wider than science or art or philosophy or all together. Mind encloses science, not the other way around. Science is a little nugget within the mind, not a vast medium encompassing its

[27]Jacques Barzun, *Science: The Glorious Entertainment* (New York: Harper & Row, 1964), 286.

thoughts." [28] Careful attention to ideas of existential thinkers like Camus may stimulate in us an awareness that science may not have the last word on what we can know—at least sufficiently to accept as credible and commit ourselves to, even if not with absolute certainty—about the human condition and what we ought to be and do within it.

Camus himself dealt scarcely at all with the potentialities of his existential method for ameliorating the deleterious effects of the logico-scientific world-view upon the cognitive status of moral norms. However, as we have noted previously at some length, he did employ his anti-abstractionism in subjecting to intensive criticism all total ideologies and utopianism. In recent years there have been a number of attempts to revive and revitalize utopian social thought, and I believe that Camus's insights can assist our efforts to evaluate this new utopianism. Here it seems appropriate to examine briefly the central ideas of two utopian writers and to seek to determine whether they have succeeded in avoiding the pitfalls which Camus believed to be endemic to any programmatic ideology.

One book, which has already been touched upon briefly, is George Kateb's *Utopia and Its Enemies.* Kateb makes no effort to validate ultimate human norms but simply sets out from the assumption that all men desire perpetual peace, guaranteed material abundance, and consistently "virtuous" behavior for themselves and their fellows. Since utopian peace and abundance hinge upon the establishment of undeviatingly virtuous patterns of social life, we shall focus only upon this fundamental requirement of Kateb's utopia. For support on this essential point, Kateb turns to behavioristic psychology, more precisely to the theories of B. F. Skinner.[29] Skinner believes that, by use of the manipulative techniques of positive reinforcement, it is possible to shape the behavior patterns of human beings—especially if the effort begins

---

[28]*Ibid.*
[29]For a clear presentation of Skinner's psychological utopianism, see his didactic novel *Walden Two* (New York: Macmillan Company, 1948).

with infants—in almost whatever way the manipulators desire. Kateb is persuaded by this argument and agrees with Skinner that if men of benevolent social vision do not exploit the possibilities of these techniques, they will be employed—as to a great extent is presently the case—by men of military and economic power for their own ends rather than for the general good of mankind.

Kateb is not entirely content with this scheme for creating conditioned virtue; he is highly critical of what he sees as Skinner's lack of appreciation for the importance of self-conscious, autonomous self-direction in the progressive development of human potentialities. Whereas, then, Skinner (or at least the psychologist-hero of *Walden Two,* Frazier) forthrightly proposes government by an elite composed of virtually all-powerful behavioral scientists, Kateb favors a political system for utopia that includes a limited and rational democratic politics and representative government. He is deeply convinced that men in utopia would be less than human—no matter how happy they might be—if they sacrificed autonomous self-awareness through submission to a virtually invisible oligarchy—however benevolent its intentions and achievements.

On this point, Skinner appears to me much more consistent and persuasive than Kateb. Skinner's basic psychological technique, positive reinforcement (rewarding desired behavior until it becomes a fixed response to particular stimuli) would seem to depend for its effectiveness upon concealing the manipulative mechanisms. His approach is designed not to give individuals a choice between virtuous and evil, or pleasurable and painful, alternatives, but to condition the individual's *un*conscious in order that he may automatically and *thoughtlessly* choose to do the good (which is whatever the manipulator decides). Skinner quite consistently denies any meaningfulness to the concept of free will, and his entire scheme is designed to effectuate this denial by relieving people of the painfulness of moral choice. It is utterly impossible to see how Skinner's theory of conditioned virtue could in any way be combined with the heightening of self-conscious awareness which Kateb views as an indispensable objective of any desirable utopia.

Kateb's strongly positive valuation of self-awareness and of autonomous choice is much more reminiscent of Camus than of Skinner. If Camus had ever given serious consideration to Skinner's utopian novel (there is no evidence that he knew of it), he almost certainly would have considered the inhabitants of *Walden Two* to be wretchedly subhuman, will-less automatons, whose pacific behavior and temperate pleasures could not begin to compensate for their inability to respond freely and self-critically to their deepest existential perceptions. It is scarcely credible that Skinner's flesh and blood mechanisms could ever experience what Camus considered the highest human good—dialogical life in communion.

The most profound and suggestive contemporary utopian thinker of the "left-Freudian" variety is undoubtedly Herbert Marcuse. In *Eros and Civilization,* Marcuse presents a Freudian analysis and indictment of contemporary society. In his view, our social and political institutions and dominant cultural values weight us down with an enormous burden of surplus-repression—that is, repression of libidinal desires in excess of what would be minimally necessary to maintain human social existence. This surplus-repression is produced by the reigning performance principle, the general belief that work and production are overriding imperatives of life itself and that all pleasures, physical and intellectual, must be subordinated to the observance of this principle.

Once functional in an age of scarcity, the performance principle is profoundly dysfunctional in an age of automation and relative affluence. Its perpetuation serves only the continued domination of the many by the politically and economically powerful few whose power and position would not survive a gradual but generalized instinctual liberation. Such a liberation, Marcuse contends, need not result in the anarchic violence and mutual destructiveness of Hobbes's "war of all against all." For, as Marcuse interprets Freud's theory, aggressiveness became incorporated into man's instinctual heritage because the condition of material scarcity *(Ananke)* forced men to struggle with one another for their very sustenance. If securely scarcity-free conditions could be created, Marcuse assumes that aggressiveness would eventually cease to be functional and the psychic purpose of relieving tension that it presently fulfills would be wholly assumed by a liberated eros.

Genuine instinctual liberation would bring about a reunification of intellect and the pleasure principle, since intelligence would no longer be compelled, as it is under the dominance of the performance principle, to do the work of repressive sublimation. Furthermore, liberated eros would be autonomously self-limiting and self-controlling; its tension-free union with intelligence would thus permit it to maximize pleasure rather than endanger its future enjoyment through involvement in orgiastic excess.

Marcuse does not deal at all clearly or specifically with the problems of attaining the utopian condition of generalized instinctual liberation which he believes Freud's theories have made not only conceivable but plausible. However, he does maintain that the "liberation [of the individual], instinctual as well as intellectual, is a political matter, and a theory of the chances and preconditions of such liberation must be a theory of social change." And further: "Where repression has become so effective that, for the repressed, it assumes the (illusory) form of freedom, the abolition of such freedom readily appears as a totalitarian act." [30] Does Marcuse believe that we must sacrifice what we consider to be political freedom in our "repressive" society in order ultimately to realize the only genuine human freedom, namely instinctual liberation? His writings do not make it possible to answer this question unequivocally, but their general tenor does seem to suggest, at least possibly, an affirmative response.

It is quite evident, from a recent essay, that Marcuse is a par-

[30] Marcuse, *Eros and Civilization,* xi, 205.

tisan of political revolution—if it is "historically progressive" and a step on the road toward the elimination of surplus-repression.[31] As presented in these pages, Marcuse's viewpoint is far from unambiguous. On the one hand, he declares: "With all its limitations and distortions, democratic tolerance is under all circumstances more humane than an institutionalized intolerance which sacrifices the rights and liberties of the living generations for the sake of future generations."[32] But on the other hand, he asserts that "extreme suspension of the right of free speech and free assembly is indeed justified only if the whole of society is in extreme danger. I maintain that our society is in such an emergency situation, and that it has become the normal state of affairs."[33] His essential message seems to be that the forces of repression are so much in control even of societies with democratic governments—particularly through the power of the mass media to shape our vision of reality—that tolerance within such a context serves only to strengthen powers which represent reaction and servitude. Hence: "Liberating tolerance . . . would mean intolerance against movements from the Right, and toleration of movements from the Left. . . . it would extend to the stage of action as well as of discussion and propaganda, of deed as well as of word."[34]

Whatever demurrers Marcuse may include about the preferability of democratic tolerance to institutionalized intolerance maintained for the sake of future generations, or about the lack of a " 'right of resistance' to the point of subversion" against "a constitutional government sustained by a majority of the population,"[35] the main thrust of his argument is directed against steadfast protection of existing democratic liberties should they

[31]Herbert Marcuse, "Repressive Tolerance," in Wolff, Moore, and Marcuse, *A Critique of Pure Tolerance.*
[32]*Ibid.,* 99.
[33]*Ibid.,* 109–10.
[34]*Ibid.,* 109.
[35]*Ibid.,* 116.

block the road to revolutionary victory for the truly progressive forces of history.

Obviously such an approach is completely incompatible with Camus's insistence upon the limitations which awareness of our finitude and fallibility impose upon our manner of treating other persons. Marcuse has manufactured a grandiose and abstractly historicist ideology from Freudian (and Marxist) materials, and to make possible its realization he calls (though cautiously and ambiguously) for the suppression, if necessary, of what we presently consider to be essential political liberties. From Camus's perspective, one might well ask what gives Marcuse so much confidence that Freud's theories, mediated through their authoritative social and political interpreter (Marcuse), have disclosed the ultimate truth about man and his potentialities— at least to the extent necessary to justify reshaping whole societies in accordance with this ideological vision? It is surely a commonplace that psychoanalysis has produced a great host of divergent and mutually incompatible interpretations of the same data.[36] Confidence in the capacity of psychoanalytic methods to produce the absolute and certain truth about human nature— much less in one particular and highly idiosyncratic interpretation of the alleged findings of psychoanalysis (Marcuse admits that Freud himself was a pessimist about man and his social future but asserts that it is possible to interpret Freud's fundamental conceptions in order to support an optimistic perspective)— would certainly seem to furnish even less reason than have the Marxists whom Camus criticized at length to sacrifice whatever freedom we believe we have attained for a promised future of freedom perfected.

Neither Kateb (along with Skinner) nor Marcuse, whose writings are among the most challenging and intellectually stimulating works representative of the contemporary revival of uto-

---

[36]For a survey of seven widely differing psychoanalytical theories, see Patrick Mullahy, *Oedipus: Myth and Complex* (New York: Grove Press, 1955).

pian thought, succeeds, it seems to me, in blunting the main thrust of Camus's arguments against totalist ideology. Kateb specifically attempts to refute Camus's contention that the human costs of efforts to attain utopia through large-scale violent revolution are excessive to an incalculable degree, but he succeeded only in misinterpreting Camus's views on revolutionary violence. And further, Kateb was forced to admit, finally, that in the fantastically complex real world the costs of such an enterprise *are* too great, particularly in view of our inability to guarantee a utopian outcome of the struggle. But even more damaging to his effort to defend utopia is his fascination with Skinner's techniques of psychological conditioning, which is fatal to Kateb's commitment to increasing self-conscious human awareness and is wholly incompatible with the ideal of free dialogue which Camus persistently defended. And Marcuse's theory is simply an updated form of that ideological arrogance which claims to know everything and which the experience of the twentieth century convinced Camus—despite its author's explicitly contrary intent— was always a threat to end up killing everything that enables us to achieve some degree of humanity here and now.

Camus remained steadfast in his conviction that true rebellion persistently struggles against evil—but without hope for utopia:

Rebellion indefatigably confronts evil, from which it can only derive a new impetus. Man can master in himself everything that should be mastered. He should rectify in creation everything that should be rectified. And after he has done so, children will still die unjustly even in a perfect society. Even by his greatest effort man can only propose to diminish arithmetically the sufferings of the world. But the injustice and the suffering of the world will remain and, no matter how limited they are, they will not cease to be an outrage.[37]

Finally, what can we say in general about the value of Camus's contributions to political thought? For the most part I have tried to permit his ideas to speak for themselves, but especially in

[37]*The Rebel,* 303.

concluding I have attempted to suggest that they are relevant to such current central problems as the validation of moral norms in politics and the revival of utopian speculation. Perhaps Camus's principal contribution in the long run will prove to be his contention that, bereft of any certainty of divine guidance or of consensus on a metaphysical system, we need not float adrift on a sea of nihilism. He not only maintained but sought vigorously to demonstrate that we can discern moral norms for ourselves and for the direction of political life through faithful attention and response to our most deeply significant experiences and perceptions. This may seem a frail reed in contrast to the vanished authority of established religions and natural-law "traditions of civility." [38] But Camus was deeply persuaded that we are capable, through open, honest, existential encounter, of validating for ourselves the simple but enormously significant human values that he explicated as constituting the meaning of "true rebellion."

Camus certainly did not begin to solve all the problems that confront contemporary students and practitioners of social and political philosophy. But in addition to demonstrating the potentialities of a thoroughly existential approach to the comprehension and evaluation of political phenomena, he left us with a set of salutary warnings which we can fail to heed only at the price of giving up on a humanly meaningful corporate life. He reminded us forcefully that life cannot be served and enhanced through alliance with forces of death and oppression, whatever the ideological justifications presented to excuse their inhumanity. And he wrote about in his essays and portrayed unforgettably in his fiction the experienced goodness and meaningfulness of life in dialogical openness and communion. Camus's efforts to transcend nihilism point toward a genuinely human social and political order which we cannot take for granted as the gift of gods or of history, but the hope and the struggle for which we can never afford to give up.

[38] This phrase is Walter Lippmann's, in *The Public Philosophy*.

Index

Abstraction: and the existential, 12, 93, 136, 201–204; and absurdity, 23; and moral values, 24, 99, 188, 191; rejected by Conqueror, 45; and totalitarianism, 94–96; and depersonalization, 126; and murder, 126, 158; endemic to bureaucratization, 135; as historicism, 136–37; opposed by syndicalism, 180–81; and science, 201–205; dangers of, for Barzun, 204

Absurdity: as Camus's point of departure, 17–18, 26–27, 43, 50; and happiness, 19, 34, 43, 47, 51; as existential reality, 22–23, 27–28, 49; and death, 28, 32, 51; in conjunction of mind and universe, 28–30, 33; and reason, 32–33; and freedom, 32, 43–45; and honesty, 35, 36; and rebellion, 36, 37, 75, 78, 136; and quantitative ethics, 37; exemplars of, 37–38; in *The Stranger*, 38, 39–43; in *Caligula*, 47–48; and nihilism, in Germany, 51–52; in *The Plague*, 54, 57–58, 63–64; in *Cross Purpose*, 65–66; and humanism, 102; and liberalism, 178

Actor: as absurd man, 37

Aggression: in Freud, 80; in Marcuse, 208

Algeria: as influence on Camus, 12, 18; French injustice toward, denounced by Camus, 46, 160–67

Algerian War: Camus's reaction to, 16, 160–67; and existential morality, 160; contrasted to Hungarian rebellion, 161–62; Sartre on violence of, 162

Alienated labor, 180

Alienation: importance of, for Marx, 17, 116*n*; from transcendence, 51; from human solidarity, in *The Plague*, 54; in recent thought, 61; abolition of, 61–62; implicit in utilitarianism, 171

American Revolution, 169

Ananke, 208

Animal laborans, 168

Aquinas, Saint Thomas, 3

Arendt, Hannah: on science and nature, 29–30; as critic of ends-means political thought, 167–69

Aristotle, 3

Artist: as absurd man, 37

Assassination, 110

Atheism: of Camus, denied by Buber, 69; of metaphysical rebel, 104–105

Augustine, Saint, 13, 96

Bacon, Francis, 187

213